Healthy Stadia

Public health is a key priority for developed and developing nations. Indeed, many countries have sought strategies to promote health and reduce health inequalities. A 'settings approach' to promoting health has been endorsed by the World Health Organization, which has seen settings such as workplaces, schools, hospitals and prisons utilised to promote health. Alongside this, sport has received increasing pressure to consider its social role within the societies and communities in which it operates. Healthy Stadia is a European focused initiative with lessons relevant for global audiences to develop: (i) healthier stadium environments for fans and non-matchday visitors (e.g. smoke-free environments), (ii) healthier club workforces (e.g. bike to work schemes) and (iii) healthier populations in local communities (e.g. child obesity interventions).

This book outlines lessons and insight from practitioners and empirical research for those seeking to learn and research stadia as a settings approach to health promotion. The areas covered include: practical considerations for health promotion in sports stadia; empirical research on the sports stadia as a setting for public health promotion; research on physical activity and health promotion programmes delivered by the outward facing community trusts attached to sports clubs; an analysis of the policy considerations for health promotion by sports clubs in school based settings and critical insight and discussion surrounding the use of physical activity and sport interventions to promote physical activity and public health.

The chapters in this book were originally published as a special issue of *Sport in Society*.

Daniel Parnell is a Senior Lecturer in Business Management. He has extensive research leadership experience with national interventions that aim to use sport to develop social and health outcomes.

Kathryn Curran is a Senior Lecturer in Physical Activity, Exercise and Health and Non-Executive Director of the NGO European Healthy Stadia Network.

Matthew Philpott is Executive Director of the NGO European Healthy Stadia Network. Matthew has worked in the area of health promoting settings for over twelve years, with an initial research background in philosophy and psychology.

Sport in the Global Society: Contemporary Perspectives

Series Editor: Boria Majumdar, *University of Central Lancashire, UK*

The social, cultural (including media) and political study of sport is an expanding area of scholarship and related research. While this area has been well served by the *Sport in the Global Society* series, the surge in quality scholarship over the last few years has necessitated the creation of *Sport in the Global Society: Contemporary Perspectives*. The series will publish the work of leading scholars in fields as diverse as sociology, cultural studies, media studies, gender studies, cultural geography and history, political science and political economy. If the social and cultural study of sport is to receive the scholarly attention and readership it warrants, a cross-disciplinary series dedicated to taking sport beyond the narrow confines of physical education and sport science academic domains is necessary. *Sport in the Global Society: Contemporary Perspectives* will answer this need.

For a complete list of titles in this series, please visit https://www.routledge.com/series/SGSC

Recent titles in the series include:

Football, Community and Sustainability
Edited by Chris Porter, Anthony May and Annabel Kiernan

From Olympic Administration to Olympic Governance
Edited by Emmanuel Bayle and Jean-Loup Chappelet

Junior and Youth Grassroots Football Culture
The Forgotten Game
Edited by Jimmy O'Gorman

Gender in Physical Culture
Crossing Boundaries – Reconstituting Cultures
Edited by Natalie Barker-Ruchti, Karin Grahn and Eva-Carin Lindgren

DIY Football
The Cultural Politics of Community Based Football Clubs
Edited by David Kennedy and Peter Kennedy

A Social and Political History of Everton and Liverpool Football Clubs
The Split, 1878–1914
David Kennedy

Football Fandom in Italy and Beyond
Community through Media and Performance
Matthew Guschwan

Numbers and Narratives
Sport, History and Economics
Wray Vamplew

Healthy Stadia
An Insight from Policy to Practice
Edited by Daniel Parnell, Kathryn Curran and Matthew Philpott

Healthy Stadia

An Insight from Policy to Practice

Edited by

Daniel Parnell, Kathryn Curran and Matthew Philpott

Routledge
Taylor & Francis Group
LONDON AND NEW YORK

First published 2018 by Routledge

2 Park Square, Milton Park, Abingdon, Oxfordshire OX14 4RN
52 Vanderbilt Avenue, New York, NY 10017

Routledge is an imprint of the Taylor & Francis Group, an informa business

First issued in paperback 2019

British Library Cataloguing in Publication Data
A catalogue record for this book is available from the British Library

ISBN 13: 978-1-138-50693-0 (hbk)
ISBN 13: 978-0-367-89191-6 (pbk)

Typeset in Minion Pro
by RefineCatch Limited, Bungay, Suffolk

Publisher's Note
The publisher accepts responsibility for any inconsistencies that may have arisen during the conversion of this book from journal articles to book chapters, namely the possible inclusion of journal terminology.

Contents

Citation Information

The chapters in this book were originally published in *Sport in Society*, volume 20, issue 2 (February 2017). When citing this material, please use the original page numbering for each article, as follows:

Introduction
Healthy stadia: an insight from policy to practice
Daniel Parnell, Kathryn Curran and Matthew Philpott
Sport in Society, volume 20, issue 2 (February 2017), pp. 181–186

Chapter 1
Perspectives from those involved in healthy stadia
Daniel Cade, Kathryn Curran, Andy Fuller, Jenny Hacker, Clive Knight, Simon Lansley, Daniel Parnell and Matthew Philpott
Sport in Society, volume 20, issue 2 (February 2017), pp. 187–201

Chapter 2
Who ate all the pies? The importance of food in the Australian sporting experience
Keith D. Parry, Timothy Hall and Alastair Baxter
Sport in Society, volume 20, issue 2 (February 2017), pp. 202–218

Chapter 3
Sport heritage and the healthy stadia agenda: an overview
Gregory Ramshaw
Sport in Society, volume 20, issue 2 (February 2017), pp. 219–225

Chapter 4
An evaluation of opportunistic health checks at cricket matches: the Boundaries for Life initiative
Chet Trivedy, Ivo Vlaev, Russell Seymour and Matthew Philpott
Sport in Society, volume 20, issue 2 (February 2017), pp. 226–234

Chapter 5
Health promotion orientation of GAA sports clubs in Ireland
Aoife Lane, Niamh Murphy, Alex Donohoe and Colin Regan
Sport in Society, volume 20, issue 2 (February 2017), pp. 235–243

Chapter 6
The community impact of football pitches: a case study of Maidstone United FC
Anthony May and Daniel Parnell
Sport in Society, volume 20, issue 2 (February 2017), pp. 244–257

Chapter 7
Improving the physical and mental well-being of typically hard-to-reach men: an investigation of the impact of the Active Rovers *project*
Colin J. Lewis, Matthew J. Reeves and Simon J. Roberts
Sport in Society, volume 20, issue 2 (February 2017), pp. 258–268

Chapter 8
Success of a sports-club led-community X-PERT Diabetes Education Programme
Angela Morgan, Dee Drew, Angela Clifford and Katrina Hull
Sport in Society, volume 20, issue 2 (February 2017), pp. 269–280

Chapter 9
Tackling mental health: the role of professional football clubs
Kathryn Curran, Simon Rosenbaum, Daniel Parnell, Brendon Stubbs, Andy Pringle and Jackie Hargreaves
Sport in Society, volume 20, issue 2 (February 2017), pp. 281–291

Chapter 10
Sport policy and English primary physical education: the role of professional football clubs in outsourcing
Daniel Parnell, Ed Cope, Richard Bailey and Paul Widdop
Sport in Society, volume 20, issue 2 (February 2017), pp. 292–302

Chapter 11
'It brings the lads together': a critical exploration of older men's experiences of a weight management programme delivered through a Healthy Stadia project
Lorena Lozano-Sufrategui, Andy Pringle, David Carless and Jim McKenna
Sport in Society, volume 20, issue 2 (February 2017), pp. 303–315

Chapter 12
Lessons from the field for working in Healthy Stadia: physical activity practitioners reflect on 'sport'
Jim McKenna, Thomas Quarmby, Nicky Kime, Daniel Parnell and Stephen Zwolinsky
Sport in Society, volume 20, issue 2 (February 2017), pp. 316–324

For any permission-related enquiries please visit:
http://www.tandfonline.com/page/help/permissions

Notes on Contributors

Richard Bailey is based at the International Council of Sport Science and Physical Education, Germany.

Alastair Baxter is a retired rugby union player, registered architect and company director based in Populous, Australia.

Daniel Cade is a Project Manager at Schwery Consulting, Biel/Bienne, Switzerland.

David Carless is a Professor at the School of Sport, Leeds Beckett University, UK.

Angela Clifford is a Research Associate at the Centre for Health and Social Care Improvement, Faculty of Education, University of Wolverhampton, UK.

Ed Cope is a Lecturer in Sports Coaching and Performance at the Department of Sport, Health and Exercise Science, University of Hull, UK.

Kathryn Curran is a Senior Lecturer in Physical Activity, Exercise and Health and Non-Executive Director of the NGO European Healthy Stadia Network.

Alex Donohoe is a Research Assistant at the Department of Health, Sport and Exercise Science, Waterford Institute of Technology, Ireland.

Dee Drew is based at the Centre for Health and Social Care Improvement, Faculty of Education, Health and Wellbeing, University of Wolverhampton, UK.

Andy Fuller is an independent researcher based at Reading Sideways, Leiden, The Netherlands.

Jenny Hacker is an independent public health consultant at Inspire Research, Training and Consultancy, UK.

Timothy Hall is the Academic Course Advisor in Hospitality and Sport Management at the School of Business, Western Sydney University, Australia.

Jackie Hargreaves is module leader for exercise psychology and physical activity modules at the Carnegie Faculty, Centre for Active Lifestyles, Leeds Beckett University, UK.

Katrina Hull works in Public Health, Stoke-on-Trent City Council, UK.

Nicky Kime is Senior Research Fellow at the Centre for Active Lifestyles, Leeds Beckett University, UK.

Clive Knight is a tennis coach at Oswestry Team Tennis, Shropshire, UK.

Aoife Lane is based at the Department of Health, Sport and Exercise Science, Waterford Institute of Technology, Ireland.

Simon Lansley is the founder of Connect Sport Ltd, London, UK.

Colin J. Lewis is based at the School of Sport Studies, Leisure, & Nutrition, Liverpool John Moores University, UK.

Lorena Lozano-Sufrategui is a Senior Lecturer at the School of Sport, Leeds Beckett University, UK.

Anthony May is based at the Department of History, Politics and Philosophy, Manchester Metropolitan University, UK.

Jim McKenna is Carnegie Professor of Physical Activity and Health, and Head of the Active Lifestyles Research Centre in the Carnegie Faculty, Leeds Beckett University, UK.

Angela Morgan is a Senior Researcher at the Centre for Health and Social Care Improvement, Faculty of Education, Health and Wellbeing, University of Wolverhampton, UK.

Niamh Murphy is a Lecturer and Researcher at the Department of Health, Sport and Exercise Science, Waterford Institute of Technology, Ireland.

Daniel Parnell is a Senior Lecturer in Business Management. He has extensive research leadership experience with national interventions that aim to use sport to develop social and health outcomes.

Keith D. Parry is a Lecturer at the School of Business, Western Sydney University, Australia.

Matthew Philpott is Executive Director of the NGO European Healthy Stadia Network. Matthew has worked in the area of health promoting settings for over twelve years, with an initial research background in philosophy and psychology.

Andy Pringle is a Reader at the Carnegie School of Sport, Leeds Beckett University, UK.

Thomas Quarmby is a Senior Lecturer in Physical Education and Sport Pedagogy at the Centre for Active Lifestyles, Leeds Beckett University, UK.

Gregory Ramshaw is Associate Professor at the Department of Parks, Recreation and Tourism Management, Clemson University, USA.

Matthew J. Reeves is based at the School of Sport Studies, Leisure, & Nutrition, Liverpool John Moores University, UK.

Colin Regan is the Community and Health Manager at the Gaelic Athletic Association, Dublin, Ireland.

Simon J. Roberts is a Reader and Associate Professor in Sport and Exercise Pedagogy at the School of Sport Studies, Leisure, & Nutrition, Liverpool John Moores University, UK.

Simon Rosenbaum is an Early Career Fellow at the Faculty of Medicine, Department of Exercise Physiology, University of New South Wales, Australia.

Russell Seymour is Sustainability Manager at the Marylebone Cricket Club, London, UK.

Brendon Stubbs is Head of Physiotherapy at the Physiotherapy Department, South London and Maudsley NHS Foundation Trust, UK, and a Postdoctoral Researcher at King's College London, UK.

Chet Trivedy is based at the Centre for Applied Health Research and Delivery, Warwick Medical School, UK.

Ivo Vlaev is a Professor at Warwick Business School, University of Warwick, UK.

Paul Widdop is a Research Fellow in Cultural and Leisure Sociology at the Sport Business Management Group, Leeds Beckett University, UK.

Stephen Zwolinsky is a Research Officer at the Centre for Active Lifestyles, Leeds Beckett University, UK.

INTRODUCTION

Healthy stadia: an insight from policy to practice

Daniel Parnell, Kathryn Curran and Matthew Philpott

Public health is a key priority across developed and developing nations. It concerns a broad range of issues that can influence both physical health and mental well-being, and it focuses on populations of people rather than on individuals. The idea of utilizing a 'setting' to promote health and reduce health inequalities has been applied to a number of everyday environments. The 'settings approach' developed after the World Health Organization's (WHO) Ottawa Charter laid the foundations for much of modern health promotion, shifting the emphasis away from the individual and concentrating upon the living environment and organizational structures as a medium to promote health (WHO 1986). This approach has already seen success in the contexts of schools, workplaces, hospitals and prisons, and has been used by public health agencies to deliver interventions aimed at tackling lifestyle issues such as smoking, poor diets and physical inactivity. As the international community and governments have turned towards business and sport for support through more ethical, sustainable or social engagement practices, the relationship between sport and its communities has come under increased scrutiny (Parnell and Richardson 2014). This volume addresses the complex reality of the relationship between sport clubs, their stadia and health.

In recent times, sport has seen a shift in pressure from government, fans and other stakeholders towards the need for a greater contribution to social agendas (Anagnostopoulos and Shilbury 2013; Parnell et al. 2013). One key area of this shift has been within the realm of stadium management, specifically, how sports stadia can provide a setting to deliver on public health outcomes. Over the last 10 years in particular, the potential for using sporting stadia as health-promoting settings has started to be realized, not only to the benefit of local communities, but also to help achieve the corporate objectives of the clubs and stadia involved (Drygas et al. 2013). Sports stadia play iconic roles amongst fans and in the communities that they are located, capable of engaging large numbers of people both in the ground and surrounding area. In addition, the demographic and age group of fans visiting stadia – largely middle-aged, working-class males – often exhibit high levels of chronic health problems such as obesity, cardiovascular disease, some types of cancer and poor mental health. However, the ability of professional and amateur sports clubs to harness their badge/brand to engage fans is almost unique (Parnell et al. 2015), thereby having the potential to provide both an excellent physical setting and communications vehicle to positively influence the behaviour of fans, including their health-related behaviours (Witty and White 2011; Curran, Bingham, et al. 2014; Curran, Drust, and Richardson 2014).

During the early to mid-2000s, a number of pioneering sports stadia in the north-west region of England hosting the sports of football, rugby league and horse racing, started to work with the cardiovascular disease prevention charity Heart Of Mersey, to trial a number of 'healthy stadia'-type initiatives. This settings-based approach emphasized the potential for sports venues to develop policies and interventions promoting healthier lifestyles across three cross-cutting themes: (i) healthier stadium environments for fans and non-matchday visitors (e.g. smoke-free environments), (ii) healthier club workforces (e.g. bike to work schemes) and (iii) healthier populations in local communities (e.g. child obesity interventions). During this trial period, a working definition of a 'healthy stadium' was established in 2005, namely:

> Healthy Stadia are … those which promote the health of visitors, fans, players, employees and the surrounding community … places where people can go to have a positive healthy experience playing or watching sport

In 2006, a successful proposal for a 'Sports Stadia and Community Health' project was made to the European Commission in the framework of its Public Health Programme. This project worked with an initial group of partner agencies in Finland, Greece, Italy, Latvia, Ireland, Poland, Spain and the UK, and was tasked with piloting the healthy stadia concept with stadia in a cross section of European countries, and developing suitable guidance documentation to enhance the future roll-out of healthy initiatives. One of the primary outcomes from this project was the founding of a 'European Healthy Stadia Network' to act as a facility for sharing good practice and emerging research amongst clubs, stadium operators, governing bodies of sport, public health practitioners and academic institutions. The European Healthy Stadia Network (hereon Healthy Stadia) is now established as a successful social enterprise based in the UK with over 300 members from a cross section of European countries, and long-term partnerships established with the World Heart Federation and the Union of European Football Associations (UEFA) (http://www.healthystadia.eu/).

Since the initial EU 'Sport Stadia and Community Health' project, Healthy Stadia has worked on another four EU-funded health and sport programmes since 2010, including work with young people not in education, employment or training – NEETs (Health 25), a programme enhancing the health and well-being education of young performance level athletes (Fit 4 Health), a new programme on health enhancing physical activity advocacy (Active Voice) and a groundbreaking five-year clinical research project entitled EuroFIT, improving levels of physical activity and reducing sedentary time in male football fans. Whilst Healthy Stadia may be considered a spearhead in advocating for spots stadia, clubs and governing bodies of sport to develop health-promoting sports settings, it is especially pleasing to see the major groundswell in healthy stadia practices, policies and research over the last 10 years across a wide number of different sports and European settings. There is now a genuine recognition amongst clubs, governing bodies of sport and – perhaps most importantly – agencies commissioning health interventions, that sports settings offer a unique opportunity for both population-level approaches to improving public health (e.g. smoke-free sports environments), and interventions attempting to change the individual behaviours of target groups (e.g. addressing low levels of physical activity and sedentary behaviour in male football fans).

There are a number of key issues that the Healthy Stadia network considers (Drygas et al. 2013), which include healthier catering (Ireland and Watkins 2010), unhealthy sponsorship (Sherriff, Griffiths, and Daube 2009), smoke-free policies (Philpott and Sagar 2014) and sport-club and foundation-led community physical activity and health engagement (Hunt et al. 2014; Parnell and Richardson 2014; Parnell et al. 2015; Parnell and Pringle 2016). Part of Healthy Stadia's role is to capture current good practices and to disseminate these case studies across its network of members and to decision-makers with governing bodies of sport. In a number of cases, good practice examples are also accompanied by practical guidelines on the website and are intended to help sports organizations develop policies and practices that are part of the healthy stadia agenda. This includes guidelines on active travel to sports stadia (2014), on the development of smoke-free and tobacco-free sports venues (2016), and online healthier catering guidance (2016) (http://www.healthystadia.eu/). On the subject of tobacco control and sports stadia, this is an area that has been of considerable success in terms of advocacy and policy change, with Healthy Stadia and World Heart Federation working closely with UEFA over the last six years to ensure tobacco-free environments at club competition finals, and the European football championships (EURO) in 2012 and 2016. In addition to this, and with the launch of its tobacco-free guidance and training documents in 2016, Healthy Stadia will be launching a major programme of work with governing bodies of sport and other key stakeholders in European sport and health advocating for all European sports venues to be completely smoke-free by the year 2020. This progressive movement from good practices, to advocacy campaigns and finally to policy change is not new to public health as a discipline, but is enhanced greatly through strong evaluation and the input of academic research.

There is a growing evidence base that recognizes the role that professional sport clubs, and their stadia, can play in improving public health outcomes across local communities, including those who interact with the stadia and sport venues (i.e. Witty and White 2011; Drygas et al. 2013; Bingham et al. 2014; Curran, Bingham, et al. 2014; Curran, Drust, and Richardson 2014; Hunt et al. 2014; Parnell and Richardson 2014; Hulton et al. 2015; Martin et al. 2016; Parnell and Pringle 2016). In order for the healthy stadia agenda to begin to be fully realized, in particular amongst commissioning agencies within local and national governments, it is vital that this rigorous evidence base is developed. Research is needed that demonstrates the impact that both population level and individual behaviour change programmes developed through sports settings can have on public health outcomes. Whilst many 'community' or 'social' programmes attached to sports clubs have included process monitoring techniques as part of their health projects, there is often still a gap in providing evidence of a project's impact that can be (sometimes at least) lacking in the internal reports produced by clubs that make up much of the grey literature in this field. It is therefore imperative that clubs, national governing bodies of sport and league operators look to work with academic partners to assist with both programme design and evaluation of projects. This will help address a common lack of 'in-house' expertise within sports organizations to address the key issue of developing an evidence base that clearly demonstrates the value (or not in some cases) of using sports settings to delivery public health programmes.

It is pleasing to see that a growing number of pioneering clubs in numerous European countries have now developed research partnerships with universities, integrating insight, design and evaluation techniques into their programmes. Indeed, a good number of the articles included in this special edition are testimony to the wider understanding of sports organizations working closely with academic partners, and it is hoped that these examples will inspire readers from sports organizations, public health and academic institutions to work more closely together in order to move the healthy stadia agenda onto the next stage. This volume examines the relationship between professional and amateur sport clubs, stadia and health promotion, through a collection of papers aligned to philosophical, political, environmental and practical health-related interventions enabled through sport stadia settings.

The volume begins with an applied contribution from a number of practitioners from across Europe who are working on, or towards, the healthy stadia agenda. In this article, contributors share findings and highlight practical considerations from the field of practice. Following this article, a number of papers and commentaries which discuss applied, practical and empirical experiences of a range of authors are presented. There is a collection of five articles that specifically consider sport stadia as a setting for public health promotion. Each of these articles enhances our understanding of how health-promoting policies and practices at sport stadia can contribute to improved levels of public health amongst fans, visitors, stadia workforces and local communities. Parry et al. discuss the satisfaction of fans regarding food and beverage offerings within Rugby Union stadiums in Australia; Ramshaw explores the relationship between sport heritage and the healthy stadia agenda and considers if they are potential partners in public health education; Trivedy and colleagues investigate the feasibility and user acceptability of offering free health checks to fans and venue staff attending cricket matches in England; Lane et al. present the health promotion orientation of Gaelic Athletic Association (GAA) clubs in Ireland and discuss the use of GAA stadia as a setting for health promotion for both its members and the wider community. Finally, May and Parnell examine the financial impact of a 3G Artificial Grass Football Pitch for a non-league football club and discuss the potential role that these pitches can play in supporting community public health objectives.

Research on the outcomes of a range of physical activity and health-promotion programmes delivered by professional football clubs Football in the Community (FitC) schemes within stadia in England are also presented through two empirical studies and one research note included in this volume. Lewis et al. examine the effectiveness of a physical activity intervention upon mental well-being, health perceptions, and lifestyle knowledge in men classed as hard-to-reach; Morgan et al. explore the effectiveness of a Diabetes Education Programme by measuring changes to participants' physical condition, knowledge of diabetes, psychological well-being, activity level, diabetes self-management and participants rating of the programme. Lastly, Curran et al. offer insights into mental health interventions delivered within and by, professional football clubs and present the available evidence concerning their reach, effectiveness and impact.

Due to the power and pull of the professional football club brand, FitC schemes in the United Kingdom now operate a broad range of activities and services broadly housed within Primary Physical Education (PE) and school sport. Parnell and colleagues critically discuss the challenges of outsourcing Primary PE to coaches who work for professional football clubs FitC schemes and offer some evidence supporting the employment and development of sports coaches. The volume concludes with two articles which outline key lessons from sport, PA and health-promotion interventions with distinctive relevance to the Healthy Stadia agenda. Lozano et al. report the experiences of older men attending a community football-led weight management programme, and in doing so, investigate the use of sports settings to facilitate health promotion with older men; McKenna et al. discuss the role that professional sport clubs have played, and continue to play, in physical activity and public health promotion with hard-to-reach groups, and consider the challenges of integrating sport into PA and health promotion.

Each article offers practical implications which can assist those who commission, manage or deliver physical activity and public health-related interventions through amateur and professional sports clubs. We anticipate that the contributions contained within volume issue will be of interest to a range of stakeholders involved in research, policy and practice. We, the editors, would like to thank the contributors for the insight into their research and their effort in developing their submission for this call for papers. We would like to extend this appreciation to the many anonymous peer reviewers who have contributed to submissions and resubmissions, helping strengthen the quality of the individual articles and thus, the overall volume.

Statement on intellectual property

The Healthy Stadia® word mark and logo mark are registered as official trademarks to the European Healthy Stadia Network CIC Ltd at EU level. Healthy Stadia CIC has granted permission for the word mark 'healthy stadia' to be used by contributing authors, editors and the journal's publication house for this special edition only.

Disclosure statement

No potential conflict of interest was reported by the authors.

References

Anagnostopoulos, C., and D. Shilbury. 2013. "Implementing Corporate Social Responsibility in English Football: Towards Multi-Theoretical Integration." *Sport, Business and Management: An International Journal* 3 (4): 268–284.

Bingham, D., D. Parnell, K. Curran, and D. Parnell. 2014. "Fit Fans: Perspectives of a Practitioner and Understanding Participant Health Needs within a Health Promotion Programme for Older Men Delivered within an English Premier League Football Club." *Soccer and Society* 15 (6): 883–901.

Curran, K., D. Bingham, D. Richardson, and D. Parnell. 2014. "Ethnographic Engagement from within a Football in the Community Programme at an English Premier League Football Club." *Soccer and Society* 15 (6): 934–950.

Curran, K., B. Drust, and D. Richardson. 2014. "'I Just Want to Watch the Match': A Practitioner's Reflective Account of Men's Health Themed Match Day Events at an English Premier League Football Club." *Soccer & Society* 15 (6): 919–933.

Drygas, W., J. Ruszkowska, M. Philpott, O. BjOrkstrOm, M. Parker, R. Ireland, and F. Roncarolo. 2013. "Good Practices and Health Policy Analysis in European Sports Stadia: Results from the "Healthy Stadia" Project." *Health Promotion International* 28 (2): 157–165.

Hulton, A., B. Drust, D. Flower, D. Richardson, and K. Curran. 2015. "Effectiveness of a Community Football Programme on Improving Physiological Markers of Health in a HTR Male Population." *Soccer and Society* 17 (2): 196–208.

Hunt, K., S. Wyke, C. M. Gray, A. S. Anderson, A. Brady, C. Bunn, and P. T. Donnan. 2014. "A Gender-Sensitised Weight Loss and Healthy Living Programme for Overweight and Obese Men Delivered by Scottish Premier League Football Clubs (FFIT): a Pragmatic Randomised Controlled Trial." *The Lancet* 383 (9924): 1211–1221. doi:http://dx.doi.org/10.1016/S0140-6736(13)62420-4.

Ireland, R., and F. Watkins. 2010. "Football Fans and Food: A Case Study of a Football Club in the English Premier League." *Public Health Nutrition* 13 (05): 682–687.

Martin, A., S. Morgan, D. Parnell, M. Philpott, A. Pringle, M. Rigby, A. Taylor, and J. Topham. 2016. "Editorial: A Perspective from Key Stakeholders on Football and Health Improvement." *Soccer & Society* 17 (2): 175–182.

Parnell, D., and A. Pringle. 2016. "Football and Health Improvement: An Emerging Field." *Soccer and Society* 17 (2): 171–174.

Parnell, D., and D. Richardson. 2014. "Introduction." *Soccer and Society* 15 (6): 823–827.

Parnell, D., G. Stratton, B. Drust, and D. Richardson. 2013. "Football in the Community Schemes: Exploring the Effectiveness of an Intervention in Promoting Healthful Behaviour Change." *Soccer and Society* 14: 35–51.

Parnell, D., A. Pringle, J. McKenna, S. Zwolinsky, Z. Rutherford, J. Hargreaves, L. Trotter, M. Rigby, and D. Richardson. 2015. "Reaching Older People with PA Delivered in Football Clubs: The Reach, Adoption and Implementation Characteristics of the Extra Time Programme." *BMC Public Health* 15. doi: http://dx.doi.org/10.1186/s12889-015-1560-5. http://www.biomedcentral.com/1471-2458/15/220

Philpott, M., and D. Sagar. 2014. "Survey of Smoke-free Policies at Football Stadia in Europe." *European Health Stadia Network*, June 01. Accessed 20 December 2015. http://www.healthystadia.eu/resource-library/alcohol-and-substance-misuse/itemlist/user/63-matthew-philpott.html

Sherriff, J., D. Griffiths, and M. Daube. 2009. "Cricket: Notching up Runs for Food and Alcohol Companies?" *Australian and New Zealand Journal of Public Health* 34: 19–23.

Witty, K., and A. White. 2011. "Tackling Men's Health: Implementation of a Male Health Service in a Rugby Stadium Setting." *Community Practitioner* 84 (4): 29–33.

WHO (World Health Organization). 1986. "Ottawa Charter for Health Promotion." *Canadian Journal of Public Health* 77: 425–426.

Perspectives from those involved in healthy stadia

Daniel Cade, Kathryn Curran, Andy Fuller, Jenny Hacker, Clive Knight, Simon Lansley, Daniel Parnell and Matthew Philpott

ABSTRACT
Healthy stadia is a growing agenda across industry and in turn academia. In this era of growth, much of the research literature is primarily sourced from academics with little contribution from applied and industry stakeholders. As such, the editors have sought to offer practitioners a platform to share novel projects, perspectives and preliminary intervention evaluation findings. This applied article intends to share evaluation and insight from applied practice, to encourage closer debate between the academic community and applied industry.

Introduction

Sport stadia and sport-oriented community-based interventions have been highlighted as vehicles to promote public health (Drygas et al. 2013; Bangsbo, Krustrup, and Dvorak 2014; Curran, Drust, and Richardson 2014; Hunt et al. 2014; Parnell and Richardson 2014; Parnell et al. 2014; Parnell and Pringle 2016). There is growing recognition of the role that amateur and professional sport clubs can play in improving public health outcomes across local communities, including those who interact with stadia and sport venues (Drygas et al. 2013; Martin et al. 2016). Indeed, it was the research of Drygas et al. (2013) that helped cement the European Healthy Stadia Network, which works with sports clubs, stadia operators and governing bodies of sport to develop stadia as health promoting environments. The European Healthy Stadia Network offers assistance through one-to-one support, guidance documents, case studies of good practice, benchmarking tools and research (Martin et al. 2016).

The purpose of this special issue is to disseminate a range of contributions from practitioners, commissioners and researchers involved in, or concerned with, the healthy stadia agenda. The editors [Parnell, Curran and Philpott] hope that by developing a platform for dissemination, it will enable those working on, and around, the healthy stadia agenda to share novel projects, stories, perspectives and insight. This applied article intends to encourage a closer debate between the academic community and applied industry. In no particular order, we are pleased to highlight the work of Ms Jenny Hacker, discussing a stadium-based approach to men's health through Albion in the Community (AITC) at Brighton Hove Albion Football Club, Dr Andy Fuller on his experiences of football and health promotion in the Netherlands, Mr Clive Knight of Oswestry Team Tennis on his experiences making community stadia accessible to the local community, Mr Simon Lansley of ConnectSport on his personal experiences on sharing the community sport message on social media, and Mr Dan Cade from Schwery Consulting on sustainable sponsorship.

Our first contributor is Ms Jenny Hacker; she is an independent public health consultant who has previously led a number of health promoting programmes at AITC, the charitable arm of Brighton and Hove Albion Football Club (England). In her contribution, Jenny discusses the *Shape Up at the Stadium* project offering both insights and preliminary evaluation findings.

Shape Up at the Stadium, AITC

Shape Up at the Stadium is a weight management programme for men delivered at the Amex, home of Brighton and Hove Albion Football Club. Targeting men with a body mass index of 25–43 kg/m^2, it is a self-referral programme for men wanting to lose weight in a supportive group environment, delivered by staff from the club's charitable arm, AITC.

Each programme lasts for ten weeks. Sessions include nutritional advice, behaviour change strategies and physical activity sessions. The programme forms part of a broader collection of Shape Up projects delivered as part of the Tier-two community-based weight management service, funded by Brighton and Hove Public Health. Additional Shape Up programmes are delivered in the city centre or community venues and include a programme for new mothers.

As part of the evaluation of the Shape Up programme, participants are weighed and measured at the start of the programme (week 1), and weighed again at the mid-point (week 5) and end of the programme (week 10). Responses to questions on behaviour were recorded at the start and end of each ten-week programme. The primary outcomes of the programmes include a 2% reduction in body weight at week ten, reductions in waist circumference, increases in physical activity levels and changes to diet, specifically increased consumption of fruit and vegetables and reduced consumption of food high in fats, sugars.

Analysis of available data shows that the programme delivered at the stadium has been the most successful of the wider local Shape Up programmes and supported many men to kick start healthier lifestyles. Data was available from 45 men. The vast majority (97%) attended more than half of the sessions. In terms of weight loss, more than a third (36%) achieved the target of 2% or greater weight loss by the end of the ten-week programme. This was more than twice the average of 15% achieved over the overall Shape Up programme. This supports a settings-based approach to promoting health (Parnell et al. 2014; Martin et al. 2016).

The overall weight reduction for the group was a loss of 84.75 kg. One participant managed to increase his weight slightly, whilst 29% experienced no change. However, 69% of men lost weight over the ten weeks, which ranged from 0.3 to 7.9 kg. The majority of men, 67%, also achieved reductions to their waist circumference, ranging from 0.8 to 12 cm. However, 30% did not achieve a change and one man increased his waist circumference by 0.9 cm.

Only around half of the sample completed both pre- and post-programme questionnaires regarding behaviour change. As such, the sample is limited to a cohort of 23 participants. Of these, the most successful behaviour change achieved was increased physical activity whereby 70% increased the number of days they were physically active for more than 30 min. This was higher than the average for the overall Shape Up programme delivered in other setting, 64%.

In terms of improving diet, 42% reported an increase in fruit and vegetables, higher than the broader programme average of 3%; and 38% reported that they consumed fewer foods that were high in fat and sugar, lower than the overall programme average of 40%. Although the collection of data on long-term changes (i.e. six- and twelve-month questionnaires) was challenging with poor completion, the current results presented are encouraging.

The stadia based approach to promoting health with men appears favourable. This is supported by feedback from participants who suggested that men liked the stadium venue, being with like-minded people, a programme tailored to a male audience, excellent motivational support from the practitioners and the banter and camaraderie of the programme. Participants highlighted:

> As an Albion fan, I got to see bits of the stadium I wouldn't normally have seen, but more importantly than that, I found the advice given from the team was invaluable. The advice on food types, portions sizes, and what was actually in what I was eating, coupled with the work-outs, saw the weight drop and the belly diminish…

> I am now a confirmed label watcher looking for the right foods and salt content has become an obsession … I will miss it when we finish in a few weeks' time, hopefully some of the guys will continue the pod sessions … I have now re-joined my local gym to progress things further.

In conclusion, this contribution offers an insight into a stadium-based health promotion programme. The majority of men taking part in AITC Shape Up at the Stadium programme lost weight over period of the programme. This compared favourably with other Shape Up programmes delivered in the city, supporting the use of sports stadia for men. The programme successfully supported the majority of men to increase their physical activity levels, with less favourable, yet positive changes in diet. Supporting men to lose weight and maintain a healthy weight remains a challenge in the context of the obesogenic environments. In terms of men's health, football stadia present opportunities to engage a traditionally 'hard to reach' group to achieve successful outcomes.

Our next contribution is from Dr Andy Fuller. Andy researches sports and urban culture and edits the Reading Sideways website. In his contribution, Andy discusses his experiences and insight into health promotion through sports clubs from both top and lower leagues in The Netherlands, and introduces the concept of 'gezellig' as a typically Dutch way of fans being emotionally involved with their clubs.

Gezellig Stadia: observations from The Netherlands

Football is an integral part of communal life in The Netherlands. The country has the world's highest participation rates in club football per capita (Kuper 2003). Although there are only four large stadia (i) Amsterdam Bijlmer Arena (on the southern fringe of Amsterdam and home to Ajax, (ii) de Kuip (in Rotterdam, home of Feyenoord), (iii) Philips Stadium (in Eindhoven, home of PSV) and (iv) Kyocera Stadium (in The Hague, home of ADO Den Haag), the Dutch landscape is marked by the rectangular shapes of football grounds and hockey grounds. These grounds are rarely open for the public and are often lined with fences and have locked gates. The grounds belong to football clubs, and if one wants to play, one must join a club, or be satisfied playing on half-sized grounds in improvised public spaces. The Netherlands has high population density, and land is at premium. Due to its low-lying geography, the landscape needs to be managed, controlled intensely, which is reflected in the highly organized nature of the country's use of public and green space: the landscape needs to serve an environmental function as well as providing a communal, recreation space.

Members are loyal to and proud of their clubs: the clubs are integral to identity formation, which goes 'hand in hand with the production of difference, for each act of inclusion and identification is based on exclusion and the making of boundaries' (van Slobbe, Vermeulen, and Koster 2013, 1364). "Many prefer watching their club's amateur teams play, rather than watching the professional Eredivisie and Jupiler Leagues. Dennis v. P., a member of Quick in The Hague says, 'the city is quite fragmented. The city's layout is clearly structured and has clear classes. Most people are far more attached to their local club, where they play or serve as volunteers, rather than supporting the city's only professional team, ADO Den Haag. If you are not from that part of town, or don't have a family connection with the club, most people don't support it, just because they play in the Eredivisie" (Interview, February 2016).

Bert V., a lifelong member of Koninklijke HFC in Haarlem, reinforces this sense of attachment to local clubs, over the more nationally or internationally prominent clubs such as Ajax, Feyenoord or PSV.

> I have little interest in the Eredivisie. I have no time for watching Ajax or whoever. Sure, at the time of the World Cup, or if a Dutch team is playing in the Champions League, I will support them in a nominal manner, but it is not something I invest in emotionally. My club is Koninklijke HFC. (Interview January 2016)

The highly valued quality of gezellig (a sense of warmth, cosiness, familiarity, belonging) is also reflected in the affection that members keep for their local club. Although the quality of gezellig generally applies to indoor spaces, the term has relevance to the feeling, atmosphere that can be generated at a football stadium. Gezellig is the feeling of warmth, that familiarity, comfort, order and security that is a result of physical conditions, personal interactions and pattern. As such, local amateur football clubs play an important role in communal life, maintaining social relations and fostering positive changes in living a healthy life.

The Netherlands has one of the most active populations in Europe. Sport is an important form of leisure activity for the Dutch: 52% of the population participate in sport on a weekly basis, well above the European Union average of 38%. This participation, but also the sports infrastructure, for example, is determined in part by social developments in the Netherlands (Tiessen-Raaphoorst and Breedveld 2007). Despite this, as in other parts of the world, fast (fried) food is very popular and is a part of Dutch lifestyle. Bitterballen, croquettes, frikandel, patates frites are staple warm and savoury snacks eaten throughout the whole year. Fast food chains, has shops at train stations, main shopping streets and also – unsurprisingly – at football stadia. Sweets such as oliebollen (deep-fried dough), stroopwafel (a waffel filled with a caramel syrup), poffertjes (small, spongy pancakes) are very popular; slaagroom (whipped cream) is offered with hot chocolates and cakes.

A healthy Dutch lifestyle seems to be characterized by eating in moderation (another important value), the use of bicycles as a main mode of transport (another important aspect to being Dutch) and being able to walk easily throughout the small city or town that one lives in. Being a member of a sports club – whether it be football, hockey or athletics – provides an important framework for structuring one's physical exercise. The clubs offer socialization, communal engagement and friendships. Members are active as volunteers even if not always intensely active as players or participants. Being Dutch, or 'acting normal' (as people say), proves at times both an impediment and encouragement to living a healthy lifestyle: oliebollen, for example, are an integral part of winter-time celebrations and festivities, just as one eats fries or croquettes (deep-fried bread-crumbed rolls, containing some kind of meat) while watching football.

I have been visiting football grounds and stadia in The Netherlands while living in Leiden 2014–2016. The observations below are drawn from a range of stadium visits, mainly conducted while going to games and talking with various club volunteers and people, who have over time, become friends. The reflections below seek to explore the notions of healthy stadia against the sense and feelings of attending games and atmospheres created. That is, I explore to what degree is the stadium, or particular football club culture, indicative of healthy social relation conditions. In this regard I am asking whether the stadia facilitate positive health and social relations.

The Amsterdam Bijlmer Arena is the most modern stadium in The Netherlands. It has its own train station and is integrated into an entertainment precinct close to restaurants, bars, cinemas and concert venues. It is the home ground of The Netherlands' most successful club, Ajax, and is walking distance from the club's training venue at de Toekomst. Ajax left de Meer stadium (their home since 1934) in 1996 to move into the multi-purpose stadium. The shift in home stadium was common throughout the 1990s amongst the Eredivisie clubs, as clubs moved out of their outdated stadiums into newer, safer and more modern facilities (Spaaij 2007). The transition to a new stadium is always a tense affair: the memories, demands and wishes of supporters need to be taken into account in order for supporters to maintain a sense of identification with the club. Ajax has struggled hard to maintain a sense of the 'Ajax feeling' after moving in to the Amsterdam Arena (Oppenhuisen and van Zoonen 2006).

The Ajax Run of 25th October 2015 sought to increase community participation and identification with Ajax football club and to promote healthy living. This was the second year of holding the event, and, unlike the previous year, the race was followed by a live-screening of an away match (against Vitesse Arnhem). Coincidentally, it was the first Ajax game to be played after news broke of legendary player Johann Cruyff being diagnosed with lung cancer. The start line of the race was just outside of Amsterdam Arena and the finishing line was at the northern end of the pitch. The Ajax Run is an initiative of Ms Eefje Schep, a press officer at Ajax, and her colleagues. I met her after the race, and we spoke during the half-time of the Vitesse-Ajax game. Eefje described the origins and purpose of the event as follows:

> I love running myself, and a couple of years ago, some of us thought of holding this event. We wanted to attract more people to come to the stadium to see what it is like and also to hold an event that would involve a broader cross-section of the nearby community. Today, we had around 3,600 runners; last year, we had about 3,300 runners. So, it has been a success. Last year we organised the event in a weekend that Ajax played no game. This year we were also looking for a free weekend but it was unfortunately not possible to find a date on which the stadium was available and Ajax did not have to play a game. Now we decided to go for this date and to broadcast the game Vitesse versus Ajax after the run on a big screen in the stadium.
>
> The participants were enthusiastic after the first event so, perhaps this is one reason for the greater number of participants for this second event. We sent out information to the media, the local athletics clubs and the local schools; we advertised it through our own website and

> social media channels. All the profits from the event go to the Foundation of Ajax and through this event we also want to promote a 'healthy lifestyle' amongst our community.
>
> We had several different communities participating in this event. Including, Ajax fans who wanted to run on the pitch and watch the event; professional runners, people from the local community and runners who were participating in the event through their work. Some former Ajax players were running as well. Sjaak Swart and the Ajax players Thulani Serero and Arek Milik who were injured were present for the award ceremony of the winners. The atmosphere was great.
>
> I sat in the northern stand watching the end of the race. Runners, sometimes bedecked in Ajax jerseys, crossed the line often full of exuberance and with arms raised. Although the top three or so runners finished with times below 35 min, the bulk of participants finished well above 40 min, and many above 1hour. It was not an elite competition, but the point was participation and creating an incentive to run, exercise, set a goal for oneself. As Eefje states above, the atmosphere was indeed great. Participants had friends and family in the crowd and there was much cheering; the gestures of runners also indicated that they were satisfied with their achievement of either finishing or getting a personal best.

Johan, an Ajax fan, took his seat up in the stand, where he was greeted by his wife and teenage daughter. During the one-minute applause for Cruyff – based on the recent news of his lung cancer diagnosis – Johan stopped our conversation in order to clap along with the rest of the crowd. Somewhat, ironically, Johan had a lit up a cigarette only a moment earlier, in this rokvrij (smoke-free) stadium. Johan described the Amsterdam Arena as 'colder' than the previous stadiums he has watched Ajax play in de Meer and the Amsterdam Olympic Stadium. He says, those stadiums are 'warm' (ie gezellig), because they are the venues in which he has seen Ajax's great victories and triumphs. That the Amsterdam Arena is clearly a warmer, more-sheltered and more luxurious venue, yet it does not trump the memories of the victories at other stadiums;

> I run perhaps once or twice a week. I am an Ajax fan, so, when there was this opportunity to run on this holy ground, of course I wanted to do it. I have also done the Amsterdam half-marathon, which starts and ends at the Amsterdam Olympic Stadium, another important stadium in Ajax's history. I am from Amsterdam; I was born here and my grandfather too, was born here. But, now, I live in Almere. For two seasons, I had membership tickets with Almere City FC, but my heart was always with Ajax. We moved to Almere because of my daughter. These days, things are different. If for example, children are mucking around and you tell them 'hey don't do that', they don't say, 'sorry sir, we won't do it again', like we used to in the past, they'll start shouting abuse and they probably have a knife. We moved to Almere where it is quieter and safer for my daughter.

Football fandom is an expression of identity, heritage and loyalty. Eefje sought to draw on the enthusiasm of Ajax fans for their club to get them involved in a healthy, sporting activity. For a fan such as Johan, finishing on the Ajax home pitch was an added incentive to link with his hobby for running. The Amsterdam Arena though in the mind of Johan lacked the gezellig-ness of de Meer and the Olympic stadium.

My second insight relates to the Middelmors Sportpark of Rijnsburg, home to the Rijnsburgse Boys, which contrasts significantly with the highly multi-functional Amsterdam ArenA. The Rijnsburgse Boys, founded in 1930, is a Topklasse team (third division) from a village outside of Leiden and has around 2000 members and about 50 different teams; most of which are youth teams. The club is a successful amateur club and has up-to-date facilities. Its home ground is used for an annual FIFPro tournament for un-contracted professional footballers. Crowds are generally around 1000, but for bigger games (such as against local rivals Noordwijk) attendance can swell to around 2000. The ground is easily reached by foot, bicycle, bus, scooter or car. The bicycle racks are largely full during games; indicating not only the Dutch habit of cycling. but also suggesting that many only make short distances.

The large yellow and black Rijnsburgse Boys flags in houses near the stadium also suggest a strong and proud support for the club. Atmosphere on game days is generally one of relaxed enthusiasm for watching a game of football coupled with bonhomie. I was introduced to Mr Lennart Paauw, a board member of Rijnsburgse Boys, by Rijnsburgse Boys press officer, Mr Henk Hogewoning. In discussing healthy stadia, we discussed the kinds of food available at the club and the challenges involved in making a shift from the traditional fast food to healthier alternatives. Lennart explained Rijnsburgse Boys situation as follows:

> Well, it is difficult. Eating fast food is a part of football culture. When people come to a game, they want to eat fast food. Perhaps, they eat well for five or six days a week, but, when they come here, they eat fast food. We recognise this, but we are doing our best to change it. Even if at the same time, we recognise that the change is going to be slow. It is very difficult to change culture. We have at the moment around 30–40 volunteers working today. We have a dozen or so working in the canteen. No-one gets paid. But, the good thing is, that we have volunteers who are very much behind promoting alternatives to fast food. At the least it is about making sure that there is whole-grain bread, that there is fruit available. Our staff do their bit to set a positive example to others: they themselves choose the healthy options. Slowly, over time, we can hopefully establish a culture that separates 'fast/junk food' from being at the football.
>
> One of the hurdles is that providing fast food is much cheaper and easier than providing healthier food, which of course, perishes quicker and requires more people involved in its serving. So, although we value fresh and good food, it still has to be balanced against what we can afford in terms of costs, with what facilities we have available and what our customers – i.e. our members and players want. Our club is also open on Thursday nights, and it is clear that people eat and drink more healthily on Thursday nights. So, it seems that the weekend is a time where people eat in a less-disciplined manner. We can see by the levels of consumption that this is a clear pattern. We have a good atmosphere at our club. People don't drink too much; we don't serve alcohol by the side of the pitch. If people drink they do so before the game or afterwards in the social club. But, while watching the game, people aren't drinking or being abusive. It is a football crowd, so of course, there are moments of tension and excitement, but, generally, there is no trouble.

In conclusion, the entrenched culture of club football and loyalty in The Netherlands means that football clubs can play a vital role in developing healthy lifestyles. Whilst this commentary offers some observational and reflective insight, it is clear that clubs with huge supporter bases like Ajax of Amsterdam are able to draw on their brand-appeal to attract participants for events they would not otherwise attract. Similarly, smaller, more-locally based clubs such as the Topklasse club Rijnsburgse Boys are able to make incremental changes to the lifestyles of their community working in consultation with them and thanks to the support of (unpaid) volunteers.

Football is an integral and all-encompassing aspect of Dutch culture that brings together many of the complexities of Dutch national identity and tradition (van Hilvoorde, Vorstenbosch, and Devisch 2010). The healthy lifestyles of walking, cycling and playing regular sport are also countered by consumption of fast food, cigarettes and large quantities of beer, often while being a spectator at a local or Eredivisie football game. Gezellig stadia are those in which the fans, supporters and volunteers can both identify with as well as contribute to. As such, football clubs and their associated stadia are positioned to play a contributing role in promoting health in their local communities.

In our next contribution, Mr Clive Knight at Oswestry Team Tennis (OTT) discusses a *community-based* tennis facility that has also taken on a healthy stadia approach, something that will be echoed in some of the full articles later in this special edition. Clive offers his personal insight into how a club originally set up to deliver a single sport has now become a multi-activity deliverer within its community, thereby contributing to its member's health and well-being. The club has also encouraged additional sports activities to take place within the adjacent town centre park, and make better use of the existing facilities to increase levels of physical activity within the local population.

Oswestry Team Tennis

Oswestry is a rural market town situated in Shropshire (England) with a population of around 40,000 including the immediate surrounding area. OTT is a junior tennis club with two floodlit courts – one macadam court for the full game, one court for multi-activity, and four smaller orange/red courts designed specifically for children aged from 4 to 9 years, in order to progress through structured mini-tennis activities, leading to the full game. OTT is based in Cae Glas Park in Oswestry which is a seven-acre site adjacent to the Town centre, and regarded by the Town Council as Oswestry's 'jewel in the crown'. The club has a long lease with Oswestry Town Council to use the tennis courts. The public can make use of the facility when the club is not occupying them.

OTT informal activities started in the 1990s when coaching of promising local juniors started at a nearby secondary school. OTT became a Lawn Tennis Association (LTA) accredited club in 2002 to meet the increasing local demand to provide tennis opportunity for juniors of all abilities in the town. In 2005, Barclays Spaces for Sports invested £100,000 – a mixture of capital and revenue into the club to fund the new facilities in Cae Glas Park and provide a revenue stream to pump prime the club in its infancy. The club is one of 202 such Barclays Spaces for Sports facilities spread across the country. The club is run by volunteers and is a charity, which is unusual for tennis clubs, but it serves the purpose well.

The club is one of 202 such Barclays Spaces for Sports facilities spread across the country. From an initial 50 members in 2002, the club now has over 200 junior members. The club provides coaching sessions throughout the week with development squads, and a full range of group sessions are on offer on Saturdays. Competition match plays are ran throughout the year for all groups from mini red through to LTA-rated players including adults. Participants' motivations to attend include exercising and consequently improving their health, to be with their friends and to become the best they can be in that sport.

Thirty years ago, there was a very different attitude with 'becoming the best you can be' being the major reason for taking part, and coaches generally only interested in players in this category. Encouragingly today, there is raised awareness that youngsters playing other sports is a good thing and will help develop their core skills, including the fitness and health agendas. OTT has a myriad of youngsters who play multi-sports and it takes great pride in its members succeeding in other sports. This holistic multi-sport approach to governance and operations has allowed OTT to look beyond its existing delivery to grow membership and participation within the club, whilst bringing it closer to the local community.

In the last few years, awareness has improved across the local community as to what a brilliant town park the tennis club operates within, and the need to deliver more structured physical activity opportunities, extending current provision in the park. Due to OTT now operating as more than just a tennis club, it has become increasingly obvious to the trustees that the club has a wider responsibility to the community than just the provision of tennis activity. Whilst its core activity is and always will be tennis delivery, the education of its overall membership and beyond to lead healthier and more social lives has become more important than just producing performance players (although this may also help produce better tennis players!).

By operating the OTT community stadia in true community fashion rather than in an isolated and protective manner, the clubs relationship with the Town Council has grown positively. Following the success of the Olympics and Paralympics in 2012, OTT was entrusted by the Town Council in 2013 to take over the whole park to deliver a pilot Oswestry Community Games to gauge interest in bringing local sports organizations from their isolated venues into a central venue to work together to deliver a fun activity day, and this worked very well on the day. The focus of these Games is very much on encouraging people whatever their age or ability to do more physically, improve their health, and the inclusion agenda is a vital ingredient to increasing participation.

Following its success in 2013, this is now a recognized annual event in Oswestry's park calendar and has grown to include our local arts organizations. Participation on the day has also grown from 500 to around 1000 people in 2015 with almost 40 local organizations coming together to deliver the Games. Organizations benefit from taking part by showing what their club offers to potential users, sharing good practice, working together, recruiting new members and having fun.

The spin off to OTT is that apart from the success of working with many sports and arts organizations from the local community and seeing the park used to its full effect, this event and our role within it support recruitment of new members. Using the park in this way has also encouraged other organizations to make use of it in a similar way.

My concluding thoughts would be to advise community stadia managers and practitioners to look at what your facility and its surrounding amenity area have to offer, work collaboratively (including other sports), and support broader community events that engage with your local community, all of which will help contribute to greater awareness of and participation in your site and provision.

Over the last decade, changes in the media landscape have given rise to new opportunities for community sport providers to market themselves at no cost. Here Mr Simon Lansley, of ConnectSport, offers an insight into how they can capitalize to share their work and help communicate the social value of their work.

Sharing the community sport message

Traditionally, the mainstream media has always relied on elite sport to satisfy their audience and drive newspaper sales or website visits. This has created the belief amongst those delivering at community or grassroots level that there is not much interest in their work amongst the general public, even when there may been tangible public health outcomes. Subsequently, with tight budgets focused on delivery, little or no attention is paid to marketing. In this short perspective, I hope to demonstrate the potential of bringing your programmes, your story and your impact to social media. This is particularly important for those working in or towards the healthy stadia agenda and are aiming to share their progress, impact or influence policy.

For many reasons the 'sport for development' sector is emerging from the shadows, as recognized by the UK Government's recent sports strategy which applauds the work of organizations which are 'outside' sport but using sport to benefit society. I worked for one of those, Street League (a major national football-based education and employment charity), for four years and witnessed first-hand the stories that are being told and the value they provide for local media. Before Street League, I also spent 15 years in the mainstream media at the UK's national news agency, The Press Association. It was a special place to work because journalistic principles, such as objectivity and the right to reply, were sacrosanct. More and more, however, it seems that in certain areas of newspaper industry, profit and loss has come to cloud editorial decision-making.

So when it comes to redressing the balance, thank goodness for social media, which has enabled community and grassroots sports providers to find and speak directly to their own audiences. For those working on, and towards, public health outcomes whether from sports stadia or from a community or grassroots sport organization, the message is simple. Sign up for free and get tweeting; stick to your key messages but be friendly, be conversational and eventually your audience – the people who care about, or benefit from what you're doing – will gravitate towards you. Most importantly, those people who follow you are your advocates. In other words, the people who will market your organization for free. This, in turn, has got even the most media-shy grassroots sport organizations thinking about how they appear to the wider world. If social media is your shop window, make sure you're selling yourself when potential customers happen to pass by. Whether it's the key messages on your website or what you're tweeting, a new funder could be checking you out at any time, while local journalists with an agenda are almost certainly scouring social media looking for someone who fits the bill.

Social media offers avenue to share your progress, your developments and your impact. If you can get your brand assets right online and this will also breed confidence amongst your delivery staff. It's almost certain that, thanks to the benefit you are bringing to the local community, they are proud to work for you and eager to 'walk the brand'. Involve them in the creation of your key messages, and encourage them to connect (online and offline) and build relationships with local journalists. Make sure they keep it short, sweet and to the point – too much jargon or detail will lose people's attention – and remember what you're selling needs to be of value to the media outlet's audience. Can your stadia provide an accessible space and place for local services? Can your programme help to solve a problem directly affecting the listeners of your local radio station? Provide case studies of real people, showing real impact in the community. We know from recent sport policy that evidencing social value is key. More than anything, remember you are having a real impact on society. So make sure you let people know.

Finally, we are pleased to receive and include a contribution from Mr Daniel Cade of Schwery Consulting. Daniel offers an insight into the challenges facing governing bodies of sport, mega events and sports venues themselves when considering the wider sustainability of sponsorship agreements, something that in addition to environmental and economic considerations, also includes social consideration such as health and well-being. Daniel will draw upon a number of examples, challenges and considerations when discussing the complex relationship between sport, sponsorship and sustainability (including health and well-being).

Sustainable sponsorship

The London Organising Committee of the Olympic and Paralympic Games (LOCOG) demonstrated sponsorship's true potential when it created an additional marketing rights designation for sustainability partners. It formed a working group among marketing partners with the aim to reach more people and inspire a step change in sustainable living. This move took LOCOG into unchartered territories for a major sport event organizer and should have paved the way for others to place sustainability issues on a higher footing. Indeed, as many would have hoped for sustainability to be considered in cooperation with sponsorship partners (London 2012 2011).

LOCOG offered each sustainability partner the opportunity to develop its own sustainability project for London 2012, in addition to assisting with the sustainability objectives of the organizing committee. BMW, for instance, through its role as 'Automotive Partner', wanted to increase public awareness of the most advanced fuel and CO^2 saving technologies. British Petroleum (BP) was the official 'Carbon Offset Partner' for the Games and was committed to offsetting all the CO^2 emissions for the 'Games Family Transport Service', as well as launching a spectator and partner activation programme and young leaders programme.

Traditional sponsorship practice is under increased scrutiny. As such, LOCOG's approach, which followed and built on that of its predecessor VANOC (Vancouver Organising Committee for the 2010 Olympic and Paralympic Winter Games), should have been among a group of good practices that triggered a renewed commitment to meaningful sponsorship deals within the sport industry that are more in tune with the times. However, there has yet to be credible progress on LOCOG's initiative in the three-and-a-half years since London 2012. Looking ahead, the Rio 2016 Sustainability Report (published in September 2014), which reports on 'detailed operational planning and pre-Games operations', highlights an acceptance of its potential influential role in raising awareness of sustainable lifestyle choices among spectators, sponsors and partners (Rio 2016 2014). The report goes on to identify sponsors as one of 12 key stakeholders, which it has engaged with 'in discussions [...] on partnerships to support [it's] sustainability objectives'. However, it did not explain any tangible outcomes of these discussions (Rio 2016 2014).

Debates surrounding the ethics of corporate sponsorship of sport and other cultural events will continue, especially surrounding companies that sell, or have sold, products that are deemed hazardous to the health of consumers and society in general. Indeed, for the London 2012 Olympics, controversy surrounded Dow Chemical, BP and Rio Tinto's partnerships due, as one campaigner put it, to the devastation these companies have caused to communities around the world. Moreover, Coca-Cola and McDonalds have resulted in criticism as sponsors due to their association and potential contribution to existing public health issues, such as obesity and diabetes, which currently plague the UK and beyond. This contribution rather focuses its attention on the practice of sustainable sponsorship. It highlights some of the challenges that other major events may have encountered in an attempt to 'clear the way' for future event organizers to continue to experiment and innovate within this field for the benefit of sponsors, organizers and society (GreenNet 2016).

Traditional sponsorship practice, that associates a brand to a particular property or event, can amass goodwill through brand association among a target population. However, it does not address this author's perception of high levels of animosity that currently perceived, developed and delivered towards the corporate sector, and may even serve to aggravate the situation. In an effort to regain trust, a more hands-on approach, as demonstrated by

LOCOG and its sponsors, can enable other sponsors and sport organizations to communicate a long-term commitment to responsible business practice to a broader target audience. This practice can be termed sustainable sponsorship. Sustainable sponsorship in sport can be defined as the sponsorship of a sport property or event whereby both parties are responsible for a long-term positive impact on society or the environment. Sustainable sponsorship can be more effective, and believable, if it is used as an expression of a long-standing commitment to corporate social responsibility (CSR) or sustainability (both terms, CSR and sustainability are used interchangeably in this section).

Establishing a sustainable sponsorship agreement without a firm CSR grounding is pointless. Social media has seen to it that customers and the general public are well-informed and can see through organizations making ambiguous claims. However, implemented under the right circumstances, sustainable sponsorship can be used as an effective means to communicate to a number of stakeholders (current and future employees, public authorities, pressure groups), helping to maximize opportunities and minimize risks. It appears important to consider the potential of operations aligned with such an approach. Indeed, many large corporate entities have now developed sound CSR practices that make up part of their DNA. Coca-Cola, for instance, has been very public about its intentions to become water neutral by 2020. Since 2004, Coca-Cola has replenished an estimated 153.6 billion litres of water back to communities and nature through 209 community water projects in 61 countries (Coca-Cola 2015).

Sport organizations are intrinsically different to companies in other industries, yet their motivation for implementing a social responsibility strategy is not. Sport's unique influence on society has helped to guide some sport organizations to identify areas in which they can harness their sport's positive values to benefit communities. For example, UEFA works with selected partners across Europe to address social issues connected to football. Since 2008, it has supported, promoted and reported on several social responsibility projects, under the umbrella slogan of 'Respect', during its EURO tournaments (Schwery Consulting 2008; UEFA 2013; EURO 2016 (2015)). However, collaboration between corporate sponsors and sport organizations on projects that create a sustainable impact on society has so far been lacking. And, until now, issues regarding the alignment of different CSR strategies have perhaps justified the relative inaction. These issues are outlined below.

Since CSR focus areas and implementation methods will vary from one organisation to the next, logic tells us that sustainable sponsorship should not be a 'one size fits all' approach. In a different approach to Coca-Cola, Nike's environmental CSR goals focus on producing environmentally friendly products. One of the initiatives it has developed is the Nike Considered Index. It uses this to rate the ecological footprint of the products that it manufactures. A Considered product is one that has been made with the fewest possible materials and can be easily recycled into a new product or 'safely returned to nature' at the end of its life (Nike 2015). These companies' choices will define their overall strategy, influencing day-to-day decisions, like sponsorship. Rather than making ad hoc charitable donations, they will support meaningful projects that meet specific business goals and stakeholder expectations. Sustainable sponsorship practitioners would need to align the CSR commitments of different organisations to enable them to support a shared, or unified, social goal.

Appearing to have good intentions does not necessarily mean that you are 'doing good'. This is one of the most widely used, and necessary, CSR industry clichés. To increase the chances of having a positive impact, and not causing harm, good things must be done well. A responsible 'do no harm' approach can only be validated by the use of an impact assessment. Both UEFA and Nike have policies that dictate the use of external evaluations to assess the social impact of projects that they support. In relation to sustainable sponsorship initiatives, this means that projects should not be designed only for their alignment with supporting partners but, primarily, because they help to combat a problem affecting society. Selecting a suitable project should be a bottom-up process that starts by assessing the potential impact of the project on its stakeholders and then looks for the alignments among partners' CSR strategies. This added variable makes the task appear slightly more tedious.

Time pressures raise the challenge of alignment if the objective is to create sustainable sponsorship agreements for a one-off event. Until LOCOG, the prospect of involving so many partners (host countries and cities, local implementing organisations, sponsors, sport federations and associations) in sustainable sponsorship project negotiations has been a deterrent, although that is not to say it has not happened on a smaller scale. The practice of effective time management is necessary to ensure that, instead of being a hindrance to progress, multi-sector partnerships are nurtured to create synergies that mobilise the skills and resources of each partner group. The potential to strengthen the impact of a project and meet the needs of all partners and stakeholders is great.

To conclude, there should be little doubt that the sponsorship industry will adapt to changing times and find the necessary solutions to sustainable sponsorship. One of which might be to empower local non-governmental organizations to determine the alignments. Given the time and funding to investigate the partners' expectations, these organizations are best placed to come up with an idea that suits everyone. Their knowledge and awareness of the issues affecting society should allow them to provide relevant and viable options to the other partners. In this new era, when the 'large and global' will be judged more and more by how they treat the 'small and local', continuing on the traditional sport sponsorship path is simply not enough. It is in the best interests of the parties involved in agreements to overcome the challenges and adopt a sustainable sponsorship approach, for their own economic benefit and for the benefit of society.

Concluding comments

The contributions presented within this applied article offer a range of perspectives from those involved in the healthy stadia agenda. Considerations from international, national and local perspectives, including operations and interventions in professional sport clubs and grassroots or community settings, have been presented. These contributions support the notion that the healthy stadia, whilst an established applied concept, is a growing research area. Moreover, a range of perspectives on the need to raise communication of the healthy stadia agenda across various media have been discussed. We hope this insight establishes further interest, discussion and research on, and around, the healthy stadia agenda. Furthermore, we hope that this insight acts as a catalyst to strengthen the dialogue and partnerships between researchers and applied practitioners.

Disclosure statement

No potential conflict of interest was reported by the authors.

References

Bangsbo, J., P. Krustrup, and J. Dvorak. 2014. "Special Issue: Football for Health – Prevention and Treatment of Non-Communicable Diseases across the Lifespan through Football." *Scandinavian Journal of Medicine & Science in Sport* 24 (S1): 1–150.

Coca-Cola. 2015. "Coca-Cola on Track to Meet 100% Water Replenishment Goal." *Coca-Cola*, August 25. Accessed January 7, 2016. http://www.coca-colacompany.com/press-center/press-releases/coca-cola-on-track-to-meet-100-water-replenishment-goal/

Curran, K., B. Drust, and D. Richardson. 2014. "'I Just Want to Watch the Match': A Practitioner's Reflective Account of Men's Health Themed Match Day Events at an English Premier League Football Club." *Soccer & Society* 15 (6): 919–933.

Drygas, W., J. Ruszkowska, M. Philpott, O. BjOrkstrOm, M. Parker, R. Ireland, and F. Roncarolo. 2013. "Good Practices and Health Policy Analysis in European Sports Stadia: Results from the 'Healthy Stadia' Project." *Health Promotion International* 28 (2): 157–165.

EURO 2016. 2015. "Social Responsibility & Sustainability – One-Year-to-Go Report, 2015." *UEFA*. Accessed January 7, 2016. http://www.uefa.org/MultimediaFiles/Download/uefaorg/General/02/26/41/78/2264178_DOWNLOAD.pdf

GreenNet. 2016. "World's Worst Polluters Sponsor 'Greenest' Olympics." *GreenNet*. Accessed January 7, 2016. https://www.gn.apc.org/network/news/worlds-worst-polluters-sponsor-greenest-olympics

van Hilvoorde, I., J. Vorstenbosch, and I. Devisch. 2010. "Philosophy of Sport in Belgium and the Netherlands: History and Characteristics." *Journal of the Philosophy of Sport* 37 (2): 225–236.

Hunt, K., S. Wyke, C. M. Gray, A. S. Anderson, A. Brady, C. Bunn, and P. T. Donnan. 2014. "A Gender-Sensitised Weight Loss and Healthy Living Programme for Overweight and Obese Men Delivered by Scottish Premier League Football Clubs (FFIT): A Pragmatic Randomised Controlled Trial." *The Lancet* 383 (9924): 1211–1221. doi: http://dx.doi.org/10.1016/S0140-6736(13)62420-4.

Kuper, S. Ajax. 2003. *The Dutch, The War*. London: Orion.

London 2012. 2011. "A Blueprint for Change." *London 2012*, April. Accessed January 7, 2016. http://learninglegacy.independent.gov.uk/documents/pdfs/sustainability/2-london-2012-sustainability-report-a-blueprint-for-change.pdf

Martin, A., S. Morgan, D. Parnell, M. Philpott, A. Pringle, M. Rigby, A. Taylor, and J. Topham. 2016. "Editorial: A Perspective from Key Stakeholders on Football and Health Improvement." *Soccer & Society* 17 (2): 175–182.

Nike. 2015. "Produce Design – Considered Design Index." *Nike*. Accessed January 7, 2016. http://www.nikebiz.com/crreport/content/environment/4-1-1-product-design.php?cat=product-design

Oppenhuisen, J., and L. van Zoonen. 2006. "Supporters or Customers? Fandom, Marketing and the Political Economy of Dutch Football." *Soccer and Society* 7 (1): 62–75.

Parnell, D., A. Pringle, J. McKenna, S. Zwolinsky, Z. Rutherford, J. Hargreaves, L. Trotter, M. Rigby, and D. Richardson. 2014. "Reaching Older People with PA Delivered in Football Clubs: The Reach, Adoption and Implementation Characteristics of the Extra Time Programme." *BMC Public Health* 15. doi: http://dx.doi.org/10.1186/s12889-015-1560-5. http://www.biomedcentral.com/1471-2458/15/220

Parnell, D., and A. Pringle. 2016. "Football and Health Improvement: An Emerging Field." *Soccer and Society* 17 (2): 171–174.

Parnell, D., and D. Richardson. 2014. "Introduction." *Soccer and Society* 15 (6): 823–827.

Rio 2016. 2014. "Embracing Change – Rio 2016 Sustainability Report." *Rio 2016*, September. Accessed January 7, 2016. http://www.rio2016.com/sites/default/files/parceiros/rio_2016_sustainability_report_sept2014.pdf

Schwery Consulting. 2008. "UEFA EURO 2008 – Football & Social Responsibility Evaluation Report." *UEFA*, October. Accessed January 7, 2016. http://www.uefa.com/multimediafiles/download/uefa/keytopics/82/57/46/825746_download.pdf

van Slobbe, M., J. Vermeulen, and M. Koster. 2013. "The Making of an Ethnically Diverse Management: Contested Cultural Meanings in a Dutch Amateur Football Club." *Sport in Society* 16 (10): 1360–1374.

Spaaij, R. 2007. "Football Hooliganism in the Netherlands: Patterns of Continuity and Change." *Soccer and Society* 8 (2–3): 316–334.

Tiessen-Raaphoorst, A., and K. Breedveld. 2007. *Sport in the Netherlands: A Short Introduction*. The Hague: Social and Cultural Planning Office.

UEFA. 2013. "Social Responsibility Report – UEFA EURO 2012 Creating History Together." *UEFA*. Accessed January 7, 2016. http://www.uefa.com/MultimediaFiles/Download/uefaorg/General/02/10/87/62/2108762_DOWNLOAD.pdf

Who ate all the pies? The importance of food in the Australian sporting experience

Keith D. Parry, Timothy Hall and Alastair Baxter

ABSTRACT

Australians watch live sport in large numbers and traditionally consume high quantities of meat pies, chips and beer within stadiums. However, the food and beverage preferences of stadium-attending Australian sports fans are not well understood, particularly in comparison to their North American and European peers. This paper utilized a survey-based approach to understand the satisfaction of fans of Australia's national Rugby Union team with stadiums in Australia. While food and beverage offerings were found to be a particular point of dissatisfaction, the price and service quality were found to be of greater concern than the healthiness of these. The study also drew on the researchers' observations and knowledge of recent Australian stadium redevelopments to examine how the traditional offerings may be changing. We conclude that in order to attract greater attendances from a wider market, stadiums in Australia need to provide more varied, higher quality, healthy food and beverage offerings that are both affordable and easy to eat.

Introduction

Every year, over two-fifths of Australians aged 15 and over attend a sporting event. This equates to almost 8 million adults attending each year (ABS 2012). However, while the average 2012 attendance figure for the Australian Football League was almost 33,000 attendees per match, the figures in other Australian sporting codes do not match this number (Sporting Intelligence 2013). For instance, the average figure in the National Rugby League was only 16,423, which falls some way short of the National Football League (NFL) (68,278), German Bundesliga (43,331), English Premier League (36,464) and the Major League Baseball (MLB) for example (30,517) (Barrett 2016). Indeed, German Association Football team Borussia Dortmund averaged 80,451, NFL American Football team Dallas Cowboys 88,531 and NCAA American Football team Michigan 112,252 fans per match in 2012 (Sporting Intelligence 2013). With the amount of sport available on television increasing (Rowe and Scherer 2014), Australian sports teams may find it increasingly difficult to encourage an increasingly sedentary population to attend live events, especially if compounded by additional negative factors such as poor quality food and beverage at the stadium venues. This inactivity creates an interesting social obligation on professional sporting bodies to not only use sport as a spectacle for television, but to also encourage fans to be an active part of a healthier, sport inspired lifestyle (Anagnostopoulos 2011; Inoue et al. 2015; Parnell et al. 2015).

Academic studies into attendance and/or spectator satisfaction at sports events have been conducted across a number of continents, including North America, Europe, Asian, and Australasia, and in a number of sports, including golf, American football, basketball, association football and rugby league. Bouchet et al. (2011) argue that sports spectators share common characteristics and so it is possible to compare spectators across sports, time and location. Analyses of these studies have revealed a number of factors influencing attendance at sporting events. In a Spanish setting it was found that attendance at sporting events was linked to social class (Lera-López, Ollo-López, and Rapún-Gárate 2012). Those spectators of middle and high social class, with average to high level of education and socio-economic status, had higher levels of attendance at professional sporting events. Gender differences have also been identified in the experiences of sports spectators. Men were more likely than women to evaluate the performance of athletes competing in the sport while fantasizing that they were a part of the action. In such a way, men would achieve a sense of flow during sporting competitions. Conversely, women were more likely to appreciate the aesthetic beauty of the sport performance, by either men or women, and to evaluate the performance of athletes (Madrigal 2006).

There are many factors that influence a person's decision to attend a sporting event, such as price, transport, and availability of competing leisure activities. One factor, which has been examined in some detail, is that of the stadium itself. A number of studies found that the physical environment of a sports stadium influenced attendance (Hill and Christine Green 2000; Wheaton 2007; Yusof and Lee 2008); however, there is also need for research into the less tangible elements of the sporting experience. Similarly, in Australia there are a range of influences which impacts on the less tangible elements of the sporting experience. This paper considers the importance of food in the Australian sporting context using a case study of fans of Australia's national Rugby Union team (commonly referred to as the Wallabies).

At the stadium

Once at a venue, perceptions of service quality will impact on a non-avid spectator's satisfaction, which in turn influences re-patronage intentions (Wakefield and Blodgett 1996) as spectators who enjoy spending time at the stadium are inclined to return to the stadium for future games (Wakefield and Sloan 1995; Greenwell, Fink, and Pastore 2002; Blank, Sweeney, and Fuller 2014). However, it is noted that most sporting teams will have a core of hardened fans who will attend regardless of factors such as team performance, weather conditions and stadium facilities. When spectators return to a stadium repeatedly over time, a sense of identification with a venue can be developed (Penny and Redhead 2009). This love of place has been termed topophilia (Bale 1996; Ramshaw and Gammon 2010) and home stadiums have been found to generate location pride, awareness and geographic memories (Ramshaw and Gammon 2010). Bale (1996, 167) suggests that stadium developers and planners have 'too often ignored the power of topophilia', including the influence of food and beverage offerings.

In terms of the venue's sportscape, it has been shown that satisfaction is influenced by whether or not spectators feel crowded or cramped, and, therefore, poorly designed seating, with limited elbow room, impact on spectator satisfaction (Lambrecht, Kaefer, and Ramenofsky 2009). Wakefield and Sloan (1995) found that perceived crowding had the strongest effect on spectators' desires to stay or leave a stadium. In addition, where spectators have difficulty reaching important destinations, including the food and beverage outlets, there is evidence of increased spectator frustration and a decreased desire to stay at the venue and to return to future games (Wakefield and Sloan 1995; Wakefield, Blodgett, and Sloan 1996; Greenwell, Fink, and Pastore 2002; Sarstedt et al. 2014). The helpfulness of employees/volunteers can also impact (both positively and negatively) on spectator satisfaction (Lambrecht, Kaefer, and Ramenofsky 2009). Wakefield and Sloan (1995) also identified stadium food prices as an area of dissatisfaction for many sports fans. Spectators with access to hospitality facilities (such as complementary refreshments, easier/closer parking, private seating) have been found to be more satisfied with the sportscape than general admission spectators (Lambrecht, Kaefer, and Ramenofsky 2009).

Food choices

Food plays an important role in the stadium experience (Sukalakamala, Sukalakamala, and Young 2013). Although there is increased awareness of the impact of diet on health, the food offered to spectators at sports stadiums continues to be of poor quality and typically is not healthy (Ireland and Watkins 2010). While there is no one definition of healthy eating options, organizations such as the World Health Organization (WHO) offer discussions around levels of fat, sugars and cholesterol in foods (WHO 2015). Lee, Heere, and Chung (2013) draw attention to the tendency of sports teams to outsource food and beverage offerings resulting in little or no influence or control over the food and beverage sold in the venues in which they play, and frequently have no healthy eating policy (Drygas et al. 2013). Stadium food has typically been similar to the high carbohydrate, fat and calorie offerings found in fast food restaurants (Sukalakamala, Sukalakamala, and Young 2013).

In MLB, as far back as the 1990s, there have been a (limited) number of healthy options available at venues, such as frozen yogurt, teriyaki bowls and fresh fruit (Roan 1997). However, the more traditional offerings of hot dogs, pretzels and peanuts have remained dominant. Newer venues such as Icahn Stadium, a multipurpose stadium in New York City that opened in 2005, offer healthier food options including pizzas made on whole-wheat pitas, wraps, grilled sandwiches and low-fat organic parfaits (Fabricant 2005). One MLB club, the San Diego Padres, has even combined in-game physical activity breaks for spectators with healthy and competitively priced foods (Yancey et al. 2009). Choices for food and delivery options have also increased in a number of venues. Yankee Stadium in the New York borough of the Bronx serves Latin food in addition to the obligatory hot dog and hamburger (Fernandez 2007). Miami's Sun Life Stadium has served multi-cultural menus including Handmade Turkey Empanadas, baked potatoes and a 'Pizza Dog' – a foot-long hot dog baked in pizza dough. This variety demonstrates that stadiums across North America seem to be changing by offering greater food diversity including some healthier options.

A number of stadiums, such as Rio Tinto Stadium in Utah, now offer in seat food delivery (PR Newswire 2009). Elsewhere in the United States, the San Francisco 49ers have developed a stadium app that shows the length of queues for beverages while the Aviva Stadium in Ireland utilizes an app that allows customers to pre-order beverages (IRFU 2014). In Australia the Penrith Panthers are introducing a digital waiter app (Jones 2015) and the Sydney Cricket Ground (SCG) has introduced Q-Hopping technology that allows fans to order and purchase food and beverage using a mobile device (SCG 2014).

Perhaps in response to the limitations of stadium food tailgating, where fans set up portable grills or barbeques in stadium car parks and cook their own food, is a popular North American alternative to in stadium dining. Tailgating has been historically associated with College football in southeastern states of North America (Keaton, Watanabe, and Gearhart 2015), but its popularity is growing. While the primary motivation for attending a tailgate may be to socialize with friends and family (Drenten et al. 2009), food is an important element (James, Steven Breezeel, and Ross 2001) and such activities allow fans to choose alternative foods, with tailgating menus now including ribs, steaks and seafood (Russell 2011).

While some North American stadiums have made moves to offer a greater range of good tasting food, many teams and stadiums still need to make greater effort to provide menus that reflect the needs of their fans (Lee, Heere, and Chung 2013). In many European countries, sports stadiums are found in less affluent areas that are often surrounded by low-quality housing (Drygas et al. 2013). The spectators that attend these venues may be more familiar and comfortable with less healthy options. In the United Kingdom (UK), Ireland and Watkins (2010) identified that healthy eating is not something that most fans associated with Association football grounds. They found that such fans described the food on offer with terms such as "awful', 'abysmal' and 'atrocious" and highlighted a lack of both choice and options for those with dietary needs (2010, 684). Moreover, according to a YouGov report, attendees at UK sports events believe that food is unhealthy (Tobin 2013). In addition to being of poor quality, food in European stadiums is also perceived to be overpriced (Miles and Rines 2004; Sukalakamala, Sukalakamala, and Young 2013). For example, in their annual survey into the price of attending football matches, the BBC (2015) reveal that a pie can cost up to £4.50 (AU$9.13 in January 2016) at some stadiums. However, it has also been found that some fans see 'the match is a place for an occasional unhealthy pie [which] means it is unlikely that football fans will take easily to pies being removed from menus' (Ireland and Watkins 2010).

In Australia meat pies are rather more than an occasional match day food. The meat pie is a traditional food at Australian sporting events and has been equated with the American hotdog (Kovaricek 2010). The meat pie is such traditional fare in Australia that in 2013 one of Australia's iconic venues, the Melbourne Cricket Ground (MCG) alone sold over 300,000 pies (Veenhuyzen 2014). The MCG also sold 600,00 servings of hot chips, 95,000 jam doughnuts, 65,000 burgers and 40,000 pizzas in 2013 (Rolfe 2014). Across Australia, stadium menus have been rather predictable with meat pies, hotdogs, chips and burgers dominating, all of which are typically washed down with beer. As with other countries, Australian venues have been criticized for over-pricing their food and beverage offerings (Tarbert 2015). However, studies into Australian fans' perceptions of these offerings are limited.

Sports fans are not homogenous and there are differences in the behaviours and attitudes of fans of different sports (Parry, Jones, and Wann 2014), and so it is important for service providers to understand the wants and needs of their particular fan base to ensure a satisfying experience. In its simplest form, service providers need to understand the different wants and needs of male, female and family spectators. With the non-homogeneity of sports fans in mind, it is important that each sporting code gains an understanding of their fans and their expectations. Furthermore, while a small number of studies have focused on Australian sports fans (for instance Hill and Christine Green 2000; Hall, O'Mahony, and Vieceli 2010), the Australian market remains poorly understood. Drawing on data from a survey of sports fans and the researchers' engagement in this field, this study aims to bridge these gaps by investigating Australian fans' perceptions of sports stadiums and the food and beverage offerings in these.

Methodology

To facilitate comparison to previous research, the methodology adopted in this study was based upon those used in the studies by Wakefield and Sloan (1995) in their study into sport service quality in Japan and America, Wakefield, Blodgett, and Sloan's (1996) investigation into spectators' desire to stay at sporting events, Yoshida and James (2011) and Byon, Zhang, and Baker's (2013) examinations of service quality. A concurrent mixed methods, survey-based design was utilized.

Participants

Supporters of the Wallabies team on one of the Australian Rugby Union's membership databases were provided with an email invitation to complete an electronic survey on behalf of the researchers. A total of 293 completed surveys were utilized as part of a pilot study in stadium satisfaction. The majority of those completing the survey were male (87.7%) and participants were primarily over the age of 41, with this category representing 95% of the sample group (mean = 57.8, SD 10.0).

The majority of participants (93.3%, $n = 249$) were located in the state of New South Wales (NSW), which is on the east coast of Australia. The two NSW-based stadiums featured in the survey were ANZ Stadium (27.1%) and Allianz Stadium (51.7%), both of which are in Sydney. However, it was noted that some of these members were prepared to travel interstate to attend games with responses from fans indicating that both Suncorp Stadium in Queensland (17.8%) and Etihad Stadium in Victoria (3.4%) were the most recently visited stadium. Of all respondents, over 60% had attended a game within one month prior to the survey. It was evident that there is a social element to attending a rugby match with 55.9% of respondents indicating that they attended a match with family, while a further 40.5% indicated that they attended with friends. Interestingly, an overwhelming majority of female respondents (73.0%) indicated that they attended with family. With sociality playing such an important role, it was hypothesized that food would also be important for these fans.

Measures

The questionnaire contained three sections. The first section asked participants to provide basic demographic information regarding gender, age, postcode and details on their most recent visit to a sports stadium. In the second section, participants indicated their agreement with a series of statements based on their feelings towards the stadium they had identified. The survey utilized eight scales; getting to and around the stadium; stadium aesthetics; entertainment; screens and scoreboards; seating; food and beverage; stadium atmosphere; and stadium management – the survey scales can be found in Appendix 1.

To enhance the reliability and validity of the research tool existing scales (that had previously been tested) were used, or adapted, for the purpose of this study. Additional questions relating to the design of the stadium and topophilia were added to scales previously utilized by Wakefield and Sloan (1995), Wakefield, Blodgett, and Sloan (1996), Yoshida and James (2011) and Byon, Zhang, and Baker (2013). Additional questions were added following discussions with a leading sport architect and based on the researchers' knowledge and observations of sports fans. The survey was then piloted with a small sample to test the face validity of the new research tool. The questionnaire was found to work well and needed few changes.

Participants were provided with multiple Likert-type scale items, with five-point response options, for each scale ranging from 1 = not at all to 5 = very much. A single pre-existing scale could not be found that covered all aspects of the sporting experience and so a new scale was developed for this study. Mean scores were calculated for each individual scale item and, to allow comparisons across scales, for each scale. Given that a five-point Likert-type system was used, a mean score of greater than 2.50 was taken to indicate that respondents were satisfied with a particular scale or item.

The final section provided respondents with the chance to provide their thoughts of the most positive and most negative aspects of the stadium via two open-ended questions: *What aspects of the stadium do you consider to be particularly positive?* and *What aspects of the stadium do you consider to be particularly negative?* Answers to these two questions were collated and then initially displayed via a word cloud, before being thematically analysed. Word clouds present the most commonly used words arranged with the size of the word corresponding to the frequency of its occurrence in responses. Such a visual trend analysis approach has been dubbed as a 'simple yet effective approach' (Hunt, Gao, and Xue 2014) that is able to provide instant insight into responses. Such an approach has been used previously in a variety of studies such as those by Ahearn (2014), Hunt, Gao, and Xue (2014) and Guggenheim et al. (2015).

Findings and discussion

As shown in Table 1, participants were most satisfied with Seating and Stadium Management and least satisfied with Entertainment and Food and Beverage offerings. The scores for the Food and Beverage scale (1.89) and the Entertainment scale (1.79) were considerably lower

Table 1. Scale mean scores.

Scale	Mean score
Seating	3.77
Stadium management	3.17
Getting to and around the stadium	3.16
At the stadium (Topophilia)	2.98
Screens and scoreboards	2.87
Aesthetics	2.79
Food and beverage	1.89
Entertainment	1.79

Table 2. Food and beverage scale item mean scores.

Food & Beverage					
	All stadiums	ANZ	Allianz	Etihad	Suncorp
This stadium offers a wide variety of food choices	2.16	2.21	2.09	2.20	2.17
This stadium offers a wide variety of beverages choices	2.14	1.94	2.13	2.67	2.29
This stadium offers good tasting food	2.03	1.97	2.03	2.00	2.02
This stadium offers fast service for beverages	1.98	1.75	1.86	2.17	2.55
This stadium offers healthy food options	1.83	1.76	1.83	1.60	1.86
This stadium offers a variety of ways to order and receive your food	1.76	1.66	1.71	2.60	1.88
This stadium offers a variety of ways to order and receive your beverages	1.75	1.55	1.68	2.40	2.05
This stadium offers reasonably priced beverages	1.70	1.43	1.72	2.67	1.81
This stadium offers reasonably priced food	1.66	1.43	1.64	2.20	1.90
Overall	1.89	1.74	1.85	2.28	2.06

Figure 1. Word cloud of responses to the questions. *What aspects of the stadium do you consider to be particularly negative?*

than other scales, and this indicates dissatisfaction with these elements. However, it should be noted that the ARU members are likely to have personal and emotional connections to the Wallabies. Therefore, such traditional spectators are likely to be less consumption

Figure 2. The Stadium Club at the Adelaide Oval.

Figure 3. 'Food court' style food area in SCG Northern Stand.

focused, with entertainment and other commodification-driven features of sport having less influence over them (Giulianotti 2002). The low score for the Food and Beverage scale was therefore identified as being the greatest point of dissatisfaction for participants and required further investigation.

Food and Beverage was the second-lowest ranked scale and no single scale items received a mean rating higher than 2.16 out of 5, with the price of food rated the lowest (mean = 1.66). Of the stadiums included within the survey, ANZ Stadium was rated the poorest in seven of the nine scale items. Etihad Stadium proved to be the 'best' performer for Food and Beverage with an overall mean rating of 2.28 Table 2.

Through an analysis of qualitative responses, it was evident that participants enjoyed those stadiums that were in close proximity to city centres, as the availability of restaurants

Figure 4. Microbrewery in SCG Northern Stand.

and bars allowed them to socialize before and after the game with friends. In terms of food and beverage offerings, positive attitudes only otherwise referred to the convenience of within-stadium outlets. However, in response to the question *What aspects of the stadium do you consider to be particularly negative?* there were numerous food and beverage-related responses and the word cloud below (see Figure 1) clearly shows food and beverage provision as a particular point of dissatisfaction.

Responses to this question indicated that there is a need for a greater variety of food options at stadiums. Some participants were looking for options that present healthier alternatives to traditional fast foods and they are also looking for increased quality in what they can buy. Comments indicated that the poor food quality and the lack of healthy options meant that some participants did not eat at stadiums:

> No healthy food options – I do not eat at the ground because of this.
>
> Terrible food choices (no fresh/healthy food at all) & exorbitant prices.

However, comments relating to the food and beverage options available, and in particular to healthy options, were far less common than comments on the price and time taken to be served. Terms such as 'extreme' and 'exorbitant' were used to describe the prices of food and beverage at venues. In addition to the price of food and beverages, respondents also indicated that there was a limited number of ways in which to order and receive food. This limited number of delivery options then results in difficulties around queuing for food and beverage that further impacts on the fan experience. The standard of service was a common theme with a number of respondents suggesting that inexperienced staff contributed towards poor levels of service quality. The frustration with the food and beverage options appears to be long-standing and was exemplified in the following comment:

> Catering has always been an issue, many surveys over the years with limited change.

The high price of food in Australian stadiums has been criticized by fans and the media alike and it is perhaps unsurprising that this should also be the case in this study. Australian fans want affordable or 'value for money' food that is served quickly, and increasingly without the need to queue. As was found to be the case with European fans, it is worrying that these considerations are believed to be more significant than healthy food options (Miles and Rines 2004; Ireland and Watkins 2010; Sukalakamala, Sukalakamala, and Young 2013). While in the UK having a pie at a sports match is seen as being a guilty pleasure (Ireland and Watkins 2010), this is not the case in Australia as pies are much more popular in the wider society. In Australia, the tradition of eating pies (and similar foods) may therefore be hard to move away from. Although this may be more evident for Australian males rather than females where there is some evidence to support Australian male's preference for both fast food and meat options (Savige et al. 2007).

Recent developments

Recent Australian stadium redevelopments may suggest that the tradition of poor food and beverage offering is changing. The Adelaide Oval and SCG Northern Stand redevelopments have included better quality food options, which spectators appear to have embraced. Between 2008 and 2014, the Adelaide Oval was redeveloped to include a new mid-price corporate product called the Stadium Club. The food offered at the Stadium Club included the 'Hill of Grace Restaurant', an à la carte restaurant specializing in local seasonal food and local beverages.

As mentioned in an email to the research team from Adam Hannon, 23 September 2015, the stadium operator took a 'leap of faith' initially in developing the Stadium Club, as nothing similar had been offered at a stadium in South Australia. It has proven to be popular as Stadium Club memberships reached 96% capacity for the 2014/15 and 2015/16 seasons, memberships were at 100% capacity (with a waiting list) for the upcoming 2016/17 season and event day attendances totalled 40,265 from March 2014 to March 2015.

The 2012–2014 SCG Northern Stand redevelopment included a 'food court' style food area and a microbrewery bar area offering higher quality and healthier food options, such as Doyles brand seafood and Noodle Shack brand Asian food, and higher quality custom beers. These healthier and higher quality food and beverage options constitute 11 of the 31 food and beverage counters in the redeveloped stand.

As with the Adelaide Oval example, the food and beverage offering in the new SCG redevelopment has also been very popular with spectators. In a conversation with the researchers SCG Trustee Stuart MacGill, 23 January 2015, revealed that food and beverage sales for the opening 2015 cricket Test match surpassed the equivalent 2012 sales by 40%, exceeding SCG Trust estimates by 30%. Interestingly, the new SCG food court still offers burgers, pizzas and pies (albeit made-to-order burgers and pizzas and high-quality gourmet meat pies). The popularity of the food at the new food court area may have as much to do with food quality as it does with being a healthy option but gourmet products may be expected to contain higher quality ingredients and should, therefore, be healthier. Despite the range of perceived healthier options, there is still only a limited vegetarian offering available with a small number of outlets; providing an inadequate range of vegetarian meals. The food court and associated outdoor dining area are also open for major events held at other venues within the SCG precinct, expanding and enhancing the food and beverage offerings at adjacent grounds and improving the pre and post-match spectator experience.

Both of these examples would suggest Australian spectators are willing to move away from low-quality unhealthy food options if given a reasonable alternative. However, as was found in Lee, Heere, and Chung's (2013) study, stadium operators in Australia commonly outsource the operation of food and beverage outlets to external contractors. By relinquishing control over these offerings, Australian stadiums do not have direct control over the choices provided to spectators and cannot ensure that healthy options are provided. In addition, external contractors typically operate a business model where costs are minimized and may prefer to offer cheap to produce food and beverages, again typified by pies, with larger returns than more expensive or more time-intensive alternatives. As sporting organizations seek to increase the stadium attendance, there may be a case for a revised business model which is driven by the need to provide a range of quality, healthy food options to meet the needs of fans of all ages, as opposed to a business model which pushes quality down in order to maximize profits.

The future for stadium food in Australia

Food and beverage offerings were found to be a point of frustration for fans of the Wallabies. From an analysis of qualitative answers, this frustration was due to a combination of the price, the ordering and delivery options, and the perceived poor service quality. In particular, food and beverage prices were seen to being too high for the quality and variety of food on offer. While the Etihad Stadium and the MCG in Melbourne have recently dropped food prices (Rolfe 2015), these are still higher than those at sporting events elsewhere. For instance the Augusta National Golf Course, home to the US Masters maintains much lower prices with the highest priced food item only US$3 (AU$4.28 in January 2016) and the most expensive beverage is US$5 (AU$7.14) for an imported beer (News Limited 2015). The variety of food available in North American venues is also certainly not seen in Australian stadiums, and Australian sports fans are not unaware of such global comparisons and are unhappy with being asked to pay AU$5 for a bottle of water or AU$5 for a pie of poor quality (Cherny 2015).

Australia lags behind other nations in terms of food and beverage offerings in its stadiums and the data from this study reveals the levels of dissatisfaction felt by Australian spectators with the traditional offerings. Our observations of recent stadium redevelopments reveal that Australian spectators have embraced changes in stadium food and beverages, as shown by membership and sales figures for the Adelaide Oval and the SCG redevelopments, respectively. The onus is now on other Australian stadiums who are yet to improved their food and beverage offerings to follow the example of the Adelaide Oval, the SCG and their North American counterparts to provide more varied, higher quality, healthier food and beverage options that represent better value for money. Australian spectators are likely to always eat all the pies but are now demanding these are high quality, healthy and value for money.

Recommendations

For stadium food options (outside of corporate à la carte offerings) to be considered realistic alternatives to the current pies, chips and pizzas we would recommend a number of principles be followed. Any alternate would need to be:

Figure 5. Food court at Westfield Miranda, Sydney.

- At a similar or better price than current offerings;
- Quick to order/be served;
- Easy to eat (ideally with one hand);
- Portion controlled meals factoring in nutritional requirements;
- An existing popular food choice in the city the stadium is located.

One suitable alternative, which seemingly follows all of these principles, is the Australian version of the Japanese Nori or sushi roll. Sushi rolls are increasingly popular in Australian shopping mall food courts (Langley 2015), they are quick and easy to order and serve (they are almost always pre-prepared), they can be eaten with one hand, are generally healthy (although this depends on filling) and at AU\$3–\$3.50 each they are cheaper than pies and burgers. One added benefit of such an offering is that non-meat fillings are common and they would provide a good option for those spectators who do not eat meat. Further research investigating female and family food preferences would benefit stadium food service providers particularly if this has been one of the barriers to attending live sport venues as reflected in low attendance figures for females.

We also recommend that future research explore the offerings found in the food courts of large shopping malls (such as Westfield shopping centres in Australia – see Figure 5). These food courts have infrastructure and patronage similarities to Australian stadiums and yet provide multiple and varied, high-quality options to customers. The SCG Northern Stand redevelopment has shown the food court layout can physically work in the stadium environment and further research should explore the feasibility and benefits of including such options in stadiums.

While these recommendations offer the potential to draw larger crowds from more diverse population groups to stadiums, there will be a minimal impact unless such changes are well marketed and communicated. This marketing also needs to take place within stadiums so that options that are healthier and family orientated are easily identified and accessible. This information should include the nutritional value of food and beverage offerings. While food may often be the focus of healthy eating, it is also important to offer healthier alternatives to beverages such as soft drinks, which contain high sugar contents. Finally, given the overrepresentation of male participants in our survey – 87.7% compared to 63.6% of spectators at rugby union in Australia generally (ABS 2012) – additional research is needed to examine the food and beverage preferences of female spectators.

Disclosure statement

No potential conflict of interest was reported by the authors.

ORCID

Keith D. Parry http://orcid.org/0000-0001-9025-9101

References

ABS. 2012. *Sport and Recreation: A Statistical Overview*, edited by ABS: Australian Bureau of Statistics. Canberra: ABS.

Ahearn, Laura M. 2014. "Detecting Research Patterns and Paratextual Features in AE Word Clouds, Keywords, and Titles." *American Ethnologist* 41 (1): 17–30. doi:http://dx.doi.org/10.1111/amet.12056.

Anagnostopoulos, Christos. 2011. "From Corporate Social Responsibility (CSR) to ... Club Stakeholder Relationship (CSR): the Case of Football." *The Social Responsibility Review* 3: 14–17.

Bale, John. 1996. ""Space, Place and Body Culture: Yi-Fu Tuan and a Geography of Sport". Geografiska Annaler. Series B." *Human Geography* 78 (3): 163–171. doi:http://dx.doi.org/10.2307/490831.

Barrett, Chris. 2016. "Big Bash League Jumps into Top 10 of Most Attended Sports Leagues in the World." Last Modified January 11th 2016, Accessed January 20. http://www.smh.com.au/sport/cricket/big-bash-league-jumps-into-top-10-of-most-attended-sports-leagues-in-the-world-20160110-gm2w8z.html

BBC. 2015. "Price of Football: Most Ticket Prices Frozen or Reduced." Last Modified 14th October 2015, Accessed October 15. http://www.bbc.com/sport/0/football/34531731

Blank, Ashley, Kristi Sweeney, and Rhema Fuller. 2014. "Room for Growth in Professional Sport: An Examination of the Factors Affecting African-American Attendance." *Sport Marketing Quarterly* 23 (4): 225–240.

Bouchet, Patrick, Guillaume Bodet, Iouri Bernache-Assollant, and Faycel Kada. 2011. "Segmenting Sport Spectators: Construction and Preliminary Validation of the Sporting Event Experience Search (SEES) Scale." *Sport Management Review* 14 (1): 42–53.

Byon, Kevin K., James J. Zhang, and Thomas A. Baker. 2013. "Impact of Core and Peripheral Service Quality on Consumption Behavior of Professional Team Sport Spectators as Mediated by Perceived Value." *European Sport Management Quarterly* 13 (2): 232–263.

Cherny, Daniel. 2015. "Etihad Stadium under Pressure after MCG Lowers Food and Drink Prices." *The Age*. Last Modified March 3rd 2015, Accessed August 10. http://www.theage.com.au/afl/afl-news/etihad-stadium-under-pressure-after-mcg-lowers-food-and-drink-prices-20150302-13sga0.html

Drenten, Jenna, Cara Okieshen Peters, Thomas Leigh, and Candice R. Hollenbeck. 2009. "Not Just a Party in the Parking Lot: An Exploratory Investigation of the Motives Underlying the Ritual Commitment of Football Tailgaters." *Sport Marketing Quarterly* 18 (2): 92–106.

Drygas, Wojciech, Joanna Ruszkowska, Matthew Philpott, Olav Björkström, Mike Parker, Robin Ireland, Federico Roncarolo, and Maria Tenconi. 2013. "Good Practices and Health Policy

Analysis in European Sports Stadia: Results from the 'Healthy Stadia' Project." *Health Promotion International* 28 (2): 157–165. doi:http://dx.doi.org/10.1093/heapro/dar088.

Fabricant, Florence. 2005. "Healthier Food Lineup at New Stadium." *New York Times*, 27th April 2005, p. 10. http://www.nytimes.com/2005/04/27/style/dining/food-stuff-healthier-food-lineup-at-new-stadium.html.

Fernandez, Manny. 2007. "Latin Food at Yankee Stadium. Now, How about That!" *New York Times*, 11th May 2007. http://www.nytimes.com/2007/05/11/nyregion/11food.html?_r=0.

Giulianotti, Richard. 2002. "Supporters, Followers, Fans, and Flaneurs." *Journal of Sport & Social Issues* 26 (1): 25–46. doi:http://dx.doi.org/10.1177/0193723502261003.

Greenwell, T. Christopher, Janet S. Fink, and Donna L. Pastore. 2002. "Assessing the Influence of the Physical Sports Facility on Customer Satisfaction within the Context of the Service Experience." *Sport Management Review* 5 (2): 129–148. doi:http://dx.doi.org/10.1016/S1441-3523(02)70064-8.

Guggenheim, Lauren, S. Jang, Soo Young Bae, and W. Neuman. 2015. "The Dynamics of Issue Frame Competition in Traditional and Social Media." *The ANNALS of the American Academy of Political and Social Science* 659 (1): 207–224. doi:http://dx.doi.org/10.1177/0002716215570549.

Hall, John, Barry O'Mahony, and Julian Vieceli. 2010. "An Empirical Model of Attendance Factors at Major Sporting Events." *International Journal of Hospitality Management* 29 (2): 328–334.

Hill, Brad, and B. Christine Green. 2000. "Repeat Attendance as a Function of Involvement, Loyalty, and the Sportscape across Three Football Contexts." *Sport Management Review* 3 (2): 145–162. doi:http://dx.doi.org/10.1016/S1441-3523(00)70083-0.

Hunt, Carter A., Jie Gao, and Lan Xue. 2014. "A Visual Analysis of Trends in the Titles and Keywords of Top-ranked Tourism Journals." *Current Issues in Tourism* 17 (10): 849–855. doi:http://dx.doi.org/10.1080/13683500.2014.900000.

Inoue, Yuhei, Sami Yli-Piipari, Todd Layne, Heather O. Chambliss, and Carol C. Irwin. 2015. "A Preliminary Study of a Professional Sport Organization's Family-centered Health Promotion Initiative." *International Review on Public and Nonprofit Marketing* 12 (2): 189–205.

Ireland, Robin, and Francine Watkins. 2010. "Football Fans and Food: A Case Study of a Football Club in the English Premier League." *Public Health Nutrition* 13 (05): 682–687. doi:http://dx.doi.org/10.1017/S1368980009991765.

IRFU. 2014. "Beat the Queue at Aviva Stadium with 'My Order App.'" Last Modified March 26th 2014, Accessed April 19. http://www.irishrugby.ie/news/30247.php-VbYQJWDoYWl

James, Jeffrey, G. Steven Breezeel, and Stephen Ross. 2001. "A Two-stage Study of the Reasons to Begin and Continue Tailgating." *Sport Marketing Quarterly* 10 (4): 212–222.

Jones, Grant. 2015. "New App Will Allow Football Lovers to Have Food Ordered and Delivered to Their Stadium Seats." Last Modified February 25th 2015, Accessed April 19. http://www.dailytelegraph.com.au/lifestyle/food/new-app-will-allow-football-lovers-to-have-food-ordered-and-delivered-to-their-stadium-seats/story-fnov1g0j-1227238025816

Keaton, Shaughan A., Nicholas M. Watanabe, and Christopher C. Gearhart. 2015. "A Comparison of College Football and NASCAR Consumer Profiles: Identity Formation and Spectatorship Motivation." *Sport Marketing Quarterly* 24 (1): 43–55.

Kovaricek, Elk. 2010. "The Glorious Meat Pie and Humble Pie Floater." *ABC Adelaide*. Last Modified 31st May 2010, Accessed July 20. http://blogs.abc.net.au/sa/2010/05/the-glorious-meat-pie-and-humble-pie-floater.html?site=adelaide&program=adelaide_afternoons

Lambrecht, Keith W., Frederick Kaefer, and Samuel D. Ramenofsky. 2009. "Sportscape Factors Influencing Spectator Attendance and Satisfaction at a Professional Golf Association Tournament." *Sport Marketing Quarterly* 18 (3): 165–172.

Langley, Sophie. 2015. "Australia: Land of the Rising Sushi (and the Falling Spring Roll)." *Australian Food News*. Last Modified January 19th 2015, Accessed September 27. http://ausfoodnews.com.au/2015/01/19/australia-land-of-the-rising-sushi-and-the-falling-spring-roll.html

Lee, Seunghwan, Bob Heere, and Kyu-soo Chung. 2013. "Which Senses Matter More? The Impact of Our Senses on Team Identity and Team Loyalty." *Sport Marketing Quarterly* 22 (4): 203–213.

Lera-López, Fernando, Andrea Ollo-López, and Manuel Rapún-Gárate. 2012. "Sports Spectatorship in Spain: Attendance and Consumption." *European Sport Management Quarterly* 12 (3): 265–289. doi:http://dx.doi.org/10.1080/16184742.2012.680897.

Madrigal, Robert. 2006. "Measuring the Multidimensional Nature of Sporting Event Performance Consumption." *Journal of Leisure Research* 38 (3): 267–276.

Miles, Louella, and Simon Rines. 2004. *Football Sponsorship & Commerce: An Analysis of Sponsorship and Commercial Opportunities in Football*. Buckfastleigh: International Marketing Reports.

News Limited. 2015. "Masters Food Prices Are Ridiculous." Last Modified April 9th 2015, Accessed April 9. http://www.news.com.au/sport/sports-life/masters-food-prices-are-ridiculous/story-fno61i58-1227296602993

Parnell, Daniel, Andy Pringle, Jim McKenna, Stephen Zwolinsky, Zoe Rutherford, Jackie Hargreaves, Lizzie Trotter, Michael Rigby, and David Richardson. 2015. "Reaching Older People with PA Delivered in Football Clubs: The Reach, Adoption and Implementation Characteristics of the Extra Time Programme." *BMC Public Health* 15 (1): 25. http://bmcpublichealth.biomedcentral.com/articles/10.1186/s12889-015-1560-5.

Parry, Keith D., Ian Jones, and Daniel L. Wann. 2014. "An Examination of Sport Fandom in the United Kingdom: A Comparative Analysis of Fan Behaviors, Socialization Processes, and Team Identification." *Journal of Sport Behavior* 37 (3): 251–267.

Penny, Simon, and Steve Redhead. 2009. "We're Not Really Here: Manchester City, Mobility and Placelessness." *Sport in Society* 12 (6): 755–764. doi:http://dx.doi.org/10.1080/17430430902944217.

PR Newswire. 2009. "In-seat Food Delivery Available Stadium-wide at Rio Tinto." *PR Newswire*, 23rd July 2009. http://www.prnewswire.com/news-releases/in-seat-food-delivery-available-stadium-wide-at-rio-tinto-62265612.html.

Ramshaw, Gregory, and Sean Gammon. 2010. "On Home Ground? Twickenham Stadium Tours and the Construction of Sport Heritage." *Journal of Heritage Tourism* 5 (2): 87–102. doi:http://dx.doi.org/10.1080/17438730903484184.

Roan, Shari. 1997. "Buy Me Some Peanuts and Yogurt? Food: Survey Finds Healthy Choices Have Become Available at All Major League Stadiums." *Los Angeles Times*, 11th June 1997, 3-C, 3:4.

Rolfe, Peter. 2014. "Price Rises for Food and Drink at MCG and Etihad Stadium Hit Footy Fans." *Herald Sun*. Last Modified March 15th 2014, Accessed August 10. http://www.heraldsun.com.au/news/victoria/price-rises-for-food-and-drink-at-mcg-and-etihad-stadium-hit-footy-fans/story-fni0fit3-1226855806466

Rolfe, Peter. 2015. "Etihad Stadium Lowers Food Prices ahead of 2015 AFL Season, following MCG." Last Modified March 26th 2015, Accessed July 20. http://www.heraldsun.com.au/sport/afl/etihad-stadium-lowers-food-prices-ahead-of-2015-afl-season-following-mcg/story-fni5ezdm-1227279029679

Rowe, David, and Jay Scherer. 2014. *Sport, Public Broadcasting, and Cultural Citizenship: Signal Lost?*. New York: Routledge.

Russell, Natalie Ermann. 2011. "Forget Stadium Food – Just Eat up at the Tailgate." *USA Today*. Accessed September 21, 2011. http://www.dailycomet.com/article/20110921/WIRE/110929934

Sarstedt, Marko, Christian Ringle, Sascha Raithel, and Siegfried Gudergan. 2014. "In Pursuit of Understanding What Drives Fan Satisfaction." *Journal of Leisure Research* 46 (4): 419–447.

Savige, Gayle, Abbie MacFarlane, Kylie Ball, Anthony Worsley, and David Crawford. 2007. "Snacking Behaviours of Adolescents and Their Association with Skipping Meals." *International Journal of Behavioral Nutrition and Physical Activity* 4 (36): 1–9.

SCG. 2014. "Fact Sheet on New Grandstands." Accessed April 19. http://sydneycricketground.com.au/news/2014-ashes-media-kit/new-grandstands/fact-sheet-on-new-grandstands/

Sporting Intelligence. 2013. "NFL Remains by Far the Best Attended Domestic Sports League in the World." *Sporting Intelligence*. Last Modified 4th January 2013, Accessed January 7. http://www.sportingintelligence.com/2013/01/04/nfl-remains-best-attended-domestic-sports-league-in-the-world-040101/

Sukalakamala, Piyavan, Sophitmanee Sukalakamala, and Pam Young. 2013. "An Exploratory Study of the Concession Preferences of Generation Y Consumers." *Journal of Foodservice Business Research* 16 (4): 378–390. doi:http://dx.doi.org/10.1080/15378020.2013.824278.

Tarbert, Kristine. 2015. "High Cost of Hydration: Sports Stadiums Facing Pressure to Reduce Food and Drink Prices." *The Daily Telegraph*. Last Modified March 3rd 2015, Accessed July 20. http://www.

dailytelegraph.com.au/newslocal/west/high-cost-of-hydration-sports-stadiums-facing-pressure-to-reduce-food-and-drink-prices/story-fngr8i5s-1227245839561

Tobin, Ben. 2013. "Stadium Food is Bottom of the League for Sports Fans." Last Modified December 19th 2013, Accessed January 20. https://yougov.co.uk/news/2013/12/19/stadium-food-bottom-league-sports-fans/

Veenhuyzen, Max. 2014. "Meat Pie: A Great Australian Dish." *The Guardian*. Last Modified 7th May 2014, Accessed July 20. http://www.theguardian.com/lifeandstyle/australia-food-blog/2014/may/07/meat-pie-a-great-australian-dish

Wakefield, Kirk L., and Hugh J. Sloan. 1995. "The Effects of Team Loyalty and Selected Stadium Factors on Spectator Attendance." *Journal of Sport Management* 9 (2): 153–172.

Wakefield, Kirk L., and Jeffrey G. Blodgett. 1996. "The effect of the servicescape on customers' behavioral intentions in leisure service settings." *Journal of Services Marketing* 10 (6): 45–61.

Wakefield, Kirk L., Jeffrey G. Blodgett, and Hugh J. Sloan. 1996. "Measurement and Management of the Sportscape." *Journal of Sport Management* 10 (1): 15–31.

Wheaton, Belinda. 2007. "After Sport Culture." *Journal of Sport & Social Issues* 31 (3): 283–307. doi:http://dx.doi.org/10.1177/0193723507301049

WHO (World Health Organisation) 2015. "Healthy Diet". Accessed January 28, 2016. http://www.who.int/mediacentre/factsheets/fs394/en/

Yancey, Antronette, David Winfield, Judi Larsen, Michele Anderson, Portia Jackson, Jeff Overton, Shawn Wilson, Allen Rossum, and Shiriki Kumanyika. 2009. ""Live, Learn and Play"." *Preventive Medicine* 49 (4): 322–325.

Yoshida, Masayuki, and Jeffrey D. James. 2011. "Service Quality at Sporting Events: Is Aesthetic Quality a Missing Dimension?" *Sport Management Review* 14 (1): 13–24.

Yusof, Aminuddin, and Hooi See Lee. 2008. "Sportscape Features and Team Quality: Implivation on Spectators Satisfaction and Future Attendance." *Journal of Global Business Management* 4 (2): 76–82.

Appendix 1. Full survey scales.

Getting to and around the stadium
The stadium is well served by public transport
Local roads make it easy to get to this stadium
This stadium has ample parking
Stadium parking is easy to get out of after the game
Stadium parking is conveniently located
Signs at this stadium help you know where you are going
Signs at this stadium give clear directions of where things are located
The stadium layout makes it easy to get to your seat
The stadium layout makes it easy to get to the restrooms or food and beverage outlets

Stadium aesthetics
This stadium is painted in attractive colours
This stadium's architecture gives it an attractive character
This is an attractive stadium
This stadium is well maintained
This stadium is modern
There is plenty of legroom in the seating area
There is plenty of elbowroom in this seating area
This stadium provides comfortable seats
The arrangement of seats provides plenty of space

Entertainment
Pregame shows/entertainment added to your experience at this stadium
Interval/halftime shows/entertainment added to your experience at this stadium
Postgame shows/entertainment added to your experience at this stadium
During game shows/entertainment added to your experience at this stadium
Shows/entertainment at this stadium provide a suitable degree of interactivity

Screens and scoreboards
The screens/scoreboards are entertaining to watch

The screens/scoreboards add excitement to the game
This stadium provides interesting statistics/information
This stadium has high-quality screens/scoreboards
The screens/scoreboards are conveniently located
You rely on the screens/scoreboards to watch the game

Seating
The whole playing area is easily visible from your preferred seating location
Your view is not obstructed from your preferred seating location
When the ball is in the air your view of it is not obscured from your preferred seating location
You are protected from the elements in your preferred seating location
Your preferred seating location is close enough to the playing field
The sound quality is good in your preferred seating location

At the stadium (Topophilia)
You enjoy spending time at this stadium
You like to stay at this stadium for as long as possible
You like to stay for the whole game
You are able to access the internet via your mobile phone or other devices at this stadium
You have a good phone signal at this stadium
You are able to access social media sites such as Twitter and Facebook at This stadium
You feel at home at this stadium
The journey to this stadium has special meaning for you
You know your way around this stadium

Food and beverage
This stadium offers a wide variety of food choices
This stadium offers good tasting food
This stadium offers healthy food options
This stadium offers reasonably priced food
This stadium offers a variety of ways to order and receive your food
This stadium offers a wide variety of drinks choices
This stadium offers reasonably priced drinks
This stadium offers fast service for drinks
This stadium offers a variety of ways to order and receive your drinks

Stadium Management
This stadium maintains clean restrooms
This stadium maintains clean food and beverage areas
This stadium maintains clear walkways and exits
This stadium makes certain that offensive fans are controlled
This stadium monitors abusive fans
This stadium is concerned about controlling abusive fans
Queues for toilets at this stadium are acceptable
Queues for food and drinks at this stadium are acceptable
It is easy to enter this stadium
It is easy to leave this stadium

Sport heritage and the healthy stadia agenda: an overview

Gregory Ramshaw

ABSTRACT
The healthy stadia agenda and sport heritage research appear to have much in common, though their relationship has not yet been explored in any detail. Many sport heritages involve playing particular sports, which may enhance physical activity aims of the healthy stadia agenda, while stadium tours – a staple of sport heritage industry – may also incorporate healthy stadia narratives. Similarly, sport heritage and the healthy stadia agenda are potential partners in public education, both through informal stadia-based public programmes and venue displays as well as more formal curriculum-based programming at sporting venues. However, the relationship between sport heritage and the healthy stadia agenda may also have some issues and challenges as well, as many sport heritages involve health risks and unhealthy behaviour. Ultimately, managers and researchers alike may wish to further consider the relationship between sport heritage and the healthy stadia agenda.

Introduction

At first glance, there appears to be little in common between sport heritage and the healthy stadia agenda. Broadly speaking, sport heritage seeks to socially construct and commodify aspects of the sporting past – be they traditions, places, events, or people – to address contemporary social, economic and political concerns (Ramshaw and Gammon 2005), whereas the healthy stadia agenda is concerned with using large-scale sports facilities as settings for health promotion, including addressing issues such as unhealthy diets, physical activity, alcohol and tobacco use, environmental advocacy, and social inequality (Drygas et al. 2011; Philpott and Seymour 2011). However, a closer look reveals that there may be many collaborative areas between sport heritage and the healthy stadia agenda. Both view sports stadia as playing iconic roles in communities with the potential for attracting many people (Gammon 2011; Philpott and Seymour 2011; Ramshaw, Gammon, and Huang 2013) and both see their role as beneficial to addressing corporate aims and considerations, including enhancing community relations and partnerships, and increasing revenue (Ramshaw and Gammon 2010; Roncarlo et al. 2015; Wright 2012). This reflective article considers the relationship between sport heritage and the healthy stadia agenda, finding that there are many potential areas of collaboration. However, there may also be potential challenges as well, as certain types of sport heritage may be incompatible with the current aims of the healthy stadia agenda.

Background to sport heritage research

Heritage is a widely used, though frequently misunderstood, term. Often employed as a synonym for a particularly normative historical viewpoint, it is best described as the present use of the past (Timothy 2011). This is to say that heritage uses various viewpoints of the past – which may include academic, popular, and personal constructions of the past – to address contemporary social, political and economic needs, circumstances, and issues (Graham, Ashworth, and Tunbridge 2000). Most often, heritage is explored through its touristic uses (Timothy and Boyd 2006) and its relationship to power structures (Smith 2006), although more recently heritage has been linked with public health initiatives such as personal well-being and life satisfaction (Fujiwara, Cornwall, and Dolan 2014).

Sport heritage too has largely been explored through its touristic uses, particularly the tourism generated by sports halls of fame and museums (Frost 2005), heritage-based sporting events (Ramshaw and Hinch 2006), and famous sports stadia and sporting venues (Gammon and Fear 2007). Yet, more research that is recent has looked at sport heritage through various non-touristic lenses including as a creator of intangible legacies such as a sense of belonging and community cohesion (Skinner and Taylor 2012). Although there has not been extensive research on the relationship between broader public health initiatives and sport heritage, projects such as the Sporting Memories Network in the United Kingdom, which was 'established to promote and develop the use of sporting memories to improve the well-being of older people and to help tackle dementia, depression and social isolation' (Projects 2015), and the proposed $75 million (USD) expansion to the Pro Football Hall of Fame in Canton, Ohio that would house a care facility for former NFL players (King 2014), demonstrates some current linkages between sport heritage and health.

Sport heritage and the healthy stadia agenda: cooperative areas

Philpott and Seymour (2011) argue that, one of the catalysts for using stadia as a vehicle for health promotion is that 'sports stadia play iconic roles in communities and are capable of reaching large numbers of people, both in the grounds and surrounding areas' (69). Gammon (2011) employs similar language when describing stadia and sporting venues from a sport heritage perspective:

> Sports sites are now perceived more than just places in which events take place; they are now places to visit, to stand near to, to touch, to record an image of or, perhaps, to experience more intimately through a tour…In short, the stadium has grown in importance, from an often aesthetically indifferent utilitarian structure into an iconic symbol of a place, team, sport and/or event (116).

Similarly, both healthy stadia agenda and sport heritage research recognize that both community *and* corporate/club agendas must be addressed in order for initiatives to be implemented (Philpott and Seymour 2011; Ramshaw 2011a; Roncarlo et al. 2015). As such, both the healthy stadia agenda and sport heritage begin with similar viewpoints about the symbolic meanings of stadia and how they might be used for broader programmes.

Ramshaw (2014) argues that what separates sport heritage from other forms and types of heritage is its sensual and corporeal nature; that is to say, sport must continue to be played and performed in order to create new heritage as sport is, ultimately, a physical practice. This is reflected in the many sport heritage experiences that involve a sense of play, often at famous sporting venues. Most notably, the fantasy camp – where participants play with their sporting heroes, often at an infamous sporting venue (Gammon 2002) – highlights the corporeal, physical nature of sport heritage. Many sports museums, which are frequently part of stadia infrastructure, have sport simulators that provide the visitor the chance to 'try' a particular sport, and experience something of an empathetic connection with elite athletes (Ramshaw 2011b). Ramshaw (2010) further notes that sports museums simulator displays also often provide information for young visitors and their parents to enrol in a particular sport or try sport 'for real' outside of the museum/stadium context. Sport heritage also promotes physical activity through more existential forms of identity, such as inspiring adults to 'take up' the sports of their youth through masters or 'old timers' leagues, often culminating in playing a match at a famous sports venue (Joseph 2011). These sport opportunities not only provide recreation and socialization, but also intimate connections to personal and collective pasts and identities. As such, sport heritage – and motivators such as sport-based nostalgia – might be used by the healthy stadia agenda to inspire physical activity.

Both sport heritage and the healthy stadia agenda are broadly interested in using sports facilities as vehicles for promoting particular ideas and, though the intentions and outcomes of these promotions may at first be dichotomous, there may be areas of collaboration. One of the most popular sport heritage experiences is that of the stadium tour, where visitors encounter the 'backstage' areas of venues normally closed to public view, including the luxury suites, media centre, team change rooms, and playing surface. (Gammon and Fear 2007; Ramshaw, Gammon, and Huang 2013). Normally, these tours are meant to both provide an enjoyable visitor experience as well as promote team or venue products and services, including retail, rental, and catering services (Leask and Digance 2002; Ramshaw and Gammon 2010). Certainly, teams and venues could promote their healthy stadia initiatives via backstage tours, both in terms of promoting products and services to a captive audience as well as highlighting the team/venue's community involvement and engagement. Furthermore, stadium tours offer visitors the opportunity to 'walk in the footsteps' of their sporting heroes. Combining some of the messages of the healthy stadia agenda, including healthy living and active lifestyles, with the backstage revelations of the training and diet regiment of elite athletes could re-enforce both heritage and health promotion. Furthermore, stadium tours re-enforce sports venues as special places, which may aid in how the public receives and reacts to healthy stadia messaging.

Finally, sport heritage and the healthy stadia agenda are potential partners in both formal and informal public education. Many venues include concourse displays and interpretive exhibits about team or facility history, including famous games, players, and events. These displays could be sponsored by health-based partners, and could include healthy stadia initiatives and messaging. Furthermore, stadia could be used as unique venues for public health activities and education, particularly during non-game days and in the off-season. For example, the Bon Secours Wellness Arena (known locally as 'The Well') in Greenville, South Carolina is sponsored by a local hospital system. Part of the sponsorship agreement includes the BeWellFans initiative, which features both health and heritage displays in the arena's concourse areas, a flu-shot programme at the arena, and the 'Well Walkers' programme which opens the arena for public walking during the warm summer months while also providing the general public opportunities to have consultations with sports medicine practitioners (BeWellFans 2015). Other venues and teams are using their venues as unique 'classrooms' for primary school programmes. The Edmonton Oilers, a National Hockey League team in Canada, created a programme called 'Ice School' where primary school classes spend a week at the team's venue, Rexall Place, where they take curriculum-based programming in local history, team heritage, mathematics, and technology (Ice School 2015). Certainly, aspects of the healthy stadia agenda might also align with regional or national curricula and may be appropriate for 'Ice School'-like venue-based school programmes.

Venue-based sport heritage attractions, such as team museums and halls of fame, could also help provide health-based public programming. Interpretive signage, audio tours, and hands-on displays could include information about healthy training regiments, athlete physiology, and diet. Exhibits such as the recent 'Science of Sport' at the Cincinnati Museum Center (Hefner 2015), which included displays about famous athletes, teams, and moments as well as health and well-being information about strength, endurance, balance, and diet, provides an example of using both sport heritage and health and well-being messaging in a museum setting. Similarly, team museums and halls of fame can be excellent venues for public talks from past and present athletes about both their careers and the approaches to health and well-being. As Gammon (2014) discusses, athletes could be considered a kind of sports artefact, and the fact that many former athletes maintain their health well after their playing careers have finished could be of potential interest to a diverse group of visitors as a public talk or seminar. Team museums and halls of fame can also be used as a meeting place between athletes, experts, and the public to share and discuss both heritage and health topics. Public programmes, such as the recent 'Anatomy of Sports' programme at the National Museum of Health and Medicine (2013) that brought together specialists, athletes, and visitors to learn about sports health, could also be created for and by sports museums in order to both attract a range of visitors as well as broaden museum narratives to include both heritage and health.

Sport heritage and the healthy stadia agenda could also use public educational forums like venue-based team museums and halls of fame to reveal historical approaches to health and wellbeing, and confront contemporary health and wellbeing issues that are created, practiced, or reflected through sport. Museum displays that reveal historical changes to venues, such as smoking, drinking, hygiene, violence, and overcrowding, and could both provide a fascinating historical glimpse into the spectator experience, as well as comparative tool with contemporary stadium practices. Similarly, venue-based museums could create exhibitions that address contemporary health issues in sport. For example, the International Tennis Hall of Fame in Newport, Rhode Island at one time addressed the physical and psychological toll of teenage players competing at the professional level (Spencer 1996). Although critically addressing health issues *generated by* specific sports is somewhat rare, particularly when most stadia-based sports museums and halls of fame are meant to celebrate particular teams, players, and sporting achievements, critical discourses about health-related issues may also provide sports organizations the chance to be proactive leaders in their community.

Sport heritage and the healthy stadia agenda: issues and challenges

Although sport heritage and the healthy stadia agenda appear to have many areas of interest in common, there are a few issues and challenges in combining sport heritage and healthy stadia initiatives. As Moore, Richardson, and Corkill (2014) argue, many sport heritages have health and safety risks and, as such, from a healthy stadia perspective may be incompatible with messages about well-being. Some stadia, such as Hillsbourough Stadium in Sheffield and the Superdome in New Orleans, have a heritage that is intimately tied to tragedy and human suffering. While tragic heritages often create a health-based legacy (eg. the Hillsborough tragedy led to strict safety and design rules for stadia in the United Kingdom) while also providing a symbol of healing for devastated communities (as was the case with the Superdome in New Orleans), the *infamy* of particularly tragic stadium heritages may dominate any positive health-based legacies. Similarly, some sport heritages and sporting venues celebrate sports, such as American football, that have caused significant long-term (and sometimes fatal) health issues for participants. Heritages of 'tough' athletes who played through injury are significant parts of sporting lore and mythology, and may undermine health and well-being narratives. Some sporting traditions and heritages also are frequently associated with consuming alcohol, often to excess (Collins and Vamplew 2002), as well as consuming mass quantities of unhealthy foods. For example, the practice of tailgating, a significant sporting tradition associated with college and professional football in the United States where fans drink, eat meat and high-calorie sides such as potato salad, and play games outside of venues for hours (and sometimes days) before kickoff (Gibson, Willming, and Holdnak 2002). Often, tailgating can result in binge drinking, and antisocial behaviour when encountering rival supporters (Neal and Fromme 2007; Oster-Aaland and Neighbors 2007). Given the fact that college football teams normally have seven to eight home games per season, while professional football clubs can have as many as twelve games per season over a five month period, tailgating can be a significant part of fans' social calendar and provides amble opportunities for unhealthy behaviour. Furthermore, traditional public holidays – such as Thanksgiving in the United States and Boxing Day in the United Kingdom – also have traditional associations with both sporting events and excessive eating and drinking. Some sports also have long-standing traditions linked to unhealthy behaviour. For example, the use of chewing tobacco by baseball players is an ingrained part of the culture and traditions of the sport, and though professional leagues have sought to limit tobacco use to protect both players from harm and young fans from taking up the habit, the practice nevertheless continues (Tawfik 2015). Finally, the globalization of sport tourism and, in particular, the wide-scale dissemination of sport heritage products and experiences (Higham and Hinch 2009) particularly at infamous sporting venues may also be incompatible with healthy stadia environmental initiatives, as international travel is required to experience some sport heritages.

Conclusion

Sport heritage and the healthy stadia agenda appear to be natural allies. They both view sporting venues as special places, and are keenly aware of proving positive outcomes for fan, club, and community alike. For sport heritage initiatives, the healthy stadia agenda provides a public health link that gives it an additional level of *gravitas* and legitimacy. For the healthy stadia agenda, sport heritage provides an interesting, engaging, and emotional vehicle for the promotion of health and well-being.

This reflective article has presented numerous examples by which sport heritage providers and the healthy stadia agenda are interconnected. Hands-on, relevant, topical, and experiential programming is key for sport heritage, whereas health and well-being might require a vehicle like sport heritage for broader public engagement. The question becomes how to integrate these two areas into broader public initiatives. The development of a sport heritage/healthy stadia intervention protocol may be appropriate, which may lead to many different programming options and outcomes. Perhaps it is the design of a specific facility tour that addresses both heritage and health topics that would target students at the primary and secondary levels. Perhaps it is a sport heritage-based programme at a venue that helps address isolation issues among seniors. Perhaps it is the use of 'athlete artefacts' such as ex-players to deliver or be the 'face' of healthy stadia initiatives. Perhaps it is the design of a 'healthy tailgate' where options and suggestions are provided that manage health risks while not diminishing the traditions and cultures of the practice. Although there may be some areas where sport heritage and the healthy stadia agenda are incompatible, more often than not the aims and agendas appear to align and could provide numerous options and opportunities for collaboration.

Disclosure statement

No potential conflict of interest was reported by the authors.

References

Anatomy of Sports. 2013. "National Museum of Health and Medicine." http://www.medicalmuseum.mil/index.cfm?p=media.events.2013.anatomy_of_sports.

BeWellFans. 2015. St. Francis Health. Accessed September 24. https://stfrancishealth.org/about-us-bon-secours-wellness-arena-bewellfans.html

Collins, Tony, and Wray Vamplew. 2002. *Mud, Sweat and Beers: A Cultural History of Sport and Alcohol*. London: Bloomsbury.

Drygas, Wojceich, Joanna Ruszkowska, Matthew Philpott, Olav Bjorkstrom, Mike Parker, Robin Ireland, Frederico Roncarolo, and Maria Tenconi. 2011. "Good Practices and Health Policy Analysis in European Sports Stadia: Results from the 'Healthy Stadia' Agenda." *Health Promotion International*. 28 (2): 157–165.

Frost, Warwick. 2005. "The Sustainability of Sports Heritage Attractions: Lessons from the Australian Football League Hall of Fame." *Journal of Sport & Tourism*. 10 (4): 295–305.

Fujiwara, Daniel, Thomas Cornwall, and Paul Dolan. 2014. *Heritage and Wellbeing*. Swindon: English Heritage. Accessed August 19, 2015. http://hc.historicengland.org.uk/content/pub/2190644/heritage-and-wellbeing.pdf

Gammon, Sean. 2002. "Fantasy, Nostalgia and the Pursuit of What Never Was." In *Sport Tourism: Principals and Practice*, edited by Sean Gammon, and Joseph Kurtzman, 61–72. Eastbourne: Leisure Studies Association.

Gammon, Sean. 2011. "Sporting' New Attractions? The Commodification of the Sleeping Stadium." In *Tourism Experiences: Contemporary Perspectives*, edited by Richard Sharpley, and Phil Stone, 115–126. London: Routledge.

Gammon, Sean. 2014. "Heroes as heritage: the commoditization of sporting achievement." *Journal of Heritage Tourism*. 9 (3): 246–256.

Gammon, Sean, and Victoria Fear. 2007. "Stadia Tours and the Power of Backstage." In *Heritage, Sport and Tourism: Sporting Pasts – Tourist Futures*, edited by Sean Gammon, and Gregory Ramshaw, 23–32. London: Routledge.

Gibson, Heather, Cynthia Willming, and Andrew Holdnak. 2002. "'We're Gators…Not Just Gator Fans': Serious Leisure and University of Florida Football." *Journal of Leisure Research*. 34 (4): 397–425.

Graham, Brian, Gregory Ashworth, and John Tunbridge. 2000. *A Geography of Heritage: Power, Culture & Economy*. London: Arnold.

Hefner, Cody. 2015. *Run, Jump, Row and Throw in New Interactive Exhibit.* Cincinnati Museum Center. https://www.cincymuseum.org/press/science-of-sports.

Higham, James, and Tom Hinch. 2009. *Sport and Tourism: Globalization, Mobility and Identity.* New York: Elsevier.

Ice School. 2015. Edmonton Oilers. Accessed September 24. http://oilers.nhl.com/club/page.htm?id=63917

Joseph, Janelle. 2011. "A Diaspora Approach to Sport Tourism." *Journal of Sport and Social Issues.* 35 (2): 146–167.

King, Peter. 2014. "The MMQB: A New Idea, and a Good One, for the Hall of Fame." Accessed November 24. http://mmqb.si.com/2014/11/24/odell-beckham-catch-new-york-giants-week-12-nfl/7

Leask, Anna, and Justine Digance. 2002. "Exploiting Unused Capacity." *Journal of Convention & Exhibition Management.* 3 (4): 17–35.

Moore, Ray, Matthew Richardson, and Claire Corkill. 2014. "Identity in the "Road Racing Capital of the World": Heritage, Geography and Contested Spaces." *Journal of Heritage Tourism.* 9 (3): 228–245.

Neal, Dan, and Kim Fromme. 2007. "Hook 'Em Horns and Heavy Drinking: Alcohol Use and Collegiate Sport." *Addictive Behaviors.* 32 (11): 2681–2693.

Oster-Aaland, Laura, and Clayton Neighbors. 2007. "The Impact of a Tailgating Policy on Students' Drinking Behavior and Perceptions." *Journal of American College Health* 56 (3): 281–284.

Philpott, Matthew and Russel Seymour 2011. "Sports Stadia, Public Health and Sustainability." In *Sustainability and Sport*, edited by Jill Savery, and Keith Gilbert, 66–77. Champaign: Common Ground.

Projects. 2015. Sporting Memories Network November 24. http://www.sportingmemoriesnetwork.com.

Ramshaw, Gregory. 2010. "Living Heritage and the Sports Museum: Athletes, Legacy and the Olympic Hall of Fame and Museum, Canada Olympic Park." *Journal of Sport & Tourism.* 15 (1): 45–70.

Ramshaw, Gregory. 2011a. "The Construction of Sport Heritage Attractions." *Journal of Tourism Consumption and Practice.* 3 (1): 1–25.

Ramshaw, Gregory. 2011b. "The Athlete Experience: Education, Economics and Interactive Sports Exhibits at the Olympic Hall of Fame and Museum, Canada Olympic Park." In *Museums at Play: Games, Interaction and Learning*, edited by Kathy Beale, 462–473. London: Museums Etc.

Ramshaw, Gregory. 2014. "Sport, Heritage, and Tourism." *Journal of Heritage Tourism* 9 (3): 191–196.

Ramshaw, Gregory, and Sean Gammon. 2005. "More than Just Nostalgia? Exploring the Heritage/Sport Tourism Nexus." *Journal of Sport Tourism* 10 (4): 229–241.

Ramshaw, Gregory, and Sean Gammon. 2010. "On Home Ground? Twickenham Stadium Tours and the Construction of Sport Heritage." *Journal of Heritage Tourism.* 5 (2): 87–102.

Ramshaw, Gregory, and Tom Hinch. 2006. "Place Identity and Sport Tourism: The Case of the Heritage Classic Ice Hockey Event." *Current Issues in Tourism.* 9 (4): 399–418.

Ramshaw, Gregory, San Gammon, and Wei-Jue Huang. 2013. "Acquired Pasts and the Commodification of Borrowed Heritage: The Case of the Bank of America Stadium Tour." *Journal of Sport & Tourism* 18 (1): 17–31.

Roncarlo, Frederico, Nicollo Lanati, Matthew Philpott, Wojceich Drygas, Joanna Ruszkowska, Robin Ireland, and Maria Tenconi. 2015. "Process Evaluation of European 'Healthy Stadia' Program." *Health Promotion International* 30 (4): 881–890. doi:http://dx.doi.org/10.1093/heapro/dau025.

Skinner, Neil, and Matthew Taylor. 2012. "'It's Nice to Belong': Boxing, Heritage and Community in London." In *Sport, History, and Heritage*, edited by Jeffrey Hill, Kevin Moore, and Jason Wood, 59–76. Woodbridge: Boydell & Brewer.

Smith, Laurajane. 2006. *Uses of Heritage.* London: Routledge.

Spencer, Nancy. 1996. "International Tennis Hall of Fame." *Journal of Sport History* 23 (3): 335–337.

Tawfik, Nadia. 2015. "Baseball's Toxic Tradition of Chewing Tobacco." *BBC.com.* January 25. http://www.bbc.com/news/health-30935685.

Timothy, Dallen. 2011. *Cultural Heritage and Tourism: An Introduction.* Bristol: Channel View.

Timothy, Dallen, and Stephen Boyd. 2006. "Heritage Tourism in the 21st Century: Valued Traditions and New Perspectives." *Journal of Heritage Tourism.* 1 (1): 1–16.

Wright, Richard. 2012. "Stadia, Identity and Belonging: Stirring the Sleeping Giants of Sports Tourism." In *International Sports Events*, edited by Richard Shipway, and Alan Fyall, 195–207. London: Routledge.

An evaluation of opportunistic health checks at cricket matches: the Boundaries for Life initiative

Chet Trivedy, Ivo Vlaev, Russell Seymour and Matthew Philpott

ABSTRACT

In 2009, a population level health screening programme was established in the UK for people over the age of 40 years. The primary aim of the service was to identify and treat the leading causes of preventable disease and death, including cardiovascular disease and diabetes. Checks are offered every five years through scheduled appointments at primary care settings, and uptake of such checks has been relatively low to date with 12.7% of those eligible to have a NHS health check receiving one between 2009 and 2013. Non-clinical settings such as sports stadia have previously been used to offer health interventions and opportunistic health checks. Despite relatively modest results in football and rugby settings, professional cricket fixtures with high footfall may offer higher levels of uptake and participant satisfaction, and provide a novel setting for engaging BME communities. This paper describes the process and results from the Boundaries For Life initiative that delivered health checks at professional cricket matches over the 2014 and 2015 seasons. Uptake of the checks was significantly high in comparison to other sports settings, with very strong feedback from participants on the convenience of service.

Background

Cardiovascular disease (CVD) including ischaemic heart disease, stroke, diabetes and obesity are major public health concerns in the United Kingdom (UK). Data showed that in 2013 there were over 3.2 million diabetics living in the UK and this figure was projected to increase to 5 million by 2025 (Diabetes UK 2013). The costs associated with treating these conditions are extremely high, with diabetes alone costing £10 billion pounds a year in the UK, equivalent to 10% of the annual NHS budget. The Centre of Economics and Business Research (CEBR) reported that the cost of treating CVD in the UK in 2014 was £14.4 billion (which equates to 1.4% of the UK GDP), predicted to rise to £17.6 billion by 2020 (CEBR 2014).

In 2009, the NHS introduced a new programme of Health Checks, defined as a: 'risk assessment, risk reduction and risk management programme' (PHE 2015). The primary aims of the programme are to identify and treat the leading causes of preventable deaths from some types of non-communicable diseases (NCDs), including CVD, diabetes, kidney disease and stroke. Members of the population aged between 40 and 74 are invited by a letter from either their general practitioner (GP) or a local government department responsible for public health to attend a health check every five years to assess their risk, and promote suitable interventions including lifestyle changes. Checks are based upon set appointments, and are usually undertaken in GP surgeries and local pharmacies, but may also be offered at other neighbourhood locations such as leisure centres, whilst in some areas, NHS Health Checks are offered by mobile units. Reminders to attend checks are sent by phone and email, whilst those with a previously diagnosed NCD are excluded from being invited to five year checks. Public Health England (PHE) has suggested that: 'each year NHS health checks could prevent 1600 heart attacks and save 650 lives, prevent 4000 from developing diabetes and detect 20,000 cases of diabetes or kidney disease earlier' (PHE 2015). Economic modelling has suggested the programme would result in savings to the NHS of £57 million per year after four years and £176 million per year after 15 years (PHE 2015).

While there is some evidence that the introduction of this programme has led to an increase in the detection of cardiovascular risk factors (Robson et al. 2016), uptake of the programme is lower than anticipated. A recent study which has evaluated the first four years of the programme found that the uptake of health checks was relatively low, with 12.7% of those eligible to have a NHS health check receiving one between 2009 and 2013 (Robson et al. 2016). There is little data to support the reasons for the significant variation in the uptake of NHS health checks, and it is possible that barriers such as the lack of awareness of the programme, appointments allocated during normal working hours, the inconvenience of appointment locations and the lack of motivation to have a health check in the absence of symptoms may have contributed to the low uptake. There is also evidence suggesting that health checks offered outside traditional clinical settings, for example the GP surgery, may be beneficial in leveraging greater levels of uptake (Visram, Carr, and Geddes 2015).

Delivery of health checks at sports settings

One non-clinical setting that may offer a useful locus of engagement for health promotion education and health interventions such health checks are professional sports clubs and their stadia. There is now an emerging body of literature demonstrating the potential for sports stadia to be used in the promotion of healthy lifestyles, highlighting the power of a club's brand and the iconic status of sports venues to engage fans and members of the local community with a view to influence changes in lifestyle behaviours (Drygas et al. 2013; Pringle et al. 2013). The majority of successful projects are those that engage target groups of fans or members of the local community on *non-matchdays*, for example work undertaken in Scotland using sports clubs and their venues for successful weight loss programme for overweight male football fans (Hunt et al. 2014), a project in Belgium using professional football settings and players to promote better diet and levels of physical activity in socially disadvantaged young people (Dubuy et al. 2014), and a project using football settings to improve levels of physical activity and social interaction in older adults over 55 years old (Parnell et al. 2015). As sporting events attract large crowds in their tens of thousands, it has been speculated that matchday sports settings may be harnessed for the purposes of health promotion and health interventions, whilst certain sports may be effective in targeting particular high risk groups. The efficacy of such projects to date has been mixed, with lower than anticipated levels of engagement from fans in health-related behaviours, and time pressures being cited as a main barrier to participation (Witty and White 2011; Curran, Drust, and Richardson 2014).

However, in distinction to sports such as football and both codes of rugby, professional cricket offers a different type of matchday experience, in terms of a much longer format (up to seven hours play), more relaxed atmosphere and a different fan demographic. The latter observation is particularly significant for targeted health interventions, for example, live cricket audiences include greater levels of black, minority and ethnic (BME) groups who have a higher prevalence of Type 2 diabetes, coronary heart disease and cancer when compared to White British populations (Gholap et al. 2011; Jin et al. 2015). Therefore, targeting cricket matches – in particular international fixtures featuring teams from South Asian and Caribbean countries – as a health promotion setting may be effective in engaging BME groups with a view to reducing the burden of these diseases in these populations. Furthermore, unlike football and rugby where the fan is in the venue for two to three hours, the long form of international cricket (Test Matches and One Day Internationals) can see fans in the venue for up to eight hours, in some cases over five consecutive days, thereby increasing the opportunity for fans to engage with health promotion interventions such as health checks without fear of missing a significant proportion of the game. In addition, scheduled breaks in play and unscheduled interruptions (for example, due to bad weather) only increase the opportunity for fans to engage with health promotion activities.

In 2010, a team of health care professionals developed a voluntary initiative known as Boundaries for Life (BFL) with the intention of offering free health checks for fans and staff attending international cricket matches. After early successes and growth of BFL to feature at more fixtures in the following years, an evaluation study of the initiative was established, with funding provided by a small research grant from Institute of Advanced Studies (IAS) at Warwick Medical School. The primary aims of the study were to explore the feasibility of offering free health checks at cricket matches with high footfall (predominantly international fixtures), and user experience data concerning suitability of using professional cricket settings for delivery of health checks. Ethical approval for the study was granted by Warwick Medical School.

Methodology

The BFL health check service was delivered at professional cricket venues by a team of clinicians, including doctors, dentists, nurses and medical students. The service was provided to participating venues free of charge over the course of the 2014 and 2015 season, and there was no cost to either fans or staff to undertake a health check. Checks either took place in a designated room within one of the venue's stands, or in a large 'gazebo' style tent near to other commercial concessions (eg food and drink stalls) positioned behind the main spectator stands. Checks were promoted to fans through web articles on the host club's website, social media channels, public address announcements, and in some cases, messages on the stadium 'big screen' and promotion through broadcast radio ('Test Match Special'). An additional promotional email was also sent to members of staff at some of the participating clubs making them aware of the free service. The service was promoted primarily to people over the age of 40, but anybody over the age of 18 wanting to have a check was allowed to participate.

Prior to undertaking a health check, participants were asked to complete a simple medical questionnaire enquiring about their health and lifestyle, including questions concerning their current health, any previous incidence of ill health, any relevant family history of ill health, as well as current levels of smoking and alcohol consumption (see Table 3). The health checks included a measurement of blood pressure, random blood sugar, random total cholesterol, random high density cholesterol (HDL), low density cholesterol, body mass index (BMI) and a screen for mouth cancer. The results were recorded onto a data card for the patient to take to their GP and each patient was signposted to an appropriate health care provider if deemed necessary. The health data were anonymously recorded onto an excel spreadsheet post-event. Participants were also asked to complete an anonymous qualitative questionnaire on their experience of the health check.

Results

Demographics

Data were available for 513 participants who completed health checks over the 2014 and 2015 cricket seasons. Seven cricket grounds participated in the health checks and the breakdown of participation is shown in Table 1.

There were 324 males with a mean age of 49 ± 15.2 years and 107 females with mean age of 47 ± 14.2 years. Gender was not recorded for 83 individuals. Of the 499 where data were available, 338 (67.7%) were fans attending the match, and another 161 (32.3%) were staff employed at the cricket ground as either club staff or event specific staff (eg security or catering staff). 84% gave their ethnicity as white (British), 14% were of Asian origin, 1% Chinese and another 1% falling into the 'other' category.

Medical history

Over two-thirds of the participants reported not having any health issues relating to high blood pressure, diabetes, high cholesterol, heart disease or mouth cancer while 43.4% had no family history of these conditions. The distribution of self-reported illness in this group is summarized in Table 2.

Table 1. Distribution of health checks conducted across cricket venues in 2014 and 2015 seasons.

Venue/locations	Number of events	Type of match	Total screened
Edgbaston (Birmingham)	1	One Day International	25
Headingly (Leeds)	1	Test Match	48
Sussex County Ground (Hove)	2	Domestic County Match	75
Lord's (London)	2	One Day County Cup Final	122
Emirates Old Trafford (Manchester)	2	Test Match and ODI	98
Kia Oval (London)	2	Test Match	97
SWALEC (Cardiff)	1	International T20 (men's and women's matches)	48

Table 2. Self-reported health status of users attending for a health checks (n = 513).

Condition	Current history	Family history*
None	339 (65.8%)	221 (43%)
High blood pressure	65 (12.6%)	123 (23.9%)
Diabetes	17 (3.3%)	113 (22%)
Heart disease	13 (2.5%)	91 (17.7%)
High cholesterol	74 (14.4%)	96 (18.7%)
Mouth cancer	1 (0.2%)	26 (5.1%)

*As many patients had multiple conditions in their family history the total percentages for these exceed 100%.

Table 3. Findings of health checks in cohort of 513 users.

Parameter	Findings
Body mass index (BMI)	28% normal 42% overweight 10% obese 10% morbidly obese
Blood pressure	High blood pressure according to measurement of systolic blood pressure (40%)
Random cholesterol >5 mmol/L (high risk)	39%
Random HDL <1.04 mmmol/l (high risk)	17%
Random blood sugar (>11 mmol/l) suggestive of diabetes	7–11 mmol/l (17.1%) >11 mmol/l (1.23%)
Mouth check	11% abnormal mouth check
Alcohol consumption	Male >21 units a week 9% Female >14 units a week 7% Non-drinkers 30%
Smoking	89% non-smokers

Health check findings

The clinical findings of the health checks is summarized in Table 3.

Feedback

The feedback for the health check initiative was very positive with all (100%) participants reporting that they would recommend the health checks to others through a qualitative feedback form. Many of those participating in health checks were made aware of the service on the day through promotional activities or had simply happened to come across the health check service when walking past, and felt that it was convenient in terms of time and location. It was interesting to note that only 1% of the users underwent a health check because they were worried that something was wrong. A summary of the feedback is provided in Table 4.

Discussion

A review of the literature found no publications that had evaluated health checks conducted in professional cricket venues around the world. As such, this pilot study has important finding and implications for health commissioners, in particular those working in the area of health checks provision, stadium managers, researchers and practitioners. The high indices for risk factors such as BMI (with 20% either obese or morbidly obese and 42% overweight) are in line with the findings of the UK's National Obesity Observatory data from 2009, which

Table 4. Summary of the feedback for the health checks.

Feedback questions	Response
How did they hear about the service?	Walking past (60%) Word of mouth (19%) PA announcement (14%) Other (7%)
Reason for attendance? (multiple answers per person)	Convenience of location (54%) Convenience of time (34%) Curious (35%) Walking past (30%) To get a clean bill of health (29%) Free Service (26%) Recommendation (7%) Worried something was wrong (1%) Unable to see GP (2%) Good previous experience (1%)
Would you recommend the health check to others?	100% yes
Were you provided an explanation of health checks?	100% yes
Were you treated with dignity?	100% yes
Did you feel to location of the checks gave you enough privacy?	86% yes, definitely 14% yes, to some extent
How would you rate the time of the checks?	99% about the right time 1% not enough time
Were you provided with any information?	56% verbal 26% written 12% none 6% non-response
Were you advised to have a follow up?	19% GP follow up 13% dentist follow up
How would you rate your experience?	83% excellent 17% very good

found that 23% of the adult UK population were obese and 38.3% were overweight (PHE 2016). This suggests that the BMI sample in this study is representative of the overall UK population. The percentage of elevated random cholesterol of 39% in this study was lower than the WHO data for Europe (54% for both sexes) but in line with the global prevalence of raised cholesterol figure of 39% (World Health Organization 2008). As blood pressure measurements are subject to fluctuations especially in uncontrolled environmental conditions such as those encountered on a match day, it is difficult to make a definitive diagnosis of high blood pressure based on a single reading. Finally, as there is no follow up data available on this cohort of users, it is difficult to quantify the actual health benefits of disease prevention, although anecdotal data suggested that a small number of individuals ($N \leq 10$) who had undertaken a BFL check three years running had demonstrated reduction in risk factors such as BMI, cholesterol and blood pressure, whilst they reported feeling healthier.

The initial data from 513 users of the service demonstrates high levels of interest amongst fans and staff undertaking opportunistic health checks offered at cricket matches, something which is substantiated further when comparing this data with the uptake of health interventions at professional football and rugby league matches (Witty and White 2011; Curran, Drust, and Richardson 2014). Whereas previous studies using football and rugby settings have cited problems of engaging fans in health interventions on matchdays (in particular men), and the complexities of implementing and delivering such interventions over a short period of time, user feedback form the BFL service was almost entirely positive, with many participants commenting on the convenience of the service and how this complemented their matchday experience. Given the overall acceptance of the initiative it is possible that the initiative could be scaled up to offer free health checks targeting cricket loving fans from South Asian and Afro-Caribbean populations who exhibit higher levels of NCD-related risk factors, and lower levels of access to traditional primary care services. Given relatively poor levels of uptake at population level for NHS health checks, it is possible that cricket may play an important role in incentivizing those attending a match to have an opportunistic health check, in part owing to the convenience of time and place. The study also demonstrates that due to the longer form of the game fans are not overtly discouraged by the 10–15 min spent having a health check. In addition, both scheduled breaks (lunch interval) and unscheduled breaks in play (rain breaks) during a cricket match also provide further opportunities for the uptake of health checks. It was also observed that many of the users had a health check because they saw others having the same.

There were also concerns that the checks would be selective and favour those who were worried about their health and would therefore be biased towards the 'worried well' or those who could not get an appointment to see their GP. However, the feedback data found that only 1% of participants attended because they were worried about their health. In addition, only 2% of participants stated that they were unable to see their GP for a check, thus suggesting that they could have seen their GP but felt a check at a cricket match was more convenient. Although the findings of this study support the acceptance of health checks outside of the traditional medical model, it is unknown whether the checks themselves can change or modify health behaviour.

A behavioural change framework, the COM-B model (Michie, Atkins, and West 2014), may be used to classify the reasons for attendance, as well as non-attendance at opportunistic health checks provided at cricket matches, based upon three broad categories: capabilities, opportunities and motivations. The BFL initiative provides users with *capability and opportunity* as there is the option for a free health check at a venue that they have already chosen to attend. Furthermore, the breaks in play provide further opportunities to have a health check. It is also possible that behaviour of the users may have been influenced through the positive association of sports and health and this may encourage them to have a health check. The authors are developing further work streams which will look at the application of the COM-B model to see if whether the NHS style health checks can modify health behaviour.

All seven cricket venues who hosted the BFL service have offered positive feedback from an organizational perspective, and additional work is underway to look at how venues can work more closely with local health commissioning groups to maximize the cost-effectiveness and sustainability of the impact of offering free health checks during cricket matches. Further work is also being planned to include greater levels of user follow up after participation in a health check, and comparisons in service uptake between different time formats of the game (T20 compared to One Day Internationals) and domestic cricket compared to international matches. Initial data suggests that it is not the format of the game but the positioning of the health checks service that prompts greater levels of uptake, something which can be attributed to the opportunistic nature of participants choosing to undertake a health check whilst passing by.

Conclusion

The findings of this initial study suggests that cricket stadia may be a feasible setting for providing health promotion interventions in populations that may not otherwise engage with primary care. Although the types of health checks illustrated are not intended to replace NHS health checks, they may play a role in augmenting the uptake of statutory checks using the power of sport to modify health perceptions and ultimately health behaviour. Further studies are required to look at the scalability and cost-effectiveness of rolling out similar initiatives on a larger scale.

Disclosure statement

No potential conflict of interest was reported by the authors.

References

Centre for Economics and Business Research. 2014. "The Economic Cost of Cardiovascular Disease from 2014-2020 in Six European Economies." *Centre for Economics and Business Research*, August 28. Accessed January 30, 2016. www.cebr.com/reports/the-rising-cost-of-cvd

Curran, K., B. Drust, and D. Richardson. 2014. "'I Just Want to Watch the Match!' a Practitioner's Reflective Account of Men's Health Themed Match Day Events at an English Premier League Football Club." *Soccer and Society* 15 (6): 919–933.

Diabetes UK. 2013. "Diabetes in the UK 2013: Key Statistics on Diabetes." *Diabetes UK*, March 01. Accessed January 30, 2016. https://www.diabetes.org.uk/About_us/What-we-say/Statistics/Diabetes-in-the-UK-2013-Key-statistics-on-diabetes/

Drygas, W., J. Ruszkowska, M. Philpott, O. BjÖrkstrÖm, M. Parker, R. Ireland, and M. Tenconi. 2013. "Good Practices and Health Policy Analysis in European Sports Stadia: Results from the 'Healthy Stadia' Project." *Health Promotion International* 28 (2): 157–165.

Dubuy, V., K. De Cocker, I. De Bourdeaudhuij, L. Maes, J. Seghers, J. Lefevre, and G. Cardon. 2014. "Evaluation of a Real World Intervention Using Professional Football Players to Promote a Healthy Diet and Physical Activity in Children and Adolescents from a Lower Socio-economic Background: A Controlled Pretest-posttest Design." *BMC Public Health* 14 (1): 1.

Gholap, N., M. Davies, K. Patel, N. Sattar, and K. Khunti. 2011. "Type 2 Diabetes and Cardiovascular Disease in South Asians." *Primary Care Diabetes* 5: 45–56.

Hunt, Kate, Sally Wyke, Cindy M. Gray, Annie S. Anderson, Adrian Brady, Christopher Bunn, Peter T. Donnan, Elisabeth Fenwick, Eleanor Grieve, and Jim Leishman. 2014. "A Gender-sensitised Weight Loss and Healthy Living Programme for Overweight and Obese Men Delivered by Scottish Premier League Football Clubs (FFIT): A Pragmatic Randomised Controlled Trial." *The Lancet* 383 (9924): 1211–1221.

Jin, L. J., I. B. Lamster, J. S. Greenspan, N. B. Pitts, C. Scully, and S. Warnakulasuriya. 2015. "Global Burden of Oral Diseases: Emerging Concepts, Management and Interplay with Systemic Health." *Oral Diseases* 24. doi:http://dx.doi.org/10.1111/odi.12428.

Michie, S., L. Atkins, and R. West. 2014. *The Behaviour Change Wheel: A Guide to Designing Interventions*. London: Silverback Publishing.

Parnell, D., A. Pringle, J. McKenna, S. Zwolinsky, Z. Rutherford, J. Hargreaves, L. Trotter, M. Rigby, and D. Richardson. 2015. "Reaching Older People with PA Delivered in Football Clubs: The Reach, Adoption and Implementation Characteristics of the Extra Time Programme." *BMC Public Health* 15: 220. doi: http://dx.doi.org/10.1186/s12889-015-1560-5. http://www.biomedcentral.com/1471-2458/15/220.

Pringle, A., S. Zwolinsky, J. McKenna, A. Daly-Smith, S. Robertson, and A. White. 2013. "Effect of a National Programme of Men's Health Delivered in English Premier League Football Clubs." *Public Health* 127 (1): 18–26.

PHE (Public Health England). 2015. "NHS Health Best Practice Guidance." *Public Health England*, January 01. Accessed January 30, 2016. http://www.healthcheck.nhs.uk/

PHE (Public Health England). 2016. "National Obesity Observatory (NOO) Obesity Observatory. UK Prevalence and Trends." *Public Health England*, January 01. Accessed January 30, 2016. www.noo.org.uk/NOO_about_obesity

Robson, J., I. Dostal, A. Sheikh, S. Eldridge, V. Madurasinghe, C. Griffiths, C. Coupland, and J. Hippisley-Cox. 2016. "The NHS Health Check in England: An Evaluation of the First Four Years." *BMJ Open* 6(1).

Visram, S., S. M. Carr, and L. Geddes. 2015. "Can Lay Health Trainers Increase Uptake of NHS Health Checks in Hard-to-Reach Populations? A Mixed-method Pilot Evaluation." *Journal of Public Health* 37 (2): 226–233.

WHO Global Health Observatory (GHO) data. 2008. *Raised Cholesterol Situation and Trends.* Accessed Jan 30, 2016. www.who.int/gho/ncd/risk_factors/cholesterol_text/en.

Witty, K., and A. White. 2011. "Tackling Men's Health: Implementation of a Male Health Service in a Rugby Stadium Setting." *Community Practitioner* 84 (4): 29–33.

Health promotion orientation of GAA sports clubs in Ireland

Aoife Lane, Niamh Murphy, Alex Donohoe and Colin Regan

ABSTRACT
In Ireland, a GAA sports club exists in almost every community. The purpose of this analysis is to present the health promotion orientation of clubs who have been recruited to a project run in partnership with the GAA and the Irish Department of Health. Clubs completed a questionnaire and took part in a focus group to explore why they were willing to take part in this initiative. Clubs viewed health promotion as a natural progression of their existing work. They scored low in relation to policy and coaching activities specific to health promotion, and higher for their ideology and environmental considerations. GAA sports clubs are already engaging in some health-related activities and are eager to engage further. Clubs require support to ensure health promotion is embedded into their core business.

Introduction

A setting is the place or social context in which people engage in daily activities where environmental, organizational and personal factors interact to affect health (Nutbeam 1998). The sports club is a setting which exists primarily to promote sport but which can be harnessed to promote health (Kokko, Kannas, and Villberg 2006) yet they are often not supportive of health. For example, among young people, involvement in sport is not always protective against overweight/obesity (Lane, Harrison, and Murphy 2014) while evidence is at best moderate for the health benefits of adult sport (Oja et al. 2015). Also, worldwide (Sønderlund et al. 2014), and in Ireland, sports participation is associated with higher alcohol consumption (O'Farrell et al. 2010). Therefore, as well as using sports clubs to promote sport by ensuring a greater and more active membership (Eime, Payne, and Harvey 2008) there is potential, and an existing orientation to promote health more broadly in the club (Kokko, Kannas, and Villberg 2006, 2009).

In 2014, Kokko and colleagues presented a conceptual framework for health promoting sports clubs (HPSC), identifying layers of activity at the macro, meso and micro level; from the policy and orientation of a club to, support for, and action around health promotion in daily club operations. Geidne, Quennerstedt, and Eriksson (2013) emphasized the role of external factors such as national level sporting and health organizations in supporting the HPSC. In Australia, Casey et al. (2012) reported increased organizational capacity among national sporting bodies, and good evidence for policy and practice at national level, but this was not always translated to club activity. In a move to provide direct support for clubs, the Healthy Sporting Environments Demonstration Project, supported by VicHealth, led to positive steps in relation to institutional change and delivery of health promotion (Nicholson et al. 2013).

Gaelic games are sports (hurling and gaelic football) that are indigenous to Ireland. The GAA, which is the national governing body (NGB) for these games, is the largest sporting organization in the country with up to one million members equating to almost 1 in 4 of the national population. The NGB oversees approximately 3000 clubs, which are volunteer-based, civic entities to the extent that the GAA plays a pivotal role in Irish society beyond the basic aim of promoting Gaelic games. Amateurism (no players of Gaelic games receive remuneration for their time and efforts); community identity and inclusion are among the core values of the organization while the GAA already promotes the health and well-being of its members and wider community. Since 2006 the GAA has promoted an Alcohol and Substance Abuse Programme, which has manifested as an officer, policy and practice in almost all clubs. This focus on a singular health topic did not adequately respond to the broad health needs of the Association's membership base, or reflect the degree of health promoting work many clubs were already engaging in so the GAA and National Health Service Executive (HSE) set out to examine the potential of the GAA club as a setting for broader health promotion. This paper presents the health promotion orientation of clubs taking part in the pilot phase of the GAA Healthy Club Project, which was established to guide the development of the HPSC in a GAA context.

Methods

Sample and design

To recruit clubs for the project, an expression of interest was disseminated nationwide by the GAA and subsequent submissions were reviewed in a selection process agreed upon by a National Steering Committee. This involved a scoring system across three criteria, which included ratings for current initiatives and community links and the location and size of each club. In total, 18 clubs were recruited from 60 who applied to participate; four from each province in Ireland and two additional mentoring clubs. These clubs were identified as mentoring clubs because they were already active in a health promotion context. Clubs were briefed on the project and asked to form a committee consisting of club members and community representatives. All clubs were invited to take part in this baseline assessment of health promotion activity in their clubs prior to the development of action plans to promote health in their club and community. Clubs were supported by three employees working in the Community and Health department at the national governance level of the GAA (their positions being supported by a Service Line Agreement with the National HSE).

Data collection

Data were collected through a questionnaire and focus group interviews. The questionnaire included a HPSC Index (Kokko, Kannas, and Villberg 2009), which was originally generated from a set of HPSC standards identified by Kokko, Kannas, and Villberg (2006). The index assesses the health promotion orientation of clubs in relation to policy, ideology, practice and the club environment. In this study, questions were adapted to better reflect the GAA setting and an additional component, the 'juvenile environment', was included to specifically address health promotion activity in this context. Participating clubs self-rated on how well their club performed on 34 different items on a five-point likert scale that ranged from 'this does not describe the club well at all' to 'this describes the club very well'. The instrument also included questions on membership and an assessment of current levels of engagement with and perception of partnerships. Questionnaires were emailed to, and completed by the healthy club committee chairperson in all participating clubs in October 2013. Regional focus group interviews with at least two representatives from each club participating in the project were carried out in January 2014 to assess why they self-selected to become involved in a HPSC project. Ethical approval for this project was granted by the WIT Research Ethics Committee.

Data analysis

Similar to analysis conducted by Kokko, Kannas, and Villberg (2009), the original likert scale used in the questionnaire was reduced to a two-point scale (0–1; 0 indicates that the factor does not describe the club at all and 1 indicates it describes the club very well) so the overall range of scores on the index was between 0 and 34. Scores for items in each component (policy, ideology, etc.) of the index were summed and mean scores were used to categorize clubs as low, moderate or high health promoting in each of the sub-indices and overall. Higher scores indicate higher levels of health promotion activity so to reach an overall high health promoting standard, clubs had to have a score of 23 or more. Scores ranging between 17 and 22.99 were deemed to indicate a moderate level of health promotion while clubs who scored lower than 16.99 were classified as low health promoting. Scores for each of the sub-indices were also categorized into low, moderate and high. For policy, scores higher than six and lower than 3.99 were deemed high and low health promoting respectively; >1.72 and >4.50 were required for a high health promotion score for ideology and practice respectively while cut points for high and low health promotion were >5.30 and <3.49 for the environment and >8.25 and <5.49 for the juvenile environment. Data collected through focus groups were analysed using thematic content analysis (Green and Thorogood 2014). Each transcription was read and re-read to ensure a thorough understanding of the data. Subsequent coding was mainly deductive as quotes related to the general topic area of the relevance of health promotion for sports clubs were coded. These were then grouped into clusters and two main themes were identified. Peer-debriefing was used to verify findings.

Results

Description of participating clubs

Sixteen clubs completed this baseline assessment, representing an 89% response rate. Clubs reported an average of 408 (range 124–1012) playing members, and 146 (range 45–322) non playing members resulting in an average total membership of 546 individuals. Clubs had approximately two playing pitches and all had changing facilities while most also owned an indoor community/club centre. On average, clubs had about 29 volunteer coaches with

Table 1. Health promotion orientation of participating clubs ($n = 16$).

	Average (Min–Max)	Health promotion category
Policy index (range 0–8.0)	3.86 (.50–7.0)	Low
Ideology index (range 0–2.0)	1.72 (.75–2.0)	High
Practice index (range 0–6.0)	3.25 (1.25–5.0)	Moderate
Environment index (range 0–7.0)	4.63 (2.5–6.0)	Moderate
Juvenile environment index (range 0–11.0)	7.05 (4.0–9.0)	Moderate
Overall HP index score (range 0–34.0)	20.5 (13.75–27.75)	Moderate

basic qualifications and an additional 14 with higher certification. The GAA club activities, including coaching are overseen and carried out entirely by volunteers.

Health promotion orientation of clubs

The average policy score was classified as 'low health promoting', ideology as 'high' and the remainder were deemed 'moderately health promoting' (Table 1). Additional analysis of these scores excluding the two mentoring clubs resulted in lower average scores across all domains but there was no subsequent impact on the overall health promotion category. Furthermore, average scores for overall health promotion and each domain were higher for the bigger clubs taking part in the study.

Analysis of individual items for the policy domain are among the lowest across all indicators of health promotion in the clubs, particularly in relation to written regulations (0.27), and acknowledgement of health and well-being in club constitutions (0.23). Highest scores are allocated to the ideology indicators, such as Go Games, which emphasizes participation for all at youth level (0.89) while issues in relation to bullying (0.73), respect (0.69), fair play (0.75), safety (0.77), and maintenance of a safe, smoke-free environment (0.73) also scored well. Lower scores were noted for engagement with coaches and parents (0.45) and the provision of health education for members (0.45). Also, health promotion does not have a particularly strong emphasis in a coaching context (0.50), and coaches are not always screened for their qualifications (0.55) and interaction skills (0.52). Finally, clubs scored poorly (0.39) on the provision of healthy food options after sporting activities (Table 2).

Partnerships

About half of the clubs have engaged with coaches and external agencies, such as youth and charity groups, on club matters. Clubs rated their agreement with several statements about partnership in a GAA context (Table 3). While approximately two-thirds (69%) of clubs did perceive partners to be an important part of the club and indicated that they should formalize the partnership process, the subsequent manifestation of the partnership in relation to meetings and recruitment of new partners was lower, ranging from 6 to 38%.

Rationale for health promotion in the club

Natural progression

GAA clubs already promote health and well-being among their members and the wider community and this project is a welcome framework to further support, harness and capture

Table 2. Sub components of health promotion orientation ($n = 16$).

	Average (0–1)
The club's regulations include a written section on well-being and/or health promotion/ health education/healthy lifestyle	0.27
The club's regulations include a written policy on substance misuse (ASAP policy)	0.52
Health and well-being ideals are written in the club's constitution and regulations	0.23
The club health promotion activities are evaluated in the Annual Report	0.36
The club collaborates with other sports clubs and/or health professionals on health issues	0.55
The club assures that its sub committees have agreed regulations and practices	0.59
Health promotion is part of the coaching practice	0.61
Training pitches and schedules are distributed fairly across all teams in the club	0.83
The club promotes the 'Go Games' principles	0.89
The club promotes the 'Respect Initiative'	0.83
The club's Executive Committee discusses its regulations with coaches and parents at regular intervals	0.45
The club pays particular attention to coaches/instructors interaction skills	0.52
The club provides education on health issues or makes provisions for its members to receive such education	0.45
The club promotes individual growth and development	0.64
Sports injuries are comprehensively dealt with (including the psychological effect of injury)	0.57
The club reviews and communicates treatment policies in the case of a sports injury	61
The club assumes its fair share of responsibility for a safe sports environment (e.g. reviews the sports environment yearly)	0.77
The club provides a sports environment that is smoke free during juvenile activities	0.73
Coaches and other officials give a good example through their own behaviour	0.77
Respect for the referee is evident at all levels in the club (players, coaches, administrators)	69
Possible conflicts (e.g. bullying) are monitored and dealt with	0.73
In coaching, there is a health promoting element beyond sports performance	0.50
Healthy food options are made available following sports activities	0.39
All juvenile events are held in an alcohol-free environment	0.81
The club promotes maximum participation adopting an 'every child gets a game' policy	0.70
The implentation of 'everybody plays' policy is dependant on the importance of the com- petition	0.59
The implementation of 'everybody plays' policy is hindered by parents expectations of success by winning	0.36
The implementation of 'everybody plays' policy is hindered by other club's reluctance to adopt a similar approach	0.52
The club measurement of success is winning underage tournaments	0.30
The club perceives that success can only be achieved by having the best players on the pitch at all times	0.28
The club selects and approves coaches who have accredited coaching qualifications	0.55
The club specifically identifies suitable and qualified coaches for juvenile coaching positions	0.69
The club does not tolerate the use of bad language	0.59
The club enforces a fair play policy	0.75

the full extent of these efforts. One club remarked that 'it had been something they had been thinking about doing anyway … to use the club to do some sort of health initiative for its members, and the community'.

Community responsibility

One of the key values of the GAA is community identity. It was noted by a club that they 'owe it to players and members to be able to help them out in other aspects of their life' suggesting an awareness of the role of the GAA club beyond playing, coaching, and administrative activities. There was a belief that 'the GAA are brilliantly positioned to get into every nook and cranny in Ireland'. The concept of taking responsibility and working towards being and remaining relevant in the community was alluded to as clubs indicated their rationale for taking part in this project.

Table 3. Perceptions of partnership in the sports club.

	% Agree (*n*)
Partners have always been an important part of the club	68.8 (11)
Roles, responsibilities and expectations are agreed with partners	50 (8)
Regular meetings are held with partners	37.5 (6)
Partners sit on committees in the club	6.3 (1)
Contact with partners is mostly informal	56.3 (9)
There is no need to formalize the partnership process	18.8 (3)
Formalizing the partnership process takes too much time	18.8 (3)
Club members actively seek new partners	37.5 (6)

> It's about making it (the club) relevant in our community and that people in our community have a better experience by getting involved in the local GAA club.

While aware of the need to extend beyond their day-to-day remit of promoting Gaelic games in their community, clubs were also cognizant of the benefits of the healthy club concept to maintaining high standards both on and off the field.

> I think that everybody's aspiration is if you have healthier players in body and mind and it's not just players, it's parents, it's mothers, it's brothers, fathers whatever. If you have a healthier community you'll want to kick on and do something on the field as well as off the field.

Discussion

The GAA club in Ireland represents an ideal setting for health promotion. This entity, which is often the central hub of social as well as sporting activity in the community, is an ideal conduit for efforts to positively influence the health of members and the general community beyond a role in providing opportunities for sport. This paper presents an assessment of the potential for health promotion in GAA clubs in Ireland, and how health is currently being integrated into the daily workings of these clubs. Results from the questionnaire showed that scores for the policy domain were among the lowest across all indicators of health promotion in the clubs. The juvenile, and overall environment was classed as moderately health promoting. In relation to a healthy coaching environment, clubs performed poorly in terms of providing healthy food options after sporting activities and also did not fully engage with health promotion, beyond sporting performance in their coaching endeavours. Partnership was evident but there was a lack of understanding about how it could work effectively. Focus group discussions revealed that engaging in this initiative was a natural progression of work already being undertaken by the club and that there was a sense of responsibility to the community to respond to their health needs. It should be noted also that all of this work takes place in a voluntary capacity in clubs, which explains the innate willingness to engage in this project, despite a lack of funding from central sources.

From a settings perspective, the GAA and its club unit are well placed for health promotion activity. Previous commentary (Casey et al. 2012) remarked on the lack of strategic planning and development plans from national sporting organizations to support the HPSC concept. The leadership and investment offered by the NGB in this initiative, in partnership with a state agency for health, reflects the perceived importance of this work. Specifically, the GAA have a Community and Health department at national level and a Healthy Club Project Steering Group with representatives from the sport, health and education sector who work to support and reinforce health promotion activity in clubs. Also, since the commencement of this work the GAA has implemented new 'health and wellbeing' structures at national, regional and club level of the Association. In this particular analysis, high scores for ideology, and action around safety, respect and fair play indicate an existing disposition for health promotion in clubs while commentary from club representatives suggest a readiness for even more activity. At this early stage, clubs scored poorly in relation to governance and coaching indicators, lacking the policy and 'whole club' approach required to support their health agenda. Low levels of activity among the layers of actors defined by Kokko, Green, and Kannas (2014) suggest that participating clubs had not yet embraced health promotion into the core business of the setting. Similarly, Kokko, Kannas, and Villberg (2009) reported that policy-level change and related practice, were limited in Finnish youth sports clubs.

Findings here and previous research have shown that sports clubs are particularly relevant settings for health promotion among youth (Geidne, Quennerstedt, and Eriksson 2013) and that coaches are well disposed to the integration of health promotion ideals into their sporting activities (Van Hoye et al. 2014). It is important to communicate to clubs that they can benefit from health promotion activities by developing a stronger and more diverse membership and potentially higher levels of performance, as well as greater support across the wider community in which the club exists (Eime et al. 2013; Nicholson et al. 2013). The latter is particularly relevant to the GAA club as a volunteer-based entity who will require further external expertise and resources to operate as a HPSC. To this end, it is important that clubs engage with stakeholders in their community who can support this work. Casey, Payne, and Eime (2009) highlighted the importance of partnerships in capacity building efforts for sports clubs, particularly with health specialists. In this analysis, partnerships were perceived well and were translated into actual engagement in some cases but there was a lack of understanding of how partnerships could and should work. Jones and Barry (2011) reported that trust, leadership and efficiency are key components of successful partnerships in health promotion to maximize the synergy and potential of partnerships between sports clubs and external entities.

There are a number of limitations attached to this study. The analysis represents a relatively small sample size of 16 clubs but this is a pilot project and it is important to assess and communicate the experience even at this initial stage. Secondly, clubs self-selected to take part in this study; so it is likely that they are already engaging in health promotion efforts and are predisposed to this type of activity, which may not be the case in other similar sports clubs. Finally, clubs self-reported their activities, leading to potential social desirability bias and the perception of the responding member may not be representative of the views of other members.

Conclusion

The project overall represents a relatively unique attempt by an NGB to formally integrate health promotion into the activities and ethos of clubs. The next phase of this project will involve a second wave of clubs who as well as directing their own health promotion activity, will take part in initiatives developed by the GAA and stakeholder groups. This will permit an assessment of the impact of this project on specific health behaviours. At this stage, it is positive that participants within this sports setting have embraced this work, identified by Kokko, Green, and Kannas (2014) as a key characteristic of a health promoting setting. Evidence shows that participating clubs are working well in their community to promote health. Moving forward, clubs need to accrue policy and executive level support, generate new and beneficial partnerships and must work to integrate health promotion into coaching and other day-to-day activities of the club.

Disclosure statement

No potential conflict of interest was reported by the authors.

References

Casey, M. C., W. R. Payne, and R. M. Eime. 2009. "Building the Health Promotion Capacity of Sport and Recreation Organisations: A Case Study of Regional Sports Assemblies." *Managing Leisure* 14 (2): 112–124.

Casey, M., J. Harvey, R. Eime, and W. Payne. 2012. "Examining changes in the organisational capacity and sport-related health promotion policies and practices of State Sporting Organizations." *Annals of Leisure Research* 15 (3): 261–276.

Eime, R. M., W. R. Payne, and J. T. Harvey. 2008. "Making Sporting Clubs Healthy and Welcoming Environments: A Strategy to Increase Participation." *Journal of Science and Medicine in Sport* 11: 146–154.

Eime, R. M., J. A. Young, J. T. Harvey, M. J. Charity, and W. R. Payne. 2013. "A Systematic Review of the Psychological and Social Benefits of Participation in Sport for Adults: Informing Development of a Conceptual Model of Health through Sport." *International Journal of Behavioral Nutrition and Physical Activity* 10: 135. doi: http://dx.doi.org/10.1186/1479-5868-10-135.

Geidne, S., M. Quennerstedt, and C. Eriksson. 2013. "The Youth Sports Club as a Health-promoting Setting: An Integrative Review of Research." *Scandinavian Journal of Public Health* 41: 269–283.

Green, T., and N. Thorogood. 2014. *Qualitative Methods for Health Research*. London: Sage.

Jones, J., and M. B. Barry. 2011. "Exploring the Relationship between Synergy and Partnership Functioning Factors in Health Promotion Partnerships." *Health Promotion International* 26 (4): 408–420. doi: http://dx.doi.org/10.1093/heapro/dar002.

Kokko, S., L. Kannas, and J. Villberg. 2006. "The Health Promoting Sports Club in Finland-a Challenge for the Settings Based Approach." *Health Promotion International* 21 (3): 219–229.

Kokko, S., L. Kannas, and J. Villberg. 2009. "Health Promotion Profile of Youth Sports Clubs in Finland: Club Officials' and Coaches' Perceptions." *Health Promotion International* 24 (1): 26–35.

Kokko, S., L. W. Green, and L. Kannas. 2014. "A Review of Settings-based Health Promotion with Applications to Sports Clubs." *Health Promotion International* 29 (3): 494–509.

Lane, A., M. Harrison, and N. Murphy. 2014. "Screen Time Increases Risk of Overweight and Obesity in Active and Inactive 9-Year-Old Irish Children: A Cross Sectional Analysis." *Journal of Physical Activity and Health* 11: 985–991.

Nicholson, M., R. Hoye, E. Sherry, S. Dyson, and K. Brown. 2013. *Healthy Sporting Environments Demonstration Project: Final Evaluation Report*. Melbourne: LaTrobe University.

Nutbeam, D. 1998. "Health Promotion Glossary." *Health Promotion International* 13 (4): 349–364.

O'Farrell, A. M., S. P. A. Allwright, S. C. Kenny, G. Roddy, and N. Eldin. 2010. "Alcohol Use among Amateur Sportsmen in Ireland." *BMC Research Notes* 3: 313. doi: http://dx.doi.org/10.1186/1756-0500-3-313.

Oja, P., S. Titze, S. Kokko, U. M. Kujala, A. Heinonen, P. Kelly, P. Koski, and C. Foster. 2015. "Health Benefits of Different Sports Disciplines for Adults: Systematic Review of Observational and Intervention Studies with Meta-analysis." *British Journal of Sports Medicine, Published Online First*. doi:http://dx.doi.org/10.1136/bjsports-2014-093885.

Sønderlund, A. L., K. O'Brien, P. Kremer, B. Rowland, F. De Groot, P. Staiger, L. Zinkiewicz, and P. G. Miller. 2014. "The Association between Sports Participation, Alcohol Use and Aggression and Violence: A Systematic Review." *Journal of Science and Medicine in Sport* 17 (1): 2–7.

Van Hoye, A., P. Sarazzin, J. Heuze, and S. Kokko. 2014. "Coaches' Perceptions of French Sports Clubs: Health Promotion Activities, Aims and Coach Motivation." *Health Education Journal* 74 (2): 1–13.

The community impact of football pitches: a case study of Maidstone United FC

Anthony May and Daniel Parnell

ABSTRACT

The use of third-generation artificial grass pitches (AGPs) is growing in English semi-professional football. As usage grows, research into the impact of AGPs is needed, in order to examine the potential impact of such surfaces for a football club and local community. This article analyses the experiences of National League South club Maidstone United through a detailed case study. The club have installed an AGP at their stadium and are able to utilize it for up to 80 hours a week. All the club's 45 teams are able to train and play on the AGP, and other local sport clubs have hired it, arguably increasing Public Health opportunities. This means that youth teams, first team club players and community participants alike have access to a high-quality playing surface. This has raised the club's profile in the local community and increased income generation, supporting the financial sustainability of the club.

Introduction

The use of third generation Artificial Grass Pitches (AGPs) for competitive football matches and training has become increasingly common over the last decade. This is particularly the case in Western Europe and Scandinavia, where pitches can be adversely affected by weather conditions and regular use (up to three matches per week) and clubs have looked for an alternative to natural surfaces. Football clubs have chosen to install AGPs at their training facilities and stadia because they are durable and usable in extreme meteorological conditions, as discussed by Andersson, Ekblom, and Krustrup (2008), Bjorneboe, Bahr, and Andersen (2010) and Almutawa et al. (2014). Very little is known about the potential impact of investment in AGP developments on the operations of a football club. This research seeks to explore the impact of investment in AGP facilities in football clubs settings, focusing on the financial health of a football club and the health of its surrounding local community.

Existing studies into the use of AGPs have tended to examine the perception that their use brings additional risks in terms of injury to players. One reason for this perception is the fact that first and second generation AGPs were sometimes unsuitable for football, and did bring risks to players in addition to the normal issues associated with playing a high intensity contact sport (Williams, Hume, and Kara 2011). However, the development of 'football turf' AGPs and the need to meet minimum standards set by FIFA and the Football Association has been aimed at reducing the risk of injury (Almutawa et al. 2014). Recent studies (Almutawa et al. 2014; Andersson, Ekblom, and Krustrup 2008; Bjorneboe, Bahr, and Andersen 2010; Kristenson et al. 2016; Soligard, Bahr, and Andersen 2010) have found no increased risk of injury when newer AGPs are compared to natural grass.

In addition to examinations of the risk of injury associated with AGPs, recent mainstream press reports in the United Kingdom have also linked the regular use of AGPs that use rubber crumb infill with an increased risk of cancer, because the recycled car tyres that are often used to make rubber crumb infill have been reported to contain potentially harmful carcinogens (*Daily Telegraph*, February 17, 2016). At the time of writing a correlation between rubber crumb infill and cancer has not been definitively proven and the Football Association (18 February 2016) have concluded that '3G pitches in the UK, which are built to industry-standard specifications, are safe'.[1] The Rugby Football Union, England Hockey and the Football Foundation have all come to the same conclusions based on available research. Should any study conclusively prove a significant risk to health presented by AGPs, the approach of these governing bodies may change but at the time of writing the use of AGPs is supported by governing bodies in the United Kingdom based on scientific research that they deem reliable.[2]

This is significant because the use of AGPs has grown exponentially over the last decade, and as such it is important to consider reasons for the high level of (planned and future) strategic investment into AGPs across the United Kingdom (UK). In order to further examine this growth, it is worth exploring the role of the Football Foundation. The Football Foundation is the UK's largest sport charity and was founded by the Premier League, The FA (Football Association) and the British Government in 2000. The main goal was to improve grassroots facilities and to get more people playing football (Martin et al. 2016). In the last 15 years the Football Foundation has awarded grants in excess of £513m and multiplied their Funding Partners' investment by attracting an additional £730m in partnership funding, which means more than £1.2bn has been invested. This investment includes refurbishment of existing facilities and developing new ones, increasing participation opportunities and supporting player retention (Martin et al. 2016).

The Football Foundation investments were made within local community facilities, in partnership with local authorities and football clubs. Despite this, the findings offer some noteworthy considerations for investment by football clubs. The Centre for Economics and Business Research (Cebr) (2013) report claimed that every pound spent on grass roots facilities generated £2.53 for the UK economy. Such positive figures offer (commercial and Government) investors serious positivity. Despite the current economic climate, and the resultant funding cuts to sport and leisure (Parnell, Millward, and Spracklen 2014) the report found investment by the Football Foundation into the development of community-based AGP facilities, not only offered positive returns for GDP (Gross Domestic Product), but also boosted employment and impacted local communities (Cebr 2013). Further, the report outlined benefits for local people including voluntary experience and qualifications, whilst also highlighting the potential multiplier consequences of such investment (Cebr 2013). However, looking beyond this hard financial return, it is pertinent to consider the softer and longer term opportunities a facility can offer. These include improved health and well-being (through the links between increased participation and physical activity), which could contribute to longer term positive impacts for Public Health.

In 2015, Sport England Active People's Survey evidenced continued declining participation across the nation. Clive Efford, the shadow Sports Minister for Sport at the time commented, 'It's a disaster. It's showing government cuts are having a major impact on facilities and participation. The last coalition government set about destroying everything that had been put in place to make the most of the legacy' (Gibson 2015). Interestingly, others have made the link between facility closure, austerity and participation (Parnell, Millward, and Spracklen 2014), especially due to the plummeting rates of participation in swimming (Gibson 2015). A report commissioned by the Football Foundation found that their investment in AGPs in local urban areas, yielded a 17.3% increase in participation (Burdsey 2011). It seems clear that investment in facilities is an important factor in participation.

At the time of the report, the Football Foundation had reached 275,000 participants (a figure that has grown year-on-year). Moreover, in a special issue on Football and Health Improvement (Parnell and Pringle 2016) the Football Foundation reported that participants were asked to score of out of five (with five being the most certain) on the question of whether they felt their health had improved as a result of playing on an AGP. Eighty-six per cent of 274 players questioned gave an answer of between three and five. This is a strong indication that they felt AGPs were contributing positively to their well-being (Martin et al. 2016).

In the light of the potential benefits of investment in AGPs, it appears timely to look closely at the role such investments can play within football stadia. This article appears in a collection entitled 'Healthy Stadia: from policy to practice'. As previous research has looked at the physical health of professional or semi-professional players, it is useful to look at the impact of AGPs. The particular aspects examined are the impact of AGPs on the financial health and sustainability of football clubs (including providing a source of revenue outside of matchdays), whether one dual youth and first team facility supports talent development. Further we intend to build on the existing research (Drygas et al. 2011) to explore whether an AGP at a sports club can provide regular football participation opportunities for their local community and support Public Health objectives.

Methodology

This article analyses ways in which the installation of an AGP can boost revenue and improve football clubs' community engagement and participation, using a detailed case study from the English non-league system. Existing academic research on the revenue potential, club and community/Public Health value of AGPs is limited, and therefore it is not possible to utilize an existing body of work on the exact topic discussed. This article adds a new strand to existing knowledge, whilst offering unique findings for those working within football and in some cases sports stadia. Moreover, research into AGPs does not include an English football club case study. Given the significance of English football within the global game, a case study examining the experiences of an English club adds an important layer to existing knowledge.

In England, AGPs are only currently used by non-league clubs, rather than football league clubs and so the club used for the case study has been selected on that basis. However, while the national context chosen adds to knowledge of football within that nation, the findings also have a potential transnational significance. AGPs are used by professional clubs across Europe and the findings in this article are applicable not just to semi-professional clubs in England, but to any football club that has an interest in exploring the possibility of maximizing their playing surface for a range of objectives from talent development, financial gain and/or community engagement.

The club chosen for this case study are one of the first in England to install an AGP, Maidstone United. In many ways, the club were pioneers of AGPs in England and were only the second to install an AGP (Sutton Coldfield Town were the first). After a period of over 20 years playing outside Maidstone at stadia including Dartford's Watling Street and Sittingbourne's Bourne Park, the club moved into the newly built Gallagher Stadium in 2012. The club's co-owner Oliver Ash is the head of 3G4US, a group of professional and semi-professional clubs, which aims to promote the benefits of using surfaces within training facilities and stadia. This group operates a website at www.3g4us.org which archives stories about pitches (both positive and negative). It also takes an active role in promoting the use of surfaces by offering consultancy and advice to clubs considering a switch to an artificial pitch (see Figure 1).

Data for this article were gathered using Maidstone United's own website, 3G4US's archive of news articles about AGPs, and through a detailed interview with Oliver Ash conducted by the lead first author on 27 April 2015. Details given by Mr Ash have been checked against available material and corroborated independently. Observation of matches played at the Gallagher Stadium was also carried out in order to independently ascertain the depth of community engagement in Maidstone United. The first author attended a number of matches at the stadium from 2012 to 2015 and has first-hand knowledge of the size and nature of the club's support (see Figure 2).

Figure 1. The AGP (non-matchday) at the Gallagher Stadium, the home ground of Maidstone United.

Figure 2. The AGP (matchday) at the Gallagher Stadium, the home ground of Maidstone United.

Context: the use of AGP surfaces in England

No full-time professional clubs in the English league system have installed an AGP. This is because they are currently banned for use in the Football League and Premier League. This means that clubs in the National League with ambitions to get promoted into the Football League have not installed AGPs either. English football represents an anomaly in its ban on artificial surfaces in full-time professional football, even within the UK. Scottish Premier League teams Kilmarnock and Hamilton Academical have installed an artificial surface, as have Scottish Championship clubs Queen of the South and Alloa Athletic. Welsh Premier League champions The New Saints also play on an AGP.

It is also the case that other professional sports in England allow the use of AGP. St Georges Park is the FA's new flagship facility, and hosts a number of AGP for their elite youth, men's and women's teams. Additionally, the English FA, the English Premier League are also strategically committed to the development of an AGP infrastructure across England through funding investment. Moreover, AGP are commonplace (and indeed expected), in Football League and Premier League elite training, youth academy facilities and a growing number of community facilities (for example, Norwich FC and Arsenal FC). Interestingly, Rugby Union's Saracens and Super League team Widnes both play on AGPs, despite the fact that both codes of rugby are high impact sports with regular heavy collisions.

A vote held in November 2014 by member clubs of the Football League on allowing AGPs was tied, with 34 clubs voting in favour, 34 voting for a continuation of the existing ban and 4 abstentions (*The Guardian*, 6th November 2014). The Professional Footballers Association (PFA) had lobbied for the ban to be upheld because many of its members feared 'they couldn't play' on artificial surfaces without risking long-term health problems (BBC Sport, 6th November 2014). The PFA's support for the ban was based on a survey taken two years before the vote itself (The PFA 2012). One anonymous respondent to the survey crystallized the reasons for opposition to AGPs in his profession, saying:

> I answered no to playing matches on artificial surfaces as I feel that it would not be a good idea for most players from about the age of 25 onwards. Once you get to mid- twenties and you have played lots of football you start to feel the effects on your joints. I really think that artificial surfaces would reduce the number of 30+ professional footballers. (The PFA 2012)

Despite significant research indicating the contrary, the report also states that 'many players believe if they had to play on artificial turf on a regular basis then their careers would be curtailed by a number of years' (The PFA 2012).

The antipathy of some players and clubs towards AGPs does not appear to extend to the English FA whose vision for the next five years of football development involves investment in up to 600 pitches in 30 cities across England. In 2014, there were 639 publicly available AGPs in England, as compared to 3735 in the World Cup winning nation, Germany (*The Guardian*, 10th October 2014). Natural grass pitches degrade more quickly, and are often of poor quality or unavailable in winter and spring due to the effect of unfavourable weather conditions. The FA's estimate is that they are typically available for only five hours per week as opposed to the 70–80 h of availability for an AGP.

Given the lack of availability and poor condition of natural grass surfaces it should come as no surprise that football participation is suffering. In the Active People Survey 9, the largest survey of sport and active recreation ever carried out in Europe (since 2005/6 to 2014/5), football presented further declines in participation. The number of 16+ and 16–25-year-olds playing 1 × 30 mins of moderate football has declined in 2014/2015 in comparison to the first survey undertaken (2005/6). In 2014, as a result of failing to reverse the participation decline, the FA were dealt a £1.6m cut from the £30million four-year investment from Sport England. At the time, poor weather conditions, facilities and increased costs for clubs and the end-user (i.e. players) were attributed as factors influencing this decline (Parnell and Widdop 2015). The FA believe that this reduced playing time is leading to English players being technically poorer than counterparts in Europe, because pitches are both of low quality and available for less time than artificial surfaces (*The Guardian*, 10th October 2014).

Given this situation, the continued ban on AGP in the Football League and Premier League seems contrary to the aims of the FA regarding increased participation through the development of AGPs. Indeed, the FA have made a recent commitment to investment in AGPs and it appears that the Premier League will continue to commit part of their grassroots investments to these facilities (*The Guardian*, 12 August 2015). To invest heavily in AGPs for recreational use but not allow them for use at a higher level would indicate muddled thinking in the English game, especially as the ban on AGPs does not extend to the FA Cup which Football League teams compete within; indeed, the subject of the case study in this article, Maidstone United, beat Football League club Stevenage in this competition during the 2014/15 season.

It is also the case that AGPs are allowed within semi-professional football. Going as far down as level eight of the English football pyramid (the Isthmian, Northern and Southern Leagues), there are currently 11 clubs within the non-league system in England that have installed an AGP. This figure has risen from just two in 2012. There are also a further 12 AGPs in use at level nine (County League level). This figure is low compared to the number of clubs who use AGPs in continental Europe, but the relatively rapid growth in use at levels eight, seven and six of the English football pyramid is worthy of investigation. As the following case study demonstrates, there are important factors both on and off-field that have influenced the decision of clubs to install AGPs.

Case study: Maidstone United

At present, Maidstone United does not play in the Football League. However, they are a club whose size and significance is appropriate for a meaningful case study. It is not possible to assess the impact of an AGP on revenue and community engagement in full-time professional football in England, but Maidstone provides a useful case study with findings applicable to small- and medium-sized football clubs. With regular attendances of over 1800, a full-time manager and professional coaching staff, plus 45 teams competing under its auspices, Maidstone has a similar profile to many clubs competing in Football League Division Two. The club also has a similar profile to most full-time professional clubs competing in the National League for their community work.

Published articles on football and community programmes at Burton Albion FC helps make a comparison, as although the two clubs compete at different levels, the size of their support and level of community engagement is similar (Martin et al. 2016; Parnell and Pringle 2016; Parnell and Richardson 2014; Pringle et al. 2014). The outward facing community programmes attached to football clubs offer an interesting and varied context for further research. Authors have outlined the growing health potential of football-based community programmes (Parnell, Pringle, McKenna et al. 2015; Pringle et al. 2014). As such, this case study will make the assumption that offering and delivering increased participation will in turn facilitate positive physical activity opportunities and contribute positively towards the Public Health agenda (Bailey et al. 2013).

Maidstone has been promoted twice since 2012, and will play in the National League South (formerly Conference South) in 2015–2016. It would be difficult to make strong claims about the use of an AGP without selecting a club that shows evidence of community engagement, but the size of Maidstone United's support and its continual growth since 2012 helps to validate any claims made. In 2015, the club extended the capacity of their stadium to 3000, executing plans made following promotion to the Isthmian League Premier Division (Maidstone United FC, 18th March 2015). Overall, as one of the first and certainly the most prominent and well-supported club to use an AGP, Maidstone is ideal for a case study examining the potential benefits of AGPs both to clubs and the communities they are based within.

When Maidstone United decided to install an AGP, the club's owners were, as Oliver Ash (2015) put it during an interview with the first author, 'in the dark' about the possible community benefits. However, as the club does not possess separate training facilities, the AGP allowed the club to both train and play on the same surface, there was a clear benefit in terms of both space utilization and the efficiency savings in making need to invest in a training ground redundant. Ash (2015) confirmed that the surface that Maidstone installed can be used between 50 and 80 h per week without significant degradation in quality. This has allowed the club to set up a football academy whose players also use the surface during the week. There are 80 students at the academy (aged 16–18) who are studying for a BTEC Level 3 qualification in sport, and are also able to take an optional A Level in Maths. The academy teams play in the National League Youth Alliance. It is apparent that the academy not only contributes to support the talent development and performance objectives of the football club, but also supports community-oriented educational outputs.

The multi-purpose facility and strategic management deployed between the football club and the academy offers a coherent message across all operations. The academy is run by first-team manager Jay Saunders, who has playing experience at a higher level than

Maidstone currently play at, and was attracted to the club by the possibility of working full-time (Maidstone United FC 2015). Saunders is also able to assess the quality of academy graduates and promote them to first-team football if suitable.

Since moving to the Gallagher Stadium, the club have seen three academy graduates move into league football; these are Aaron Simpson (Wolverhampton Wanderers), Ben Swift (Aston Villa) and Alfie Pavey (Millwall). A number have also progressed to the club's first team, including midfielder Charley Robertson (Maidstone United FC 2015). Compared to other local clubs, Maidstone is at a significant advantage in terms of developing an academy because every player at the club has a high quality surface to train upon. The dual training facility offer an interesting context for those involved in talent development. Indeed, Relvas et al. (2010) have highlighted the importance of congruence between youth and first team training proximity, structures and culture for effective talent development.

The high quality playing facility attracts good players to the club, and in turn the academy squads become progressively stronger. Maidstone has been promoted twice in the last four seasons. They have also signed a number of players from higher levels – Jay May from Ebbsfleet United, Frannie Collin and Lee Worgan from Tonbridge Angels, Joe Healy from Welling United and Jack Parkinson from Woking have all been notable additions and well known within non-league football (Maidstone United 2015). In addition to the academy squad, the club has a further 45 teams. These are all able to train on the AGP. Maidstone has youth squads from under-16 to under-6 levels, and also has women and girls teams and a disability section. As Ash (2015) states, all of these squads bring in footballers from the local community and support from parents and family members. This in turn leads to increased awareness of the club in the community.

While it is certainly possible for clubs in non-league football to have as many squads as Maidstone does, only clubs with an AGP can have them all using one surface, interacting with each other and developing a sense of belonging to one club. There is a clear advantage to an AGP in developing and maintaining a community around a non-league club. There are also community health benefits to having a facility like Maidstone's available. Young people are able to use a high quality facility to develop their football skills and also to take part in regular physical activity outside of a school setting, just as they do with clubs higher up the football pyramid (Martin et al. 2016).

When the club's 45 squads are not using the AGP. Maidstone is also able to rent out their facilities to local businesses and football teams during the evening. This brings in revenue from the cost of renting out catering facilities, the bar area, and of course the pitch. It also increases awareness of the club amongst businesses and local footballers. Ash (2015) said that 'the surface was the only way we could see of bringing the community into the club'. The local community are able to use the stadium late into the evening, a situation that not only increases possible revenue streams but also allows people to feel a part of the club. A community has developed around the shared use of the surface. Over 1000 people per week use Maidstone's AGP and other facilities (Interview with Oliver Ash 2015). Again, there are clear potential health benefits to facilitating regular physical activity on a high quality surface. A rise in participation is indeed what Sport England and other national governing bodies and the Football Foundation are in pursuit of (Lansley and Parnell 2015; Martin et al. 2016).

Installing an AGP required an outlay of £350,000. The surface itself cost £160,000, which Ash (2015) confirmed with the first author is the average price for a pitch that meets FIFA and The FA standards. Given that Maidstone was moving into a new stadium and had to pay costs for installing the base and drainage, and also making the ground ready for a football pitch, the cost was higher than it would be for a club installing a surface at an existing football stadium with drainage and infrastructure already in place. The stadium is entirely owned and managed by the football club and although Gallagher Construction has bought the naming rights until 2022, no third party owns any part of the stadium (Maidstone United FC 2015). This meant that the club bore all the costs of installing the surface. This is significant because Maidstone's owners had no alternative but to go with if they wanted to pay off the costs of building the Gallagher Stadium.

Ash (2015) told the first author that it is hard to say definitively at this stage whether the cost of installing the surface has already been paid off. He did, however, confirm in his interview that Maidstone United runs at a profit, and is a sustainable business. He also confirmed that the club have experienced 'growth season upon season' and said that given the need for a significant outlay on the new stadium, the installation of the AGP surface was ultimately the 'only way for the club to survive'. The club have met their aim of bringing the local community into the stadium and the pitch that they have installed has played a significant part in that. In an environment where few clubs are able to make a profit, the health of Maidstone United as a business is comparatively good. While survival was the initial aim, the club have thrived both on and off field and as Ash (2015) confirms, the decision to install an AGP has played a key part in that.

The growing financial and footballing case for investment in an AGP is clear, yet the importance and potential impact of this facility to the community and the Public Health agenda may be the most valuable. Due to the durability of the surface, clubs are able to use AGPs on a daily basis to widen their reach into the local community offering key participation and physical activity opportunities supporting Public Health outcomes. Maidstone has also been able to expand their youth, ladies and disability teams, considerably increasing the number of players directly involved in the club, and also increasing the number of people who become aware of it as a parent or supporter. This not only offers a positive contribution to Public Health, but also offers revenue and is a way of developing awareness of the club within the local community that it represents.

The level of participation within Maidstone United's grassroots and community-oriented activities is providing accessibility where there was previously none. The attractiveness of the football club has been proven as favourable to community participants (Parnell, Pringle, McKenna et al. 2015). The need for better quality playing facilities is a national and urgent issue (Parnell and Widdop 2015). Playing recreationally has proven health and social benefits (Krustrup and Bangsbo 2015; Parnell, Pringle, Widdop and Zwolinsky 2015). As such, Maidstone United FC is providing local, accessible, much needed, recreational football opportunities for its local community.

A settings-based approach to health promotion is based on the assumption that the more supportive social and physical environment is for healthy lifestyle choices makes for easier individual healthy decision-making (Whitelaw et al. 2001). Indeed, research has explored Healthy Schools (Clift and Jensen 2005), Healthy Cities (de Leeuw and Skovgaard 2005), Healthy Prisons (Whitehead 2006) and more recently Healthy Stadia (Drygas et al. 2011). Whilst sports stadia are often characterized with fast food and alcohol, opening up the playing surface via an AGP is associated with increased accessibility and participation for those sometimes considered hard-to-reach (Drygas et al. 2011). This research allows for a new understanding around the potential health promoting prospects of a football clubs through the introduction of an AGP. Not only does football plays an important role within society, but now football/sports stadia can provide a positive setting for Public Health strategies (Drygas et al. 2011). This is important for both investors and Public Health commissioners.

Further developments in the use of AGP surfaces

Ash's (2015) view is that growth in the use of artificial surfaces in English football is inevitable due to the off-field benefits that such pitches can bring, as exemplified by Maidstone United. As he puts it, 'other clubs have come to the same conclusion that Maidstone did', and they see the installation of an AGP as a positive route towards increasing community engagement for a multitude of reasons from increased revenue, talent development and health improvement. Ash (2015) also feels that clubs will 'begrudgingly accept' playing on artificial surfaces more often but there will be 'a lot of emotion and prejudice' against change. This was demonstrated by the reaction of then Stevenage manager Graham Westley to his club drawing Maidstone in the FA Cup. 'As a surface it doesn't work', he said. 'When you're playing on it players' safety is in jeopardy' (*The Guardian* 15th November 2014). Westley made these emotive comments despite the fact that Stevenage's first team squad trains on an AGP surface every day (*Kent Sports News*, 12th November 2014).

In an English context, community engagement is particularly important for semi-professional clubs whose revenue and turnover is often low, and whose visibility in the local and national media is limited. Clubs playing below the Football League need to find innovative ways to attract new supporters and increase their revenue, and AGPs can be used for both of these purposes. Further, building on their ability to promote health in the local community may attract Public Health commissioners looking to invest in effective programmes. A key underlying principle for investment in an AGP will be the financial benefits. Sutton United are one of the clubs who have decided that installing an AGP is a good way to attract new supporters, with the club's manager Paul Doswell saying that one of the key benefits would be that all 28 of the club's junior teams would be able to train on the same surface as the first team. Doswell outlined, 'That's 28 sets of parents who maybe have never been to Gander Green Lane [Sutton's stadium]', adding 'they'll hopefully bring their child to training and think "maybe we'll come down on Saturday and check it out for a game"'(*Non League Football Paper*, 8th March 2015).

Doswell went on further to highlight the importance of expanding the accessibility of their operations, 'as a football club we need to be more than simply a one day a fortnight operation' (*Non League Football Paper*, 8th March 2015). He sees the introduction of an AGP as a method of ensuring that the club's stadium is used more regularly, bringing in greater revenue and raising the profile of the club in the local community. This has been the case for Maidstone United. Sutton are not alone in installing a new AGP; Oxford City FC of the National League North have also spent £300,000–£400,000 on a new pitch, which they argue will allow up to 40 local clubs the opportunity to play all year round on a high quality, FIFA rated surface (*Oxford Mail*, 10th April 2015). Lewes FC of the Isthmian League have also spent £850,000 on a new facility incorporating an AGP for community use, which opened in July 2015 (*Sussex Express*, 14th July 2015). There is a real opportunity to explore whether investment in these facilities can result in opposing the trend of declining participation in football.

These are just three examples of clubs following Maidstone's example; further down the football 'pyramid' in England there are also clubs planning to install an AGP, including Ashford United who play in the Southern Counties East League (*Kent Online*, 23rd April 2015), and Redditch United of the Southern Premier League (*Redditch and Alcester Advertiser*, 6th November 2014). The latter club are unable to fund the cost of installing the surface themselves and have launched a public appeal for help in developing a facility for the whole local community to use (*Redditch and Alcester Advertiser*, 6th November 2014). The principal barrier to the installation of an AGP surface is the cost and not every club in non-league football will be able raise £300,000 (as a minimum) to pay for a new surface. It is clear that amongst those who do have this spending power, however, an increasing number are choosing to install an AGP surface in the hope that, similarly to Maidstone United, the increased use of their pitch will boost their revenue, community engagement and fan base. Additionally, clubs are installing an AGP in the hope that this will increase participation and community reach and social impact (including Public Health), and in the process support talent identification and development, all of which will help build the case for investment.

Conclusions

There is very little research on the value of investment in AGPs within football clubs settings. Little is known on how AGPs can help contribute towards the financial health of a football club, through increased fan revenue and talent development. Further, little is known about the role of AGPs in creating opportunities for increased participation and in turn their potential contribution to the Public Health agenda. As the case study of Maidstone United demonstrates, there are benefits to installing an AGP, which go beyond the on-field performance of the first team squad. Whilst more research is needed to fully understand the potential, there remains an interesting and reasonable opportunity for successful outcomes from a financial perspective through to a Public Health perspective.

From a performance perspective players from local clubs (both at youth and adult level) are able to use the surface and become familiar with the club structures and culture, which appears to be coherently and strategically managed. Furthermore, Maidstone has been able to rent out their facilities to businesses, football schools, the local authority, and other sports clubs and bring in revenue as a consequence. This means that the stadium and its pitch are not just used on matchdays, but are available to the local community as an accessible resource. This increases the 'health' of the club in terms of sustainability and provides a high quality surface for regular use by the local community.

A number of clubs in non-league football are now following Maidstone's example and the use of AGP surfaces looks set to increase in the English game. Sutton United, Lewes and Oxford City all installed new artificial surfaces during 2015 in a bid to increase their revenue and community engagement. The example set by Maidstone seems set to be followed by an increasing number of clubs who wish to have a sustainable financial future, and provide a high quality facility for use by the local community. Given this, it is apparent that the potential benefits of AGPs within football stadia needs to be examined in depth. Case studies such as the one in this article could offer a meaningful approach to capture this impact. Indeed, regular case studies to monitor the financial, talent development and Public Health potential of clubs who install AGPs would be recommended to further understand the impact of pitches.

Notes

1. Coverage of work in this area can be found in the work of Ruffino, Fiore, and Zanetti (2013). The work of Schilirò et al. (2013), Llompart et al. (2013) and Birkholz, Belton, and Guidotti (2003) may also be useful for those with an interest in the link discussed by the *Daily Telegraph*.
2. Research in this area continues to move forward. The authors of this article are in no position to argue that AGPs are definitively 'safe' – to do so is beyond their expertise and without total research consensus it is impossible to definitively make that argument in any case. The risks presented by inhalation or dermal exposure to rubber crumb infill seem likely to continue to be measured. The authors make no prediction about the direction this research will move in and suggest that this is an area that will require continual monitoring by governing bodies and other stakeholders.

Acknowledgements

The authors wish to thank all the individuals and agencies who partnered these programmes and all the organizations who supported this work.

Disclosure statement

No potential conflict of interest was reported by the authors.

References

Almutawa, M., M. Scott, K. P. George, and B. Drust. 2014. "The Incidence and Nature of Injuries Sustained on Grass and 3rd Generation Artificial Turf: A Pilot Study in Elite Saudi National Team Footballers." *Physical Therapy in Sport* 15: 47–52.

Ames, N. 2014. "Will Artificial Become a New Reality as FA Cup Makes Its Debut on Pitch?" *The Guardian*, November 15. Accessed June 15, 2015. http://www.theguardian.com/football/2014/nov/15/fa-cup-artificial-pitch-maidstone-stevenage-football-league

Andersson, H., B. Ekblom, and P. Krustrup. 2008. "Elite Football on Artificial Turf versus Natural Grass: Movement Patterns, Technical Standards, and Player Impressions;." *Journal of Sports Sciences* 26 (2): 113–122.

Ash, O. 2015. *Interviewed by May, A*. April 27, 2015.

Bailey, R. P., C. Hillman, S. Arent, and A. Petitpas. 2013. "Physical Activity: An Underestimated Investment in Human Capital?" *Journal of Physical Activity and Health* 10: 289–308.

BBC Sport. 2014. "Artificial Pitches: Clubs Fail to Vote for a Return to Artificial Surface." *BBC Sport*, November 6. Accessed June 15, 2015. http://www.bbc.co.uk/sport/0/football/29919748

Birkholz, D., K. Belton, and T. Guidotti. 2003. "Toxicological Evaluation for the Hazard Assessment of Tire Crumb for Use in Public Playgrounds." *Journal of the Air and Waste Management Association* 53: 903–907.

Bjorneboe, J., R. Bahr, and T. E. Andersen. 2010. "Risk of Injury on Third-Generation Artificial Turf in Norwegian Professional Football." *British Journal of Sports Medicine* 44: 794–798.

Burdsey, D. 2011. "Understanding Sustainability in Relation to Football Foundation and Barclays Spaces for Sports Facility Projects." *A Report for the Football Foundation*.

Centre for Economics and Business Research (Cebr). 2013. "The Macroeconomic Benefits of Investment in Grass Roots Facilities: An Assessment of the Economic Impacts on the UK of Delivering New and Improved Local Sports Facilities at the Grass Roots Level." *A Report for the Football Foundation*.

Clift, S., and B. B. Jensen. 2005. *The Health Promoting School: International Advances in Theory, Evaluation and Practice*. 1st ed. Copenhagen: Danish University of Education Press.

Daily Telegraph. 2016. "Football Association's Project to 'transform Football' with 3G Pitches is Overshadowed by Cancer Fears." February 17. Accessed February 24, 2016. http://www.telegraph.

co.uk/sport/football/12162217/Football-Associations-project-to-transform-football-with-3G-pitches-is-threatened-by-cancer-fears.html

Drygas, W., J. Ruszkowska, M. Philpott, O. BjOrkstrOm, M. Parker, R. Ireland, and F. Roncarolo. 2011. "Good Practices and Health Policy Analysis in European Sports Stadia: Results from the 'Healthy Stadia' Project." *Health Promotion International* 28 (2): 157–165.

The Football Association. 2016. "FA Statement: Safety of Artificial 3G Football Pitches in the UK." February 18. Accessed February 24, 2016. http://www.thefa.com/news/thefa/2016/feb/statement-3g-pitches-180216

Gibson, O. 2014. "FA Reveals Its 2020 Vision: Football Hubs and Pitches for All." *The Guardian*, October 10. Accessed June 15, 2015. http://www.theguardian.com/football/2014/oct/10/fa-football-hubs–pitches-grassroots

Gibson, O. 2015. "Olympic Legacy Ends in Lethargy as Sporting Participation Plummets." *The Guardian*, June 11. Accessed June 20, 2015. http://www.theguardian.com/sport/2015/jun/11/olympic-legacy-sport-participation-plummets

Gidley, A. 2015. "Ashford United Owner Don Crosbie Excited by Pitch and Stadium Development at Homelands." *Kent Online*, April 23. Accessed June 15, 2015. http://www.kentonline.co.uk/ashford/sport/united-plans-have-the-wow-35632/

The Guardian. 2014. "No Return for Artificial Pitches after League One and League Two Clubs Split Vote." *The Guardian*, November 6. Accessed June 15, 2015. http://www.theguardian.com/football/2014/nov/06/artificial-pitches-league-one-two-chairmen

The Guardian. 2015. "Football Association Announces Extra £60m Investment in Grassroots." *The Guardian*, August 12. Accessed August 20, 2015. http://www.theguardian.com/football/2015/aug/12/football-association-extra-60m-grassroots-investment

Hammonds, S. 2015. "Shrewd U's on a Winner." *Non League Football Paper*, March 8. Accessed June 15, 2015. http://4us.org/Presentations/150308nlp.pdf

Kristenson, K., J. Bjørneboe, M. Waldén, J. Ekstrand, T. E. Andersen, and M. Hägglund. 2016. "No Association between Surface Shifts and Time-Loss Overuse Injury Risk in Male Professional Football." *Journal of Science and Medicine in Sport* 19 (3): 218–221.

Krustrup, P., and J. Bangsbo. 2015. "Recreational Football is Effective in the Treatment of Non-Communicable Diseases." *British Journal of Sports Medicine*. doi: http://dx.doi.org/10.1136/bjsports-2015-094955.

Lansley, S., and D. Parnell. 2015. "Football for Health: Getting Strategic." *Soccer & Society* 17 (2): 259–266. doi: http://dx.doi.org/10.1080/14660970.2015.1082764.

de Leeuw, E., and T. Skovgaard. 2005. "Utility-Driven Evidence for Healthy Cities: Problems with Evidence Generation and Application." *Social Science and Medicine* 61: 1331–1341.

Llompart, M., L. Sanchez-Prado, J. Pablo-Lamas, C. Garcia-Jares, E. Roca, and T. Dagnac. 2013. "Hazardous Organic Chemicals in Rubber Recycled Tire Playgrounds and Pavers." *Chemosphere* 90: 423–431.

Maidstone United F. C. 2015. "Fantastic News as Expansion Plans Are Agreed." March 18. Accessed June 15, 2015. http://www.maidstoneunited.co.uk/2015/03/fantastic-news-as-expansion-plans-are-agreed/

Martin, A., S. Morgan, D. Parnell, M. Philpott, A. Pringle, M. Rigby, A. Taylor, and J. Topham. 2016. "Editorial: A Perspective from Key Stakeholders on Football and Health Improvement." *Soccer & Society 17* (2): 175–182. doi: http://dx.doi.org/10.1080/14660970.2015.1082751.

Oxford Mail. 2015. "Forty Teams Could Benefit from Oxford City's Planned Pitch." *Oxford Mail*, April 10. Accessed June 16, 2015. http://www.oxfordmail.co.uk/news/12882299.Forty_teams_could_benefit_from_Oxford_City_s_planned__pitch/

Parnell, D., P. Millward, and K. Spracklen. 2014. "Sport and Austerity in the UK: An Insight into Liverpool 2014." *Journal of Policy Research in Tourism, Leisure and Events* 7: 200–203. doi:0.1080/19407963.2014.968309.

Parnell, D., and A. Pringle. 2016. "Football and Health Improvement: An Emerging Field." *Soccer and Society* 17 (2): 171–174.

Parnell, D., Pringle, A., McKenna, J., Zwolinsky, S., Rutherford, Z., Hargreaves, J., Trotter, L., Rigby, M., and Richardson, D. 2015. "Reaching Older People with PA Delivered in Football Clubs: The Reach,

Adoption and Implementation Characteristics of the Extra Time Programme." *BMC Public Health* 15: 25. doi: http://dx.doi.org/10.1186/s12889-015-1560-5. http://www.biomedcentral.com/1471-2458/15/220.

Parnell, D., A. Pringle, P. Widdop, and S. Zwolinsky. 2015. "Understanding Football as a Vehicle for Enhancing Social Inclusion: Using an Intervention Mapping Framework." *Social Inclusion* 3 (2): 200–203.

Parnell, D., and D. Richardson. 2014. "Introduction." *Soccer and Society* 15 (6): 823–827.

Parnell, D., and P. Widdop. 2015. "Postponed due to Pitch Conditions." *Leeds Beckett University*, March 31. Accessed June 15, 2015. http://mediacentre.leedsbeckett.ac.uk/post/postponed-due-to-pitch-conditions/

Pringle, A., D. Parnell, S. Zwolinsky, J. Hargreaves, and J. McKenna. 2014. "Effect of a Health-Improvement Pilot Programme for Older Adults Delivered by a Professional Football Club: The Burton Albion Case Study." *Soccer and Society* 15 (6): 902–918.

The Professional Footballers' Association. 2012. "Football League Consultation on Artificial Surfaces." *The Professional Footballers' Association*, May 12. Accessed June 15, 2015. https://www.thepfa.com/news/2014/10/9/~/media/Files/PFA%20-%20Football%20League%20Consultation%20on%20Artificial%20Surfaces.ashx

Redditch and Alcester Advertiser. 2014. "Pitch the Catalyst to Spark Reds' Revival." *Redditch and Alcester Advertiser*, November 6. Accessed August 15, 2015. http://www.redditchadvertiser.co.uk/sport/11583659.print/

Relvas, H., M. Littlewood, M. Nesti, D. Gilbourne, and D. Richardson. 2010. "Organizational Structures and Working Practices in Elite European Professional Football Clubs: Understanding the Relationship between Youth and Professional Domains." *European Sport Management Quarterly* 10 (2): 165–187.

Ruffino, B., S. Fiore, and M. C. Zanetti. 2013. "Environmental-Sanitary Risk Analysis Procedure Applied to Artificial Turf Sports Fields." *Environmental Science and Pollution Research* 20 (7): 4980–4992.

Schilirò, T., D. Traversi, R. Degan, C. Pignata, L. Alessandria, D. Scozia, R. Bono, and G. Gilli. 2013. "Artificial Turf Football Fields: Environmental and Mutagenicity Assessment." *Archives of Environmental Contamination and Toxicology* 64 (1): 1–11.

Soligard, T., R. Bahr, and T. E. Andersen. 2010. "Injury Risk on Artificial Turf and Grass in Youth Tournament Football." *Scandinavian Journal of Medicine and Science in Sports* 22: 356–361.

Sussex Express. 2015. "Club's New 3G Pitch Will Be an Asset to Lewes Community." *Sussex Express*, July 14. Accessed January 11, 2016. http://www.sussexexpress.co.uk/news/county-news/club-s-new-3g-pitch-will-be-an-asset-to-lewes-community-1-6842299

Whitehead, D. 2006. "The Health Promoting Prison (HPP) and Its Imperative for Nursing." *International Journal of Nursing Studies* 43: 123–131.

Whitelaw, S., A. Baxedale, C. Bryce, L. Machardy, I. Young, and E. Witney. 2001. "Settings' Based Health Promotion: A Review." *Health Promotion International* 16: 339–354.

Williams, S., P. A. Hume, and S. Kara. 2011. "A Review of Football Injuries on Third and Fourth Generation Artificial Turfs Compared with Natural Turf." *Sports Medicine* 41 (11): 903–923.

Young, M. 2014. "Stevenage Boss Critical of 3G." *Kent Sports News*, November 12. Accessed July 15, 2015. http://www.kentsportsnews.com/stevenage-boss-critical-of–12-11-2014/

Improving the physical and mental well-being of typically hard-to-reach men: an investigation of the impact of the *Active Rovers* project

Colin J. Lewis, Matthew J. Reeves and Simon J. Roberts

ABSTRACT

Strong associations exist between physical activity (PA) levels and incidence morbidity and mortality. Evidence suggests that PA levels decline with age but incidence of sedentary behaviour is high. This paper examines the effectiveness of a PA intervention hosted by a professional football club. It explores the impact of the intervention upon mental well-being, health perceptions, and lifestyle knowledge in men often classed as hard-to-reach (HTR). Data were collected through a shortened version of the Warwick-Edinburgh Mental Well-Being Scale, and a longitudinal self-report questionnaire. Pre- and post-intervention changes were determined by a Wilcoxon signed rank test ($p < .05$). Data indicated that the intervention was successful in improving aspects of mental well-being amongst the male client group. The qualitative findings revealed a less successful transfer from the intervention to more casual PA engagement. Professional football clubs appear to be appropriate environments to promote physical and mental well-being. However, behaviour change away from the football club was less obvious, suggesting further research in this area is required.

Introduction

Current health recommendations state that adults and older adults (50+) should do at least 150 min of moderate-intensity exercise or at least 75 min of vigorous-intensity aerobic exercise per week (World Health Organisation 2010). Yet, evidence would suggest the majority of older adults are not sufficiently active, and consequently fail to meet recommended levels of PA (Ward-Thompson et al. 2014). In the United Kingdom (UK), less than 25% of adults meet the recommended daily levels of physical activity, and thus are considered to be at a greater risk of induced medical conditions including: cardiovascular disease, type 2 diabetes mellitus, obesity, and some associated cancers (Fife-Schaw et al. 2014). A physically inactive lifestyle is also associated with poor skeletal health, debilitating mental ill health, and increased premature mortality (Hakola et al. 2015). Despite the reported positive associations between PA and health, epidemiological evidence suggests that PA levels decline with age (Sartini et al. 2015). Furthermore, PA levels of older adults are typically low and levels of sedentary behaviour high.

Older men (50+) are reported to be at the most risk from the 15 leading causes of death, and life expectancy is reported to be less than that for women, thus placing an increased burden on health services, and creating challenges for public health (Hunt et al. 2013). Despite the increase in health promotion campaigns, especially within male populations, adult male health continues to be a concern. When compared to that of women, the avoidable mortality rate for men remains disproportionately high (Robertson and Williamson 2005), though it is important to note that this gap is closing, due to significant improvements in health interventions for men. One probable explanation for this trend is the reluctance of HTR men (as defined by unemployment, low educational attainment, poor income and social isolation) to engage with mainstream health promotion services (Robertson et al. 2013). Typical barriers for these men engaging in healthy lifestyle interventions include time, motivation and access (Morgan et al. 2011). From a health consumption perspective, frequent attendance to health care provision is typically considered a feminine construct (Branney et al. 2012). For instance, a study conducted by Seymour-Smith, Wetherell, and Phoenix (2002) revealed how GPs and practice nurses considered male attendance to be driven by a female lead. For example, a common phrase used by the men who attended the practice included 'she told me to come and see you'. The implication of this discourse is that women are considered to be active, autonomous, and conscious of self-health promotion (Seymour-Smith, Wetherell, and Phoenix 2002). Thus, men have been regarded as reluctant to discuss serious health concerns (Birdis, Boggess, and Katsuranis 1998), though evidence now suggests that men address actual symptoms around the same time as their female counterparts. However, men are less likely to engage in health promotion and preventative practices than women (Carroll, Kirwan, and Lambe 2014). The inability to influence men's ill health through traditional health avenues is often attributed to the failure of health promoting programmes meeting men's needs, especially around improving awareness and knowledge of key health issues (Zwolinsky et al. 2013).

Due to the difficulties associated with recruiting HTR men via traditional health care initiatives, and in an attempt to engage men in positive health-related behaviours, the UK Government has recently financed and supported a number of alternative health-related promotions (Department of Health 2007). One such alternative includes targeted community health promotions, working in partnership with professional sports organizations. For instance, Bingham et al. (2014) conducted an older men's health intervention promotion, targeting men over the age of 55 years, within an English Premier League Football Club located in the City of Liverpool. The study did not provide any physiological evidence of change over the course of the intervention; however, the study did report some positive social and psychological benefits of the programme.

It is widely suggested that social relationships and affiliations are key determinants in positive engagements in both physical and mental health. Consequently, health promotion programmes in community settings, that promote social interaction and support are considered a viable public health option. However, despite sporting organizations providing an important social setting for health promoting policies, the dearth of controlled studies evaluating their effectiveness remains problematic (Priest et al. 2008). A notable exception, however, is the Football Fans in Training (FFiT) programme (Hunt et al. 2014). This study followed a mixed-method approach and succeeded in attracting 747 men who were at very high risk of ill health. This particular study illustrated how professional football clubs have the potential to support health-related initiatives, including weight management (Hunt et al. 2014).

Since the Priest and colleagues' review in 2008, a number of studies have demonstrated that health interventions conducted in partnership with professional sports organizations can recruit, retain and improve aspects of physical and mental health. The Premier League Health football 12-week intervention programme is one such example. This particular health programme was delivered through 16 English Premier League football clubs and attempted to improve the holistic health and well-being of men. Despite drawing solely on self-report measures, the study demonstrated how men from diverse backgrounds, with less than optimal lifestyles, improved their health behaviour (Zwolinsky et al. 2013).

More recently, Parnell et al. (2015) conducted a secondary analysis of a PA-led health improvement programme delivered by professional football clubs for older adults aged 55 + years. Results suggested that associations with the club badge were important in accessing this participant group along with enhancing adoption and satisfaction associated with the programme.

In an attempt to better understand the effectiveness of community health promotion programmes within professional football environments, and to improve service amongst some client groups, researchers have adopted increasingly novel data collection protocols. For example, Curran, Drust, and Richardson (2014) advocated the adoption of a practitioner-researcher approach; in their study, the research team examined the effectiveness of a men's health campaign during match day at Everton Football Club. However, in contrast to previous football stadia methodologies, the lead author adopted an auto-ethnographic line of enquiry. Observational data, personal reflections and autobiographical notes captured first-hand, were reflexively transformed in order to give the reader a unique insight into what aspects of the FitC health programme worked, and what did not work (Curran, Drust, and Richardson 2014).

The purpose therefore of this paper is twofold: The first aim is to evaluate the effectiveness of a HTRmen's health physical activity intervention programme, known as *Active Rovers.* Specifically, the project aim was to trial a physical activity lifestyle knowledge programme, with respect to changes in mental well-being, health perceptions, and lifestyle knowledge in older HTR men living in Wirral, North West England. Secondly, the paper intends to include experiences of a practitioner researcher responsible for the planning and the delivery of the *Active Rovers* programme.

The practitioner researcher

In an attempt to adhere to previous practitioner-research methodologies conducted within professional football settings (Curran, Drust, and Richardson 2014), it is suggested that a profile of the researcher is provided. The practitioner researcher (first author) was initially employed as a full-time member of Tranmere Rovers 'Football in the Community' department, based at Prenton Park, before securing a PhD studentship in 2013 at Liverpool John Moores University (LJMU), in the School of Sport Studies, Leisure & Nutrition. The first author's role whilst employed at Tranmere Rovers FC involved coordinating the *Active Rovers* programme, and the day-to-day management of its delivery. This included *inter alia* programme design, programme development, physical activity session organization and client satisfaction. In addition, the first author was also responsible for liaising with NHS England, with the collection of quantitative and qualitative data surrounding participant attitudes of physical, mental health and well-being.

Methods

Setting and context – Tranmere Rovers FC

Tranmere Rovers FC is situated within the borough of Wirral, northwest England. Wirral is a borough of contrast and diversity in terms of both its physical characteristics and social demographics. Rural areas, urban, and industrialized areas sit side by side in a compact peninsula of approximately 60 square miles. According to ONS (2012), data Wirral's population stands at 320,200 and has a relatively high, older population and a relatively low proportion of people in their twenties and thirties, when compared to England and Wales (ONS, 2012). For instance, Wirral has a higher proportion of its population over 45 years (male) when compared to England as a whole. Using data from the 2001 Census, over 98% of the population classified as white. In 2010–12, life expectancy in Wirral was 77.9 years for men and 81.9 years for women, compared to 79.2 years for men and 83.0 years for women in England (Wirral Economic Profile, 2014).

Within Wirral, Lower Super Output Areas (LSOAs) range from the 24th most deprived in England (i.e. Birkenhead, Tranmere, Rock Ferry, Seacombe, Bidston, and St. James) to one of the least deprived in England (i.e. Heswall). According to The Index of Multiple Deprivation (IMD) (2015), Wirral is the 2nd least deprived authority in the Liverpool City Region (IMD, 2015). Wirral is currently ranked as the 66th most deprived Local Authority (out of 326 Local Authorities in England) when ranked by average score (IMD, 2015). In the 2007 IMD, Wirral was ranked 8th worst nationally for employment deprivation. According to IMD 2015 data, the geographic location of Tranmere Rovers FC is within the 5% most deprived category nationally (IMD, 2015).

Characteristics of the physical activity intervention

Active Rovers is a unique community PA-led intervention programme, designed in partnership with the 'Football in the Community' department of Tranmere Rovers FC, and NHS England. The intervention aims to improve holistic health and well-being of HTR men. The Football Foundation (http://www.footballfoundation.org.uk), who are the UK's largest sports charity and are financed by the Premier League, The Football Association and the Government, funded *Active Rovers* initially in 2010. However, the programme is now fully funded by NHS England on a yearly rolling contract.

The *Active Rovers* health intervention comprises a series of mixed exercise programmes delivered on a weekly basis at Prenton Park, the home of Tranmere Rovers FC. The activities include football, walking football, yoga, and Tai Chi. The associated football activities were delivered by the community coaches of Tranmere Rovers 'Football in the Community' department, whose qualifications ranged from 1st4Sport Level 2 Certificate in Coaching Football to the Union of European Football Association (UEFA) B Certificate. Fully qualified health care professionals, who worked for NHS Wirral, were responsible for delivering the remaining activities (i.e. yoga and Tai chi). In addition, fully qualified staff from NHS Wirral attended weekly to conduct health checks (i.e. blood pressure, cholesterol levels, and body mass index).

Since the *Active Rovers* programme commenced in 2010, over 15,000 participants have registered and taken part in the designated activities. The participants were initially recruited via advertisements in Tranmere Rovers FC match-day programmes, social media outlets, and from NHS referral schemes for hard-to-reach (HTR) men. In addition, adverts were placed in the two local newspapers (i.e. The Wirral Globe and The Wirral News).

Data collection

Initially, participant demographic data were collected at registration and programme participation was tracked via attendance and the completion of a questionnaire designed in partnership with the research team. The questionnaire included questions such as men's motivations for participation, the activities they performed, their perception of current fitness levels, and any actions taken as a result of taking part in the programme (e.g. a reduction in alcohol consumption, improved dietary choices, attempting more exercise, giving up smoking, *etc.*). Demographic data on name, gender, date of birth, and postcode were also requested. For the purpose of this study, longitudinal data, captured from 16 men who have engaged weekly with the *Active Rovers* programme since its inception in 2010 were analysed.

Secondly, in order to capture the associated mental health benefits of being involved in the *Active Rovers* programme, a shortened scale version of the Warwick-Edinburgh Mental Well-Being Scale (SWEMWBS) was used (Stewart-Brown et al. 2009). The original 14-scaled Warwick-Edinburgh Mental Well-Being Scale (WEMWBS) was an instrument designed to enable the measurement of mental well-being of adults in the UK (ibid). WEMWBS differs from other scales of mental health as it focuses only on positive aspects of mental health. Consequently, the 14 phrased Likert-style items are positively phrased (e.g. I've been thinking clearly, I've been dealing with problems well). Despite accepted levels of face validity, the original WEMWBS, however, did not meet the accepted criterion levels for measurement, as demanded by the RASCH model (ibid). The shortened, 7-item Likert scale (SWEMWBS) however is reported to confirm to the RASCH model criteria, with an interval level transformation correlation of 0.954 to the original full scale (ibid). The final SWEMWBS scale included the following items (i.e. I've been feeling optimistic about the future, I've been feeling useful, I've been feeling relaxed, I've been dealing with problems well, I've been thinking clearly, I've been feeling close to other people, I've been able to make up my own mind about things) (ibid). Respondents completing the SWEMWBS indicated their response to a question by entering a score between 1-none of the time to 5-all of the time. For this paper, a total of 80 men who provided contact details, informed consent, and verbal assent completed the pre and post SWEMWBS. Ethical approval for the study was obtained from a local university ethics committee.

Data analysis

The SWEMWBS data were entered into a spreadsheet designed specifically by Wirral Public Health for the Cheshire and Merseyside public health network (ChaMPs). Each respondent was issued with a unique alphanumeric code, which corresponded to the hard copy of the

Table 1. Participants' overall SWEMWEBS mental well-being results.

	Total number of respondents	Pre-intervention	Post-intervention	Change
Demographics				
Gender (male)	$n=80$	$n=80$	$n=80$	
% low well-being		10.0%	0.0%	−10%
% moderate well-being		83.8%	78.8%	−5%
% high well-being		6.3%	21.3%	15%
Mean score		27.3	30	3.08
Standard deviation		3.4	2.7	2.0

Table 2. Participant SWEMWBS response scores pre-intervention.

	Total number of responses	Mean	Standard deviation
SWEMWBS questions			
I've been feeling optimistic about the future	$n=80$	3.93	0.67
I've been feeling useful	$n=80$	3.81	0.71
I've been feeling relaxed	$n=80$	3.85	0.62
I've been dealing with problems well	$n=80$	3.89	0.64
I've been thinking clearly	$n=80$	3.95	0.61
I've been feeling close to other people	$n=80$	3.91	0.66
I've been able to make up my own mind about things	$n=80$	3.91	0.66
TOTAL SWEMWBS score		27.25	3.42

survey the respondent completed. Data were then cleaned and missing and implausible values were removed. Mean descriptives of high and low well-being were then calculated for before and after the project. Pre- vs. post-intervention changes were determined by a Wilcoxon signed rank test. The probability value was set at $p < .05$. All analyses were performed using the Statistical Package for Social Science (SPSS) version 20.

Results and discussion

The demographic data captured from the 80 men (48 ± 13 years) who completed SWEMWBS were consistent with the term HTR. From this group, 53% reported being unemployed and a further 12% had part-time employment; 77% had completed formal secondary school education; 63% were registered for social welfare payments; 27% were single; 17% reported being separated or divorced; 18% reported living alone.

Active Rovers: participants well-being

The overall SWEMWBS mental well-being results are displayed in Table 1. The results in Table 1 illustrate that the mental well-being of the participants positively increased during the course of the *Active Rovers* programme. The adjusted mean SWEMWBS values increased from 27.3 points to 30 points. The reported 15% increase in high levels of mental well-being was statistically significant ($p < .05$).

Table 2 provides a more detailed breakdown into the individual mean SWEMWBS responses pre-intervention. The highest recorded mean score of (3.95 points) was associated

Table 3. SWEMWBS participant scores post-intervention.

	Total number of responses	Mean	Standard deviation
SWEMWBS questions			
I've been feeling optimistic about the future	$n=80$	4.35	0.55
I've been feeling useful	$n=80$	4.33	0.52
I've been feeling relaxed	$n=80$	4.25	0.52
I've been dealing with problems well	$n=80$	4.36	0.56
I've been thinking clearly	$n=80$	3.95	0.50
I've been feeling close to other people	$n=80$	3.91	0.56
I've been able to make up my own mind about things	$n=80$	3.91	0.50
TOTAL SWEMWBS score		30.33	2.74

with the question 'I've been thinking clearly'. In contrast, the lowest recorded score of (3.81 points) was associated with the question 'I've been feeling useful'.

Table 3 shows how four of the SWEMWBS items increased from pre- to post-intervention. For instance, item 1: 'I've been feeling optimistic about the future' improved from a pre-intervention mean score of (3.93 points) to (4.35 points). At pre-intervention, Item 2: 'I've been feeling useful' was reported at (3.81 points) this figure improved to (4.33 points) post-intervention. There were also pre- and post-adjusted mean differences in item 3: 'I've been feeling relaxed' (3.85 points) increased to (4.25 points) and item 4: 'I've been dealing with problems well' increased from (3.89 points) to (4.36 points).

Absence of behaviour change away from Prenton Park

The longitudinal questionnaire data and the face-to-face conversations revealed that the vast majority of the men now have a different perspective about the dangers associated with excessive alcohol consumption and smoking. The data also revealed the men acknowledged the positive benefits of health eating. Unfortunately, a less successful outcome of this study was the lack of PA transfer from the *Active Rovers* project into more casual forms of PA and associated exercise. Whilst the questionnaire data suggested that their fitness levels had increased since attending the *Active Rovers* sessions, it was interesting to note how a large proportion of the participants were not engaged in any additional PA externally.

From a more positive perspective, it may be that the environment (i.e. Prenton Park), or the allure of the football club, and representing the badge that was the key to maintaining the participant's motivation to engage in PA. Other professional football community-based health studies would certainly support this supposition (i.e. Parnell et al. 2015). However, from a more pessimistic perspective, we would have anticipated any proxy measure of success, to be the participants intrinsically engaging in PA away from the *Active Rovers* environment. Judging by the number of men who stated that their only PA in the week was during the *Active Rovers* sessions – then this was not the case.

Although the SWEMWBS revealed some objective statistical data to support the success of the *Active Rovers* project, what we were also interested in establishing was 'why?' The participant feedback questionnaire was particularly useful in this aspect, as it yielded far more detailed information surrounding the motives for continued engagement in the programme. Typically, we expected the answers to mirror the original aims of the project. To some extent, this was the case, and a number of the participants' comments were aligned with project brief. For example, we found evidence of participants reporting positive changes in mental well-being, health perceptions, and lifestyle knowledge especially in the older aged men (i.e. 50 years+).

Whist this was the case for some, it must also be noted that there were many additional motives for maintaining interest within the project. For example, when prompted to comment on the *Active Rovers* questionnaire regarding why they attend, the most commonly repeated responses included: 'love being a part of a group', 'like playing football and getting to know the fellas', 'to keep playing and see my mates', 'to just be active for once', and 'to lose a bit of timber of the gut'. In particular, one attendee provided feedback to the first author during a verbal dialogue:

Ian (51 years) *Active Rovers* Participant:

> In the last questionnaire you gave us where we had to fill in our fitness levels, or well what we thought they would be at this moment in time. I put down like an 8 [Valued 1–10, 1 representing the lowest level of fitness and 10 the highest]. If I looked back at what I first put when I started taking part I'd have been lucky if I had reached 2 … so I stop and think why would I stop. If I am honest this is the best I've felt in years. What's great is that, okay, it's great for fitness and let's be honest we all need it! If we weren't here we would just be sitting at home. But the impact that it's had on me, since I started coming and listening to you guys, it's been life changing. I'm even eating more healthily, after me and you had that chat a while ago. Plus mentally it has been great and making me feel more confident to take part and getting to know new people, some of which have become good friends of mine. You can't put a price on that!

The narrative above helps to showcase the potential positive impact of the *Active Rovers* programme. Interestingly, the participant reveals how the programme has helped improve aspects of both physical and mental health. However, it is perhaps the suggestion that the social aspect of the intervention, which is also illuminating.

The purpose of this particular study was to evaluate the effectiveness of *Active Rovers,* a PA-led health improvement intervention delivered by Tranmere Rovers FC. The findings from the SWEMWBS statistical data indicate the programme was successful in improving aspects of mental well-being amongst its HTR male client group. For instance, there were statistically significant differences from pre-intervention to post-intervention. However, we do add a cautionary note here, as the sample size of 80 participants is modest at best, and may not be generalized to other PA-led health improvement projects. However, these findings do support previous PA-led health improvement projects conducted within professional football clubs (Hunt et al. 2014; Pringle et al. 2014).

Practitioner-based reflections

The success of the *Active Rovers* project was largely due to the vigorous nature of the marketing campaign. The project team targeted typically HTR areas, and we were genuinely encouraged by the attendance figures, and perhaps, more importantly the high levels of retention. Football in the Community departments such as the one at Tranmere Rovers FC should, therefore, consider a range of multi-media recruitment strategies, such as social media, local newspaper articles and radio stations adverts, as an effective recruitment tool and not just rely on adverts in and around the ground.

In addition, the practice of a multi-method approach to data capture was successful. Interestingly, what was effective, and helped ensure the longevity of the *Active Rovers* programme, was understanding the attendees' motives for their sustained engagement in the programme. Therefore, moving forward, it would be worthy to continue to acquire this data to ensure that practitioners can comprehend and appreciate this evidence and utilize it for the benefit of their future physical activity intervention programmes. In addition, measuring objective levels of physical activity may offer further insights into the impact of such programmes. Finally, the research has helped, from a practitioner perspective at least, to recognize that there needs to be more of an emphasis placed on tackling key health messages, and PA levels away from the 'magnetism' of the professional football ground. As for football clubs' community departments, perhaps branching out and delivering supplementary sessions in additional LSOAs could help to facilitate this ambition.

Conclusion

The findings from this study suggest that PA-intervention programmes such as *Active Rovers*, can help support associated health agencies improve aspects of health and mental well-being amongst typically HTR men. The use of a professional football ground, as a non-traditional health venue, appeared to act as an incentive to attract, recruit and retain this priority group in the health-based programme. However, future research should also consider how these priority groups could also be supported away from the professional football environment. Furthermore, the multi-method approaches to data capture, as advocated by previous studies (i.e. Hunt et al. 2013; 2014; Pringle et al. 2014; Parnell et al. 2015; Rutherford et al. 2014) are recommended for future studies in this area.

Acknowledgements

The author(s) would like to acknowledge the staff at Tranmere Rovers FC for all their support with this research project and permission to identify the club explicitly in this publication. The author(s) would also like to thank Becky Mellor the public health manager for Wirral Council for kindly supporting the data capture process and publication plan. Furthermore, thanks must also be given to the reviewers of this paper whose comments have improved its overall quality.

Disclosure statement

No potential conflict of interest was reported by the authors.

References

Bingham, D. D., D. Parnell, K. Curran, and D. Richardson 2014. "Fit Fans: Understanding the Issues and Effectiveness of a Health Promotion Programme for Older Men Delivered within an English Premier League Football Club." *Soccer & Society* 15 (6): 883–901. doi: http://dx.doi.org/10.1080/14660970.2014.920624.

Birdis, C., J. Boggess, and F. Katsuranis. 1998. "A Profile of the Adolescent Male Family Planning Client." *Family Planning Perspective* 30: 63–66.

Branney, P., K. Witty, A. Bagnall, J. South, and A. White. 2012. "Straight to the GP; That Would Be Where I Would Go: An Analysis of Male Frequent Attenders' Constructions of Their Decisions to Use or Not Use Health-care Services in the UK." *Psychology and Health* 27: 865–880.

Carroll, P., L. Kirwan, and B. Lambe. 2014. "Engaging 'Hard to Reach' Men in Community Based Health Promotions." *International Journal of Health Promotion Education* 52: 120–130.

Curran, K., B. Drust, and D. Richardson. 2014. "'I Just Want to Watch the Match': A Practitioner's Reflective Account of Men's Health Themed Match Day Events at an English Premier League Football Club." *Soccer and Society* 15: 919–933.

Department for Communities and Local Government. 2015. *Index of Multiple Deprivation*. London: DCLG.

Department of Health. 2007. *Healthy Weight, Healthy Lives. London*. London: HMSO.

Fife-Schaw, C., S. de Lusignan, J. Wainwright, H. Sprake, S. Laver, V. Heald, J. Orton, M. Prescott, H. Carr, and M. O'Neill. 2014. "Comparing Exercise Interventions to Increase Persistence with Physical Exercise and Sporting Activity among People with Hypertension or High Normal Blood Pressure: Study Protocol for a Randomised Controlled Trial." *Trials* 15: 336.

Hakola, L., M. Hassinen, P. Komulainen, T. A. Lakka, K. Savonen, and R. Rauramaa. 2015. "Correlates of Low Physical Activity Levels in Aging Men and Women: The DR's EXTRA Study (ISRCTN45977199)." *Journal of Aging and Physical Activity* 23: 247–255.

Hunt, K., C. McCann, C. M. Gray, N. Mutrie, and S. Wyke. 2013. ""You've Got to Walk before You Run": Positive Evaluations of a Walking Program as Part of a Gender-sensitized, Weight-management Program Delivered to Men through Professional Football Clubs." *Health Psychology* 32: 57–65.

Hunt, K., C. Gray, A. Maclean, S. Smillie, C. Bunn, and S. Wyke. 2014. "Do Weight Management Programmes Delivered at Professional Football Clubs Attract and Engage High Risk Men? A Mixed-methods Study." *BMC Public Health* 14: 50. doi:http://dx.doi.org/10.1186/1471-2458-14-50.

Office for National Statistics mid-year Estimates. 2012. Accessed February 2016. http://www.ons.gov.uk/

Morgan, P. J., D. R. Lubans, R. Callister, A. D. Okely, T. L. Burrows, R. Fletcher, and C. E. Collins. 2011. "The Healthy Dads, Healthy Kids Randomised Controlled Trial: Efficacy of a Healthy Lifestyle Program for Overweight Fathers and their Children." *International Journal of Obesity* 35: 436–447.

Parnell, Daniel, Andy Pringle, Jim McKenna, Stephen Zwolinsky, Zoe Rutherford, Jackie Hargreaves, Lizzie Trotter, Michael Rigby, and David Richardson. 2015. "Reaching Older People with PA Delivered in Football Clubs: The Reach, Adoption and Implementation Characteristics of the Extra Time Programme." *BMC Public Health* 15: 220. http://bmcpublichealth.biomedcentral.com/articles/10.1186/s12889-015-1560-5.

Priest, N., R. Armstrong, J. Doyle, and E. Waters. 2008. "Interventions Implemented through Sporting Organisations for Increasing Participation in Sport." *Cochrane Database of Systematic Reviews*. 1–17, 3Art No: CD004812. doi: http://dx.doi.org/10.1002/14651858.CD004812.pub3.

Pringle, A., D. Parnell, S. Zwolinsky, J. Hargreaves, and J. McKenna. 2014. "Effect of a Health-improvement Pilot Programme for Older Adults Delivered by a Professional Football Club: The Burton Albion Case Study." *Soccer and Society* 15: 902–918.

Robertson, S., and P. Williamson. 2005. "Men and Health Promotion in the UK: Ten Years Further on?" *Health Education Journal* 64: 293–301.

Robertson, S., K. Witty, S. Zwolinsky, and R. Day. 2013. "Men's Health Promotion Interventions: What Have We Learned from Previous Programmes?" *Community Practitioner* 86 (11): 38–41.

Rutherford, Z., B. Gough, S. Seymour-Smith, C. R. Matthews, J. Wilcox, D. Parnell, and A. Pringle. 2014. "'Motivate': The Effect of a Football in the Community Delivered Weight Loss Programme on over 35-year Old Men and Women's Cardiovascular Risk Factors." *Soccer & Society* 15 (6): 951–969.

Sartini, C., S. Wannamethee, S. Iliffe, R. W. Morris, S. Ash, L. Lennon, P. H. Whincup, and B. J. Jefferis. 2015. "Diurnal Patterns of Objectively Measured Physical Activity and Sedentary Behaviour in Older Men." *BMC Public Health* 15: 609. http://bmcpublichealth.biomedcentral.com/articles/10.1186/s12889-015-1976-y.

Seymour-Smith, S., M. Wetherell, and A. Phoenix. 2002. "My Wife Ordered Me to Come!: A Discursive Analysis of Doctors' and Nurses' Accounts of Men's Use of General Practitioners." *Journal of Health Psychology* 7: 253–267.

Stewart-Brown, S., A. Tennant, R. Tennant, S. Platt, J. Parkinson, and S. Weich. 2009. "Internal Construct Validity of the Warwick-Edinburgh Mental Well-being Scale (WEMWBS): A Rasch Analysis Using Data from the Scottish Health Education Population Survey." *Health and Quality of Life Outcomes* 7 (1): 15. doi: http://dx.doi.org/10.1186/1477-7525-7-15.

Ward-Thompson, C., A. Curl, P. Aspinall, S. Alves, and A. Zuin. 2014. "Do Changes to the Local Street Environment Alter Behaviour and Quality of Life of Older Adults? The 'DIY Streets' Intervention." *British Journal of Sports Medicine* 48: 1059–1065.

World Health Organisation. 2010. *Global Recommendations on Physical Activity for Health*. Geneva: WHO.

Zwolinsky, S., J. McKenna, A. Pringle, A. Daly-Smith, S. Robertson, and A. White. 2013. "Optimizing Lifestyles for Men Regarded as 'hard-to-reach' through Top-Flight Football/Soccer Clubs." *Health Education Research* 28: 405–413.

Success of a sports-club led-community X-PERT Diabetes Education Programme

Angela Morgan, Dee Drew, Angela Clifford and Katrina Hull

ABSTRACT

This study examined the effectiveness of a sports-club-led X-PERT Diabetes Programme, measuring changes to participants' physical condition, knowledge of diabetes, psychological well-being, activity level, diabetes self-management and participants' rating of the programme. In this mixed-method, repeated measures evaluative study, data were gathered at baseline (T0), six weeks (T1) and 6 months (T2) using the Diabetes Health Profile, General Practice Physical Activity Questionnaire, Diabetes Empowerment Scale – Short Form, Participant Evaluation Questionnaire and focus groups. Over three years, 260 individuals with type 2 diabetes provided data for the evaluation. The sports-club-led X-PERT Diabetes Education Programme was successful in achieving its targets with improvement in clinical outcomes including significant reductions in BMI, waist circumference, total cholesterol, LDL cholesterol, triglycerides and glycated haemoglobin by T2. Positive changes were also evident in relation to participants' health profile, self-management and empowerment. This study illustrates the important role that European sports stadia can play in community health through delivering targeted programmes beyond general health promotion activities.

Introduction

It is becoming increasingly recognized that sports clubs and their stadia can play an important role in communities and their health behaviours (Healthy Stadia 2015). From being an example of good practice, such as providing healthy catering and having smoking restrictions onsite, to offering open sports facilities for the public, stadia across the UK have pursued an agenda in recent years to improve the health of their fans and the wider community. Some football clubs have also offered targeted community health programmes at their stadia. For example, football clubs across the Scottish Premiership League hold Football Fans in Training weight loss and healthy living programmes, funded by the Scottish Government, finding significant reductions in attendees' weight, blood pressure and other clinical outcomes (Hunt et al. 2014).

Sports clubs and their stadia are considered 'icons' in the local area and have unique relationships with the public through their community engagement work, lacking the stigma of a healthcare setting and providing a focus of shared interest (Bunn et al. Forthcoming; Spandler, Roy, and Mckeown 2014). They therefore have the potential to support healthcare services in promoting public health and reducing the cost of chronic illness. One such example can be seen in the work of Pringle et al. (2014) who assessed the effect of a programme of men's health delivered in/by English Premier League football clubs. In this study, men attended match-day events and/or weekly classes involving physical activity and health education. Men were attracted through football and/or the clubs, and intention-to-treat analysis showed significant improvements in lifestyle profiles. The concept of football clubs delivering health initiatives is relatively recent in comparison to some of the more obvious and established work such as community sports programmes. Nevertheless, the success of such initiatives has paved the way for a constantly evolving health programme at many clubs across the country.

Diabetes is estimated to affect 346 million people worldwide and associated with negative health outcomes and comorbidities including cardiovascular disease, kidney failure and mortality (World Health Organisation 2009), unless the disease is effectively controlled (Skylar et al. 2009). Prevalence of diabetes in the UK was 3.65 million in 2010, with only 2.8 million being aware they have the condition (Diabetes UK n.d.). More than a decade ago, it was estimated that the prevalence of patients diagnosed with diabetes in the UK has doubled in less than 20 years (Harvey, Craney, and Kelly 2002). Only one in five people in England and Wales reach targets for keeping their diabetes under control. In England, 19.9% of people with diabetes meet recommended targets for blood glucose, blood pressure and cholesterol; in Wales, this figure is 18.5% (Diabetes UK n.d.).

The health of the population of Wolverhampton (currently at approximately 250,000 – mid-2012 population estimate (Office for National Statistics n.d.)) is worse than the national average, and local prevalence of diabetes reflects national figures (Department of Health 2012). In Wolverhampton, the number of people diagnosed with diabetes in 2010–2011 was 14,846; in total, 7.1% of people on GP registers in the town had a recorded diagnosis of diabetes (Department of Health 2012; National Health Service 2012). This was significantly worse than the England average, which for that same year was 5.5%, and substantially similar to the indicator proposed in the Public Health Outcomes Framework (Department of Health 2012).

Diabetes healthcare is an urgent priority and treatment/self-management needs to be improved if a public health disaster is to be avoided (Diabetes UK n.d.). The sharp rise in incidence of type 2 diabetes in the UK is linked to the Westernized lifestyle (Orozco et al. 2008), a term describing the increasingly poor dietary habits and level of physical activity. Current public health initiatives encompass measures to combat obesity, therefore helping to prevent diabetes (Department of Health 2012). Clinical trials have shown that although strengthening glycaemic control can reduce the onset of diabetes-related complications, glycaemic control in diabetic patients has seen no improvement in the last decade (Stratton et al. 2000), whilst prescription costs for diabetes have almost doubled (Currie, Gale, and Poole 2010). Controlling blood glucose levels with insulin and sulfonylureas can also lead to serious health challenges attributable to associated weight gain and hypoglycaemia (Fonseca 2003; Amiel et al. 2008; Duckworth et al. 2009; Holman et al. 2009). Evidence clearly demonstrates the need for intervention and education to improve self-management of diabetes. Self-management programmes for diabetes are recognized as the gold standard in treatment (Dinneen 2008).

The benefits of self-management programmes are twofold: they empower patients by giving them tools to manage their condition; and they relieve strain exerted on front-line primary healthcare practices and hospital emergency departments (Department of Health and Diabetes UK 2005). The X-PERT Diabetes Education Programme is a self-management programme that aims to help people with type 2 diabetes control many risk factors associated with poor outcomes and to improve their well-being (Department of Health 2001; Deakin et al. 2006). The programme involves group education delivered by trained facilitators, with sessions covering topics such as general awareness, weight management and complications of the disorder. The X-PERT Patient Programme is used by various Clinical Commissioning Groups (CCGs) throughout the UK and, on a national level, has established that it is cost-effective, empowering and clinically effective in helping people with type 2 diabetes control many risk factors associated with complications (X-PERT Health n.d.). However, local evaluation is necessary to ensure that it responds to the needs of individual communities and to share good practice.

Methods

Intervention context

The present study describes the implementation and evaluation of the X-PERT Diabetes Education Programme on a local level by Wolves Community Trust, in partnership with the then Wolverhampton Primary Care Trust (now the CCG) as part of the Tackle Diabetes initiative. This is one of the Trust's most significant health initiatives. The project was supported by Wolverhampton Wanderers Football Club; the initial project launch was held at Molineux Stadium with WWFC first team players in attendance and as a result attracted local media attention helping to raise the profile of the project. The project also featured on the BBC's Match of the Day's community feature.[1] Wolves Community Trust is a registered charity and an independent organization. However, it operates as an extension of Wolverhampton Wanderers Football Club, using the brand of the football club, and is based at Molineux Stadium, the home of the football club. The Trust runs a range of health programmes to deliver health education and promote physical activity across all ages. The X-PERT programme was delivered as a three-year local pilot as a practical intervention for diabetes and was delivered at the football stadium and other local settings. The initial project plan included delivery of X-PERT at a number of venues across the city including Molineux Stadium. However, the courses offered at the Stadium were most popular so delivery was predominantly at Molineux with occasional courses delivered in other areas of the city when required. Molineux Stadium is located in a central location of the city with bus stops nearby and free parking was provided for X-PERT participants.

On award of the funding, a Project Manager was recruited to deliver the 'Tackle Diabetes' project to develop and implement services to support residents who had type 2 diabetes. Following a mapping exercise, a review of research and recommendation from NICE (CG87 now updated to NG28), the Tackle Diabetes project offered three key components; X-PERT diabetes education programme, Physical Activity and practical Healthy Eating sessions. The Tackle Diabetes project was supported by a full time project administrator employed by the Trust. The role involved processing referrals, arranging courses, dealing with bookings and all other administrative responsibilities for the project.

Project plans were discussed and reviewed with the Steering Group which had representation from the local Public Health and Healthy Lifestyle teams, NHS Trust and Wolves Community Trust.

The Diabetes Project Manager and a Dietitian from the local NHS Trust were trained to deliver the X-PERT programme. The training was delivered by X-PERT Health a nationally registered charity committed to providing X-PERT Educator courses to healthcare professionals and lay educators to develop their competencies in evidence-based care, enabling them to deliver structured patient education to people with, or at risk of, diabetes (X-PERT Health 2016). Referrals were received from Primary Care, Dietetics and Health Trainers. Self-referrals were also received.

The evaluation of the pilot was conducted by the University and aimed to appraise the effectiveness of a local X-PERT Diabetes Programme in improving participants' physical health, knowledge of diabetes, well-being, physical activity and self-management of their diabetes.

Participants

Participants were recruited via a letter of invitation following a GP referral, Health Care Provider referral or self-referral. The X-PERT programme was designed specifically for the needs of patients having type 2 diabetes therefore those with type 1 diabetes were excluded. However, so as to be as inclusive as possible, no other exclusion criteria were placed on potential participants. A total of 394 eligible people with type 2 diabetes completed the programme over the three-year pilot period. Each X-PERT group contained an average of 16 participants, with at least 6 groups running each year. All groups completed the same programme with no control groups used. During the six-week course, participants were given the opportunity to opt in to the programme's evaluative component. Written informed consent was obtained from participants after a full verbal explanation of the evaluation, including identification of any inherent benefits and risks, an explanation of the procedure and a reminder that their participation in the evaluation was entirely optional and that they may discontinue their participation at any point without explanation and without penalty. The evaluation was reviewed and approved by the University's Faculty of Education, Health and Wellbeing ethics committee.

Design and procedure

The X-PERT programme consists of six sessions spread over six weeks and the evaluation employed a mixed-method, within-subjects repeated-measures design with three data collection points. Participants who took part in the evaluative component were invited to complete a range of measures pre-programme (T0), post-programme six-week follow-up (T1) and post-programme six-month follow-up (T2). The Diabetes Health Profile was completed at T0 and T2 – this is a validated measure that accurately records an individual's medical status (eg height, weight, BMI, cholesterol levels, blood pressure, high- and low-level lipoprotein, etc.) (Diabetes Profile n.d.). The General Practice Physical Activity Questionnaire (GPPAQ) was also completed at T0 and T2 – this is a tool to assess level of physical activity, including employment, exercise and walking pace. The Diabetes Empowerment Scale – Short Form (DES-SF) was completed at T0, T1 and T2 – this is a validated tool (Anderson et al. 2003) with eight statements, used to measure participants' level of perceived control over their diabetes over time. The Participant Evaluation Questionnaire (PEQ) was completed at T1 – this is a tool designed to assess the benefit of the programme to participants by rating each week's content and lifestyle experiment (goal setting) on enjoyment, degree of self-management, impact on health and impact on living with diabetes (World Health Organisation 2009). Comments were also invited on the venue, length of programme, most enjoyable or useful weeks and most unhelpful weeks.

Two focus groups (Wilkinson 1998) were held at T1 with participants to capture more nuanced qualitative data usually difficult to obtain with questionnaire-based measures. The first focus group comprised six participants, the second included six participants and one carer. Discussions promoted open and frank conversations of issues that participants felt were of particular importance to them during the programme. They provided a wealth of qualitative data with which to analyse participants' perceptions of the programme. In addition, the discussions acted as a method of evaluating the links the programme has made with various support services across the region, determining the utility of their inclusion within the programme, including local Healthy Lifestyle, Dieticians and Healthy Minds services.

Data analysis

Quantitative data were analysed using the Statistical Package for Social Sciences (SPSS) v16. A range of descriptive and comparative statistical techniques used a within-subjects repeated measures design (t-test and Analysis of Variance [ANOVA] for continuous data, Wilcoxon Signed Rank Test for ordinal data), wherein participants' baseline and follow-up measures (pre- and post-programme) were compared. An intention-to-treat analysis was used in which all participants were included in the final analysis even if they missed more than one session of the programme. Qualitative data obtained from the focus groups and PEQ were analysed using thematic analysis, a technique that focuses upon understanding and interpreting informants' experiences of any given issues (Braun and Clarke 2006). This data-set was analysed by two researchers without the use of computer-assisted qualitative data analysis software due to the relatively small sample size. Initial basic coding procedures were followed by more complex interpretive analysis and corroboration of themes by the two analysts.

Results

Of 394 participants who completed the X-PERT programme during the study period, 260 agreed to take part in the evaluative component. Of those, 252 (99%) participants attended four or more sessions and 150 (58%) attended all six. A total of 296 participants provided data for analysis. Table 1 shows the gender, age and ethnicity of participants. Black and Asian groups were underrepresented but there was an even split for gender. Median age fell within the 61–70 year age group for men and the 51–60 year age group for women, with the age distribution skewed towards the middle- to older-age groups.

Table 1. Demographic information of participants.

	N	%[a]
Gender		
Male	119	42.7
Female	160	57.3
Age		
20–30	1	0.3
31–40	10	3.5
41–50	42	14.7
51–60	88	30.9
61–70	96	33.7
71–80	45	15.8
81–90	3	1.0
Ethnicity		
Asian	74	25.3
Black	20	6.8
White	197	67.5
Mixed ethnicity	1	0.3

Note: Values do not add up to total $n = 296$ due to missing data.
[a]Valid per cent.

Table 2. Changes in key physiological measurements from T0 to T2.

	T0		T2		
Measurement	Mean	SD	Mean	SD	*t*
Weight (kg)	88.2	22.7	87.5	20.0	0.36
Waist (cm)	103.2	16.8	95.4	22.0	2.38*
BMI	32.0	6.5	31.1	6.2	3.33*
Total cholesterol	4.7	1.3	4.3	1.1	2.87*
HDL	1.4	0.5	1.4	0.9	−0.82
LDL	2.8	1.2	2.5	1.1	2.90*
Triglycerides	1.7	1.0	1.4	0.8	2.54*
HbA1c (%)	9.8	1.5	8.3	1.2	3.33*

*$p \leq .05$.

Changes in physical activity

Scores on the GPPAQ showed that, at T0, nearly half of participants (46.2%) scored as 'inactive', whilst 19.8% scored as 'active'. 11.5% of participants spent 3 h or more per week in physical exercise (eg swimming, jogging, aerobics, football, tennis, gym) and 20.5% spent 1 h or more per week in physical exercise. Nearly half (46.7%) spent 1 hour or more per week walking, though walking pace was mostly slow or steady (79.7% of participants). Wilcoxon Signed Ranks Tests (for ordinal data) found no statistically significant differences in activity levels ($Z = -1.446, p = .148$), time spent in exercise per week ($Z = 0.148, p = .879$), time spent walking ($Z = -0.170, p = .865$) or walking pace ($Z = -0.626, p = .532$) between T0 and T2 (missing data meant that <86 participants were included in each comparison).

Physiological changes

Table 2 shows physiological measurements at baseline and follow-up, compared using paired-samples t-tests (due to missing data, there was insufficient power to conduct an ANOVA). All measurements except HDL cholesterol showed modest movement in the desired direction between T0 and T2 and this change was statistically significant for waist circumference, BMI, total cholesterol, LDL cholesterol, triglycerides and HbA1c. After adjusting the alpha value for multiple comparisons using the Holm-Bonferroni method, observed changes in BMI, total cholesterol, LDL and HbA1c remained statistically significant.

Use of medication

Of 47 participants providing data regarding medication use, most remained stable during the course of the programme. Two participants reported a decrease in medication and four reported an increase in medication use. A further two participants who had not previously taken medication for their diabetes started doing so during the programme. The reasons for alterations in medicinal treatment were undetermined.

Diabetes Empowerment Scale – Short Form

Mean scores on the DES-SF at T0, T1 and T2 increased between baseline and post-intervention (Figure 1). Repeated Measures ANOVA showed that this increase was statistically significant ($F(2170) = 40.00$, $p = .000$). The small drop-off between T1 and T2 was not statistically significant and may reflect the small number of participants at T2 (n = 63).

Participant evaluation questionnaire

212 participants completed the PEQ at T1 covering the topics from weeks 1–6. Responses are described here briefly. Over 92% of participants responded favourably to the weekly topics being 'really enjoyable and really useful'; 'will improve their self-management skills'; 'will greatly improve their health'; and 'will help them to live with diabetes'. Comments on all weekly topics were positive and participants stated how much they valued the programme, organization, venue, group dynamics and personal skills of the Educators. Most participants thought that the lifestyle experiment was 'really enjoyable and really useful' (92%), will 'improve self-management skills' (88%), will 'greatly improve their health' (85%) and will 'help them to live with diabetes' (84%).

179 (84%) respondents stated that they found the diabetes handbook 'really useful' and 175 (82%) stated that the handbook will help a lot with their self-management of diabetes. Overall, it was felt by participants that the handbook on diabetes is an excellent reference

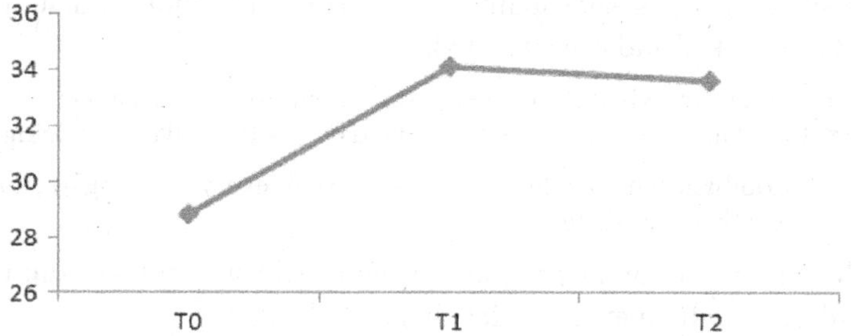

Figure 1. Scores on the DES-SF at T0, T1 and T2.

resource both during and after the programme, but one participant reported that the handbook could be improved using larger font for those with a visual impairment. 161 (82%) participants stated that the length of the programme was just right, though some participants indicated that a refresher course would be valued. Some recommendations were made regarding accessibility and comfort of the venue.

Focus group data

A number of themes were generated through the focus groups. The key reason for attending the course was that it was considered the best place to obtain specialist information that was not available elsewhere. For example, one participant stated,

> Well, when I was diagnosed, the doctor told me nothing. She just told me 'you're borderline diabetic'. I've learned since that there is no such thing as 'borderline', so for the past six years I really didn't know what to do.

General experiences of the course were entirely positive, with some participants stating that they are now recommending the course to others who have diabetes. The delivery of the programme was said to be interesting and effective for participants, with many participants praising the Educator,

> Just as I said before, in just two words, [The Educator]. Because she is the person who puts it over in the way we can understand, she isn't regimental in the programme step-by-step. You can ask her anything, she'll give you the answer, she'll give you advice and you gain confidence to go back to the people who you need to speak to in the surgery and query what's happening … But definitely, [The Educator] … because all the people that have not been diagnosed or coming up to being diagnosed need to come through her programme.

Key lessons learned included myth-busting as a way of changing to a healthier lifestyle. Acceptance was a major theme to develop with the focus group discussions, with many participants stating that they had at first not entirely believed their diagnosis of diabetes and had gone into a state of denial. The information presented reduced and allayed their fears about their current and future health.

Positively having and maintaining control over their diabetes was another major theme to emerge from the data, especially in terms of dietary self-control and medication side effects. One participant stated,

> They [doctors] give you tablets but rarely tell you how it operates. On this course, you can find out what they do and it helps you to deal with it.

The involvement of a local sports club in its support and sharing resources was particularly valued by participants; being aligned with the legendary and celebrated nature of the club has its own rewards for some participants. One participant reported that 'it felt special to be at the [sports] complex' and others stated,

> I thought it was rather nice when [footballer] came…and then we had a day session; some of the footballers, they came and they were doing the dance with us, we were doing the Zumba.

> When I spoke to [footballer] he said he had a glass of water every morning to clear his system out, and I have done that ever since!

This view on the importance of the programme being held at a sports stadium reflects those of previous studies (Bingham et al. 2014; Curran et al. 2014).

Discussion

This study identified positive outcomes from the sports-club-led X-PERT Diabetes Education Programme in terms of participants' physiological and psychological factors as well as satisfaction with the programme. The programme was well attended and impacted positively upon participants' confidence and self-empowerment. Participants considered the programme to be a valuable source of information, guidance and support for maintaining control of one's own diabetes that was widely felt was not available elsewhere. Significant reductions were observed in some, though not all, risk factors for diabetes complications (eg waist circumference, BMI, total and LDL cholesterol, triglycerides and blood glucose), which may be due to the relatively small sample size and short timescale. Participants were generally inactive at baseline, but physical activity levels did not change over the course of the programme. However, with physical activity being a key intervention for preventing or delaying the onset of type 2 diabetes (World Health Organisation 2009), further considerations for others working in this area are that football clubs and their stadia might play an additional and important role in addressing this part of diabetes self-management in the future through their general sports facilities.

These outcomes and indicators of effectiveness of the X-PERT programme appear to be comparable to those shown nationally (Deakin et al. 2006) though a direct comparison in clinical outcomes is difficult due to different follow-up timescales and baseline measurements. National data on 16,919 participants have shown the effectiveness of the X-PERT Patient Programme in many areas. For example, a very high total participant evaluation score at 94%; an increase in empowerment score by 23% post-programme and 26% at 1-year follow-up; reduction in glycated haemoglobin (HbA1c), weight and waist circumference at 6 months and 14-month follow-up; and reduction in both systolic and diastolic blood pressure and lipids (Deakin et al. 2006). Compared to 82% in the national evaluation who attended four or more sessions, 99% of participants in the present study attended four or more sessions. Although only 4% of participants in the present study showed reduction in medication use compared to 16% in the national evaluation, this was over a much shorter time span and data were based on a low response rate. This comparability between local and national outcomes suggests that sports clubs can be at least as effective as other healthcare providers in delivering structured health education.

The location of the programme within Wolverhampton Wanderers Football Club was extremely important and had a positive impact on participants. This was reflected in their comments during the focus groups which highlighted how the location within a prominent and important local venue impacted on their sense of pride and belonging and may have explained the higher rate of attendance in comparison to the national evaluation. These findings concur with Pringle et al. (2014). This reflects the importance of the football club as a symbol of the city, and it was further reinforced to participants when players from the football team joined them on the programme. Previous studies such as FITT (Hunt et al. 2014) and an Improving Access to Psychological Therapies funded mental health project in North West England (Spandler et al. 2013) have shown similar benefits of utilising sporting venues as health intervention settings with positive clinical outcomes and service user feedback. This emphasizes the importance of utilising spaces and possibly engaging public figures, which have resonance with the local target population. This should encourage service providers to consider popular venues which may not be immediately identified as 'health centres' but which have a currency with the groups they are aiming to target.

Wolverhampton CCG identified 14,000 patients diagnosed with diabetes living in the city, and the programme has the potential to be offered to all patients through the practitioner referral system. Annual inpatient care to treat short- and long-term complications of diabetes is estimated at between £1800 and £2500 per patient (Diabetes UK n.d.), in contrast to annual outpatient costs (including costs of medications and monitoring supplies) estimated at between £300 and £370 per patient. Crude estimates of costs savings from this cohort suggest that if the need for inpatient care has reduced in 50% of the sample due to reduction or stabilization of medication (n = 130), there is a potentially large saving each year from this sample alone. In addition to the health economic considerations, the findings also highlight other opportunities relating to the planning and delivery of community-based interventions to reduce diabetic risk and optimize self-agency and self-care among people living with diabetes. As a short intervention (six weeks), the X-PERT programme shows significant economic and social cost savings, although the effectiveness of the programme in maintaining these behaviours long term requires further evaluation.

Some limitations of the current study were identified that should be addressed in the future work around the X-PERT Diabetes Education programme, whether led by sports clubs or by other providers. Young people and some ethnic groups were underrepresented in this particular cohort; the majority were aged 51–70 years and less than one-third were from BME populations. Further evaluation is needed to ensure that the positive outcomes are observed in these groups and further iterations of the programme should aim to reach a diverse audience, especially since participants were effectively self-selected. Targeting younger people (those diagnosed when under the age of 25) with diabetes often referred to as having 'maturity onset diabetes of the young' (MODY) for the X-PERT programme will also give them the opportunity to learn about self-management sooner following diagnosis, thus maximising the health and well-being benefits of the programme. However, MODY is different to type 1 and type 2 diabetes and thus young patients will need specialist advice and care within such a self-management programme.

Some participants reported that they found out about the programme themselves and had to request a referral from their GP. A clear and robust referral process including education and information for primary care practitioners and diabetes specialist nurses as to the programme on offer is thus recommended to reach as many people as possible. Advertising of the programme could also be maximized through sport clubs' own community engagement channels, given their visible presence in the local area. One practical limitation of evaluative work of a non-NHS provider was that the programme organizers reported difficulty obtaining participant data directly, instead relying upon participants to bring that data to them. This resulted in fewer data at follow-up compared to baseline and represents an ongoing challenge for collecting data from non-NHS services.

Conclusion

In conclusion, this study has illustrated an effective partnership between a sports club and its stadium and a healthcare provider to improve the health of the community, using an existing targeted programme with measureable benefits. The delivery of this programme by sports clubs elsewhere could play an important role in the care of people living with type 2 diabetes locally by reducing risk factors for complications without the need for pharmacological interventions, and in doing so relieving pressure upon primary care services.

Note

1. https://www.youtube.com/watch?v=7zc19t4i2s0.

Acknowledgements

The authors wish to thank Wolves Community Trust and all the individuals who gave of their time to support and contribute to this work.

Disclosure statement

No potential conflict of interest was reported by the authors.

Funding

This work was supported by the Wolves Community Trust.

References

Amiel, S. A., T. Dixon, R. Mann, and K. Jameson. 2008. "Hypoglycaemia in Type 2 Diabetes." *Diabetic Medicine* 25 (3): 245–254. doi: http://dx.doi.org/10.1111/j.1464-5491.2007.02341.x.

Anderson, R. M., J. T. Fitzgerald, L. D. Gruppen, M. M. Funnell, and M. S. Oh. 2003. "The Diabetes Empowerment Scale – Short Form (DES-SF)." *Diabetes Care* 26 (5): 1641–1642. doi: http://dx.doi.org/10.2337/diacare.26.5.1641-a.

Bingham, D. D., D. Richardson, K. Curran, and D. Parnell. 2014. "Fit Fans: Perspectives of a Practitioner and Understanding Participant Health Needs within a Health Promotion Programme for Older Men Delivered within an English Premier League Football Club." *Soccer and Society* 15 (6): 883–901.

Braun, V., and V. Clarke. 2006. "Using Thematic Analysis in Psychology." *Qualitative Research in Psychology* 3 (2): 77–101. doi: http://dx.doi.org/10.1191/1478088706qp063oa.

Bunn, C., S. Wyke, C. M. Gray, A. Maclean, and K. Hunt. 2016. "'Coz Football is What We All Have': Masculinities, Practice, Performance and Effervescence in a Gender – Sensitised Weight-loss and Healthy Living Programme for Men." *Sociol Health Illness*. doi: http://dx.doi.org/10.1111/1467-9566.12402.

Curran, K., D. D. Bingham, D. Richardson, and D. Parnell. 2014. "Ethnographic Engagement from within a Football in the Community Programme at an English Premier League Football Club." *Soccer and Society* 15 (6): 934–950.

Currie, C. J., E. A. Gale, and C. D. Poole. 2010. "Estimation of Primary Care Treatment Costs and Treatment Efficacy for People with Type 1 and Type 2 Diabetes in the United Kingdom from 1997 to 2007." *Diabetic Medicine* 27 (8): 938–948. doi: http://dx.doi.org/10.1111/j.1464-5491.2010.03040.x.

Deakin, T. A., J. E. Cade, R. Williams, and D. C. Greenwood. 2006. "Structured Patient Education: The Diabetes X-PERT Programme Makes a Difference." *Diabetic Medicine* 23: 944–954. doi: http://dx.doi.org/10.1111/j.1464-5491.2006.01906.x.

Department of Health. 2001. *The Expert Patient: A New Approach to Chronic Disease Management in the 21st Century*. London: The Stationery Office.

Department of Health. 2012. *Improving Outcomes and Supporting Transparency: Part 1: A Public Health Outcomes Framework for England, 2013–2016*. Accessed January 6, 2014. https://www.rcpsych.ac.uk/pdf/The%20Public%20Health%20Outcomes%20Framework.pdf

Department of Health and Diabetes UK. 2005. *Structured Patient Education in Diabetes: Report from the Patient Education Working Group*. London: Crown COI for the Department of Health.

Diabetes Profile. n.d. Accessed August 1, 2014. http://www.diabetesprofile.com/

Diabetes UK. n.d. *Cost of Diabetes*. Accessed December 20, 2013. http://www.diabetes.co.uk/costof-diabetes.html

Dinneen, S. F. 2008. "Structured Education for People with Type 2 Diabetes." *British Medical Journal* 336 (7642): 459–460. doi: http://dx.doi.org/10.1136/bmj.39478.693715.80.

Duckworth, W., C. Abraira, T. Moritz, D. Reda, N. Emanuele, P. D. Reaven, F. J. Zieve, J. Marks, S. N. Davis, R. Hayward, S. R. Warren, S. Goldman, M. McCarren, M. E. Vitek, W. G. Henderson, G. D. Huang, and VADT Investigators. 2009. "Glucose Control and Vascular Complications in Veterans with Type 2 Diabetes." *New England Journal of Medicine* 360 (2): 129–139. doi: http://dx.doi.org/10.1056/NEJMoa0808431.

Fonseca, V. 2003. "Effect of Thiazolidinediones on Body Weight in Patients with Diabetes Mellitus." *The American Journal of Medicine* 115 (8): 42–48. doi: http://dx.doi.org/10.1016/j.amjmed.2003.09.005.

Harvey, J. N., L. Craney, and D. Kelly. 2002. "Estimation of the Prevalence of Diagnosed Diabetes from Primary Care and Secondary Care Source Data: Comparison of Record Linkage with Capture-recapture Analysis." *Journal of Epidemiology and Community Health* 56: 18–23. doi: http://dx.doi.org/10.1136/jech.56.1.18.

Healthy Stadia. 2015. *The Healthy Stadia® Concept*. Accessed September 14, 2015. http://www.healthystadia.eu/about.html

Holman, R. R., A. J. Farmer, M. J. Davies, J. C. Levy, J. L. Darbyshire, J. F. Keenan, et al. 2009. "Three-year Efficacy of Complex Insulin Regimens in Type 2 Diabetes." *New England Journal of Medicine* 361 (18): 1736–1747. doi: http://dx.doi.org/10.1056/NEJMoa0905479.

Hunt, K., S. Wyke, C. M. Gray, A. S. Anderson, A. Brady, C. Bunn, P. T. Donnan, et al. 2014. "A Gender-sensitised Weight Loss and Healthy Living Programme for Overweight and Obese Men Delivered by Scottish Premier League Football Clubs (FFIT): a Pragmatic Randomised Controlled Trial." *The Lancet* 383: 1211–1221. doi: http://dx.doi.org/10.1016/S0140-6736(13)62420-4.

Office for National Statistics. n.d. Accessed December 14, 2013. www.ons.gov.uk

Orozco, L. J., A. M. Buchleitner, G. Gimenez-Perez, M. R. Figuls, B. Richter, and D. Mauricio. 2008. "Exercise or Exercise and Diet for Preventing Type 2 Diabetes Mellitus (Review)." *The Cochrane Collaboration* 3 (2): CD003054. doi: http://dx.doi.org/10.1002/14651858.CD003054.pub3

Pringle, A., S. Zwolinsky, J. McKenna, S. Robertson, A. Daly-Smith, and A. White. 2014. "Health Improvement for Men and Hard-to-engage-men Delivered in English Premier League Football Clubs." *Health Education Research* 29 (3): 503–520.

Skylar, J. S., R. Bergenstal, R. O. Bonow, J. Buse, P. Deedwania, E. A. Gale, B. V. Howard, M. S. Kirkman, M. Kosiborod, P. Reaven, and R. S. Sherwin. 2009. "Intensive glycemic control and the prevention of cardiovascular events: Implications of the ACCORD, ADVANCE, and VA Diabetes Trials." *Diabetes Care* 32 (1): 187–192.

Spandler, H., M. Mckeown, A. Roy, and M. J. Hurley. 2013. "Football Metaphor and Mental Well-being: An Evaluation of the It's a Goal! Programme." *Journal of Mental Health* 22 (6): 544–554. doi: http://dx.doi.org/10.3109/09638237.2013.819420.

Spandler, H., A. Roy, and M. Mckeown. 2014. "Playing by the Rules? Gender Relations in a Football and Mental Health Project." *The Journal of Men's Studies* 22 (2): 140–154. doi: http://dx.doi.org/10.3149/jms.2202.140.

Stratton, I. M., A. I. Adler, H. A. Neil, D. R. Matthews, S. E. Manley, C. A. Cull, D. Hadden, R. C. Turner, and R. R. Holman. 2000. "Association of Glycaemia with Macrovascular and Microvascular Complications of Type 2 Diabetes (UKPDS 35): Prospective Observational Study." *British Medical Journal* 321 (7258): 405–412. doi: http://dx.doi.org/10.1136/bmj.321.7258.405.

Wilkinson, S. 1998. "Focus Groups in Health Research Exploring the Meanings of Health and Illness." *Journal of Health Psychology* 3 (3): 329–348. doi: http://dx.doi.org/10.1177/135910539800300304.

World Health Organisation. 2009. *WHO Diabetes*. Accessed November 2, 2010. http://www.who.int/mediacentre/factsheets/fs312/en/

X-PERT Health. n.d. Accessed August 1, 2014. http://www.xperthealth.org.uk/X-PERT Health. Educating for Better Health. Accessed April 11, 2016. http://www.xperthealth.org.uk/

X-PERT Health. *Educating for Better Health*. Accessed April 11, 2016. http://www.xperthealth.org.uk/

Tackling mental health: the role of professional football clubs

Kathryn Curran, Simon Rosenbaum, Daniel Parnell, Brendon Stubbs, Andy Pringle and Jackie Hargreaves

ABSTRACT

In the UK, professional football clubs are being used as settings for the delivery of interventions that promote mental health in a number of ways including (i) the delivery of physical activity interventions to improve the mental health of the general population, (ii) the delivery of physical activity interventions for people experiencing mental illness, and (iii) the delivery of community mental health services within the confines of the football club. This research note offers insights into mental health interventions delivered within, and by, professional football clubs and the available evidence concerning their reach, effectiveness and impact. The findings suggest that professional football clubs can help to facilitate access to mental health services, particularly among young people, for whom accessing such services may be highly stigmatized. Furthermore, the findings highlight that such interventions have a positive impact on health. However, in order to capitalize on this opportunity funding agencies and commissioners must provide appropriate resources (human and financial) for effective delivery and evaluation. Furthermore, a more strategic approach to working towards the mental health agenda must be adopted. It is argued that this change in practice would allow professional football clubs to offer those in need access to high-quality interventions.

Background

Mental health is more than simply the lack of mental illness. Rather, it is a positive concept related to the social and emotional well-being of both individuals and communities and relating to the enjoyment of life, ability to cope with stress and sadness, the fulfilment of goals and potential, and a sense of connection to others (Hunter Institute of Mental Health 2015). A mental illness is a disorder diagnosed by a medical professional that significantly interferes with an individual's cognitive, emotional or social abilities. Mental illnesses can include mood disorders (such as depression, anxiety, and bipolar disorder), psychotic disorders (such as schizophrenia), eating disorders and personality disorders (Hunter Institute of Mental Health 2015).

Mental illness is a considerable burden on public health; depression alone accounts for one of the top five most commonly managed conditions in general practice (Cooke et al. 2012). In addition to negatively impacting upon quality of life, well-being and psychosocial functioning, there is irrefutable evidence demonstrating a strong association between mental illness and poor physical health such as obesity, diabetes and cardiovascular disease (Vancampfort et al. 2015). Collectively, the great increase in co-morbid somatic conditions contribute to a 15–20-year gap in life expectancy compared to the general population (Laursen, Munk-Olsen, and Vestergaard 2012; Lawrence, Hancock, and Kisely 2013), a finding that has been coined a *scandal of premature mortality* (Thornicroft 2011).

Factors contributing to the increased burden of poor physical health among people experiencing mental illness include psychotropic medication (Alvarez-Jimenez et al. 2008; Perez-Iglesias et al. 2008) and lifestyle-related modifiable risk factors, such as physical inactivity (Nyboe and Lund 2013; Vancampfort et al. 2012), poor dietary intake (Dipasquale et al. 2013), and high rates of smoking (Britton 2015). While physical activity remains the cornerstone of cardiovascular disease treatment in the general population (Thompson et al. 2003), people experiencing mental illness engage in less physical activity and frequently do not meet physical activity recommendations (Gardner-Sood et al. 2015; Nyboe and Lund 2013; Snethen, McCormick, and Lysaker 2014; Vancampfort et al. 2012).

In addition to the range of physical health benefits of regular physical activity participation, a growing body of evidence has demonstrated that physical activity has both protective (Mammen and Faulkner 2013) and treatment effects for people with mental illnesses (Rosenbaum et al. 2014). Importantly, even modest increases in physical activity are associated with improved mental health outcomes (Vancampfort et al. 2015a), with available recommendations regarding intervention variables comparable to those applicable to the general population (Stanton and Reaburn 2014; Stanton et al. 2014; Vancampfort et al. 2012). Considerable evidence has demonstrated both an anti-depressive (Schuch et al. 2016) and anxiolytic (Jayakody, Gunadasa, and Hosker 2013) effect of physical activity, in addition to improving symptoms of other conditions, such as schizophrenia (Firth et al. 2015; Vancampfort et al. 2012). Furthermore, physical activity has been found to be beneficial for promoting quality of life and recovery in people experiencing mental illness (Carless and Douglas 2008; Holley et al. 2011).

Despite recent and ongoing calls for physical activity to be an integral component of psychiatric care (Rosenbaum et al. 2015; Stanton et al. 2015; Vancampfort and Faulkner 2014; Vancampfort et al. 2015a,b) universal access to physical activity programmes for people experiencing mental illness remains ad hoc in many jurisdictions, often with limited funding and resources available to support clinical exercise programmes (Medicine, Society of Behavioral Meidicine & American College of Sports 2015).

The efficacy of physical activity for improving mental health of the general population and people experiencing mental illness has been established (Rebar et al. 2015; Rosenbaum et al. 2014). However, there is an urgent need to ensure that these findings are translated into real-world programmes capable of engaging and motivating people experiencing mental illness to participate in regular physical activity (Vancampfort et al. 2015a,b). One potential and highly scalable approach to promoting physical activity among people with mental illness is the utilization of professional football clubs to deliver pragmatic, community-based interventions (Parnell and Curran 2015; Pringle 2009).

In the UK, professional football clubs have received an increasing amount of attention with regard to their potential ability to contribute to the public health agenda. Over the past three years, there have been a rolling number of research articles discussing the role of professional football clubs in health improvement. The publication of a special issue on *'Football and Inclusivity'* in the peer-reviewed journal *'Soccer and Society'* (Parnell and Richardson 2014), for example, housed a number of key articles which highlighted professional football clubs as a vehicle for health promotion (Bingham et al. 2014; Curran, Drust, and Richardson 2014; Curran et al. 2014; Pringle et al. 2014; Rutherford et al. 2014).

Further developments in the football and health movement have been led by colleagues in Scotland (Hunt et al. 2014), who recorded significant biopsychosocial outcomes emerging from a randomized control trial related to a physical activity-led weight management programme for men, delivered through professional football clubs. Moreover, articles related to football and health-related programmes for men and older adults have also emerged (Pringle et al. 2014). Most recently, Parnell and Pringle (2016, 171–174) released a special issue on football and health improvement, which housed an eclectic mix of research articles and commentaries related to the role of professional football clubs in health improvement (Hulton et al. 2015; Lansley and Parnell 2015; Pringle et al. 2015).

Professional football clubs' Football in the Community (FitC) programmes often use football as an activity to engage participants in mental health interventions (Henderson et al. 2014). Research provides evidence of how football can support the prevention, early intervention, treatment and rehabilitation of a range of diseases across the lifespan (Bangsbo et al. 2014; Krustrup et al. 2010). The current understanding shows that football can be a valuable and acceptable health improvement activity, that has the potential to reach those at-risk of, and those diagnosed with, mental illness and improve mental health and well-being (Krustrup et al. 2013; Ottesen, Jeppesen, and Krustrup 2010).

Professional football clubs' community physical activity and health programmes have demonstrated huge success in both engaging and retaining their target audiences (Curran et al. 2014; Pringle et al. 2014, Pringle et al. 2015). Promoting and engaging the public in public health messages during leisure time has also been successfully achieved through associations with professional football clubs (Pringle et al. 2011, Curran et al. 2014). For example, awareness and engagement in positive health behaviours and messages has been achieved with men on English Premier League match days through a variety of approaches (Curran et al. 2014). These approaches were based on the assumption that the men would respond to health messages, seek help and discuss taboo issues in places that they feel comfortable (Pringle et al., 2011). The culture of football clubs therefore, can create an environment with the potential to address and ameliorate poor mental health among the community.

Research reflects an increasing interest and evidence for professional football clubs as a vehicle for health promotion. At present, in the UK, there are an increasing number of applied interventions targeting mental health promotion, or specifically tackling mental illness. Offering such interventions is a valuable, normalizing and non-stigmatizing approach to increasing physical activity. Professional football clubs have been used as settings for the delivery of interventions that promote mental health in a number of ways including (i) the delivery of physical activity interventions to improve the mental health of the general population, (ii) the delivery of physical activity interventions for people experiencing mental illness, and (iii) the delivery of community mental health services within the confines of the football club. Despite this growing investment, there is very little evidence surrounding the impact of such interventions.

Programmes and evidence

The delivery of physical activity interventions to improve the mental health of the general population

The delivery of lifestyle interventions which include a physical activity component have included the assessment of mental and social well-being. Premier League Health (PLH) for example, was a three-year national programme of men's health delivered in, and by, professional football clubs in England. Through their evaluation of PLH, White et al. (2012) highlighted that 15% of participants showed a positive change in social support, with 7% of participants moving to a level where they felt that they had forged social support networks that they could rely on in times of trouble (White et al. 2012). While some men self-reported reductions in social support pre-versus-post intervention, overall there was a statistically significant improvement in the social support networks of completers engaging in PLH. Further, interviews ($n = 57$) with participants supported that those individuals completing interventions reported positive psychological well-being, including achievement, feelings of well-being and social support (Pringle et al. 2014).

Older adults represent a core priority group for physical activity, mental health and public health policy (DH 2015). Professional football clubs have featured in many approaches to tackle public health priorities in this group (Bingham et al. 2014; Pringle et al. 2014). An example is Extra Time (ET), a national programme of physical activity interventions, delivered in professional football clubs, for older adults aged 55 + years. ET engaged older adults in weekly classes of a broad menu of physical and social activities, delivered primarily within football stadia. Participants reported that the link with the professional football club made ET more appealing. The most frequently self-reported benefits of engaging with ET were making friends, having fun and feeling happier with life (Parnell et al. 2015).

The delivery of physical activity interventions for people experiencing mental illness

The '*Imagine Your Goals*' (IYG) programme (Henderson et al. 2014) in an ongoing mental health intervention which aims to improve social inclusion and well-being for people with mental illnesses, as well as tackle mental health stigma and discrimination. The programme was pioneered by Everton in the Community (Everton Football Club's FitC programme) and adopted and rolled out by the Premier League in 2011. IYG is now delivered by 16 English Premier League football clubs, in conjunction with England's Time to Change programme (Barclays Premier League 2016). A mixed methods evaluation captured pre-versus-post-intervention data on pa\rticipants' well-being, and access to social capita (Henderson et al. 2014). Results indicated significant improvements in personal and individual skills, post-intervention. Focus groups were conducted with participants at the outset and the end of the two-year programmes. Participants reported that the programme had met their expectations in a number of areas including socializing, health and fitness. The authors of the report (Henderson et al. 2014) concluded football clubs can successfully deliver programmes to people with mental illness which improve access to personal skills, social capital and have other potential benefits.

Notts County Football in the Community located in the English East Midlands, established a weekly group providing sport and physical activities for men with early onset dementia. Participants engaged in a wide range of gentle and easy-to-follow weekly activities including walking football, bowls, cricket, basketball, table tennis, volleyball and badminton. Participants and their carers were consulted about what activities they would like to take part in prior to the session (Notts County Football in the Community 2016). In contrast, the social part of the session gave participants the chance to engage in conversation, create social connections and relax in the company of others while having refreshments. Investigating this intervention, Carone, Tischler, and Dening (2014) reported enjoyment and positive anticipation related to attending the group for all involved. The 'brand' of the football club (named the *'The Notts County Effect'*) and the personalized service in a 'dementia-free' environment was attributed to the reach, adoption and adherence of the programme (Carone, Tischler, and Dening 2014).

It is important to note that recovery from mental illness refers to not only a reduction in symptoms, but achieving functional recovery through improvement in psychosocial functioning (Anthony 1993). Given that recovery is not a linear process, and community support has been identified as a fundamental component of recovery (Anthony 1993), the delivery of such programmes via professional footballs clubs are a promising intervention to help achieve improvements in psychosocial functioning and hence, recovery.

The delivery of community mental health services within the confines of the football club

One such programme that was delivered within the grounds of professional football clubs was the *'It's a Goal'* programme (Pringle and Sayers 2004). The intervention typically targeted men aged 18–35 years and aimed to improve mental well-being. Using group-based interventions, and utilizing football as a metaphor, helped young adult men with mental illness to improve self-esteem, aid inclusion, and address the subject of suicide. This intervention did not include a physical activity element, however, professional football clubs were regarded as an innovative approach to making services accessible and promoting the uptake of mental health facilities with participants.

Practical implications

Despite limited published research on the outcomes of football-led mental health interventions, professional football clubs' FitC organizations are a growing delivery agent for mental health-oriented programmes. There appears to be four major challenges however which warrant consideration in order to maximize successful implementation. These include facilitating partnerships with service providers, providing relevant continuing professional development of community coaches, adopting monitoring and evaluation frameworks, and the commissioning of interventions. Each potential challenge will briefly be considered.

Facilitating partnerships with service providers

A number of mental health interventions have been commenced without appropriate partnerships or strategies in place. As such, an open-door or walk-in approach to intervention design has resulted in uncertain group numbers, as well as a mix of participant conditions and therefore, needs. Where programmes have excelled, it has been a result of strategic and coherent partnership working. For example, Everton in the Community's *IYG* programme worked in partnership with Mersey Care NHS Trust. Working in partnership with Everton in the Community football coaches, Mersey Care ensure all participants' conditions and needs are met. This ensures that the participants most 'in need' are provided with consistent and quality care. Facilitating bilateral referral between mental health services and football-led interventions may also help to increase uptake and attendance, while ensuring adequate risk management strategies are followed whereby football programmes can deal with adverse events or escalation in symptoms appropriately. Recruitment strategies such as this should be viewed as best practice, in order to protect all stakeholders, and to ensure a consistent quality service for all participants.

Continued professional development

There is an acknowledgement of the lack of physical activity and health-based qualifications by commentators and stakeholders concerned with the practice and engagement of professional football clubs on social agendas. Previous evidence has highlighted a lack of professional development opportunities for community football coaches working on the health agenda (Lansley and Parnell 2015). While effective partnership working allows for informal, and formal, education exchanges between mental health organizations and community coaches there remains a need for an industry qualification. Football in the Community coaches, in this instance, should be skilled in mental health first aid and be aware of pathways by which adverse outcomes and/or increased symptoms can be reported and followed up. Given the scope and growth of this it would appear relevant to look towards sport national governing bodies, government departments for health, and related agencies involved in sport, health, and physical activity (i.e. in the United Kingdom, SportsCoachUK), to address this issue. This is not a concern isolated to mental health promotion; indeed, evidence suggests that community coaches and practitioners working towards a health agenda require professional development (Bingham et al. 2014; Curran et al. 2014; Parnell et al. 2015) This remains an ongoing concern for those seeking high quality and effective delivery of interventions.

Monitoring and evaluation

Football-led interventions have the capacity to improve both physical and mental health outcomes of people experiencing mental illness (Parnell and Curran 2015). With growing interest in the utility of football-led interventions, ensuring appropriate evaluation frameworks are in place is fundamental to demonstrating efficacy and justifying funding (Pringle et al. 2015). Researchers should consider non-traditional outcomes that may change in response to football-led interventions including (i) reduced stigma associated with mental health services, and any subsequent increase in traditional service utilization, especially among young people, (ii) cardiorespiratory fitness which is known to be reduced among people experiencing mental illness and a key modifiable risk factor in response to physical activity (Stubbs et al. 2016; Vancampfort et al. 2015, 2015), (iii) social connectedness, and (iv) self-confidence, quality of life and motivation (Vancampfort et al. 2015, 2015). Ensuring that evaluation of interventions also extends to those involved in the design and delivery (i.e. coaches) must also be a fundamental consideration (Pringle et al. 2015).

Commissioning of interventions

It appears that, in general, football-led mental health programmes have been commissioned like other, more typical, sport development programmes. Recent evidence (Lansley and Parnell 2015) provide an example from a football-led mental service. The authors detail the process whereby:

> funding has been provided to [a professional] football club community foundation to deliver a new area of work in football health improvement. This involved the community foundation delivering a 10-month football programme for participants with mental health issues on a budget of £10,000 without consideration of process or impact evaluation. This was not only a new area of work for the community foundation [i.e. working with participants with mental health issues], but also an agenda the current staff had little or no experience or any requisite skill for delivering.

It is important for health care to be equitable and effective. Commissioners may drive towards inflating programme targets in attempt to increase value for money. Therefore, as football and football settings are utilized as a vehicle for improving mental health outcomes, it is clear that policy-makers, commissioners and managers need to be realistic about the associated costs and practical implications of delivering effective and equitable services (Lansley and Parnell 2015). Given that projects are often under-resourced and under-supported, this is something that is both urgent and important for all stakeholders to consider.

Commissioning could be the single most important factor in stimulating change in the area of mental health football-led interventions. This process could enact a situation whereby recipients of funding must evidence partnership working, continuing professional development planning for community coaches and evidence a clear monitoring and evaluation framework. For this to occur, it appears that commissioners must also consider their role within the process, reflect, and in some cases *engage* in their own professional development to enhance the effectiveness of their practice.

Conclusion

Moving forward, can professional football clubs' FitC organizations play an integral role in promoting mental health and increasing physical activity among people at-risk of developing, and people diagnosed with, mental illness? Indeed, the evidence suggests that professional football clubs can offer a potentially valuable ground for the delivery of applied PA interventions targeting mental health promotion or specifically tackling mental illness. Professional football clubs may also help facilitate access to mental health services, particularly among young people for whom accessing such services may be highly stigmatized. However, to capitalize on this opportunity funding agencies and commissioners must provide appropriate resources (human and financial) for effective delivery and evaluation.

Furthermore, a more strategic approach to working towards the mental health agenda must be adopted. This change in practice will offer professional football clubs a genuine opportunity to offer those in need access to high-quality interventions. While professional football clubs may not be the panacea regarding improving mental health outcomes for all, the acceptability and scalability of football-based interventions warrants further investigation and investment from researchers and clinicians across the globe.

Acknowledgements

The authors would like to thank the peer reviewers of this article for the structured and critical feedback on the revisions and their continued support.

Disclosure statement

No potential conflict of interest was reported by the authors.

References

Alvarez-Jimenez, M., C. Gonzalez-Blanch, B. Crespo-Facorro, S. Hetrick, J. M. Rodriguez-Sanchez, R. Perez-Iglesias, and J. L. Vazquez-Barquero. 2008. "Antipsychotic-Induced Weight Gain in Chronic and First-Episode Psychotic Disorders." *CNS Drugs* 22 (7): 547–562.

Anthony, William. 1993. "Recovery from mental illness: The guiding vision of the mental health service system in the 1990s." *Psychosocial rehabilitation journal* 16 (4): 11.

Bangsbo, Jens, A. Junge, Jirí Dvorák, and Peter Krustrup. 2014. "Executive Summary: Football for Health–Prevention and Treatment of Non-Communicable Diseases across the Lifespan through Football." *Scandinavian Journal of Medicine & Science in Sports* 24 (S1): 147–150.

Barclays Premier League. 2016. *Imagine Your Goals*. Available at: http://www.premierleague.com/en-gb/communities/2011-12/imagine-your-goals.html [Last accessed on 20/03/16].

Bingham, Daniel David, Daniel Parnell, Kathryn Curran, Roger Jones, and Dave Richardson. 2014. "Fit Fans: Perspectives of a Practitioner and Understanding Participant Health Needs within a Health Promotion Programme for Older Men Delivered within an English Premier League Football Club." *Soccer & Society* 15 (6): 883–901.

Britton, John. 2015. "Treating Smoking in Mental Health Settings." *The Lancet Psychiatry* 2 (5): 364–365.

Carless, David, and Kitrina Douglas. 2008. "The Role of Sport and Exercise in Recovery from Serious Mental Illness: Two Case Studies." *International Journal of Men's Health* 7 (2): 137.

Carone, Laura, Victoria Tischler, and Tom Dening. 2014. "Football and Dementia: A Qualitative Investigation of a Community Based Sports Group for Men with Early Onset Dementia." *Dementia* 1471301214560239.

Cooke, Georga, Lisa Valenti, Paul Glasziou, and Helena Britt. 2012. "Common General Practice Presentations and Publication Frequency." *Australian Family Physician* 42 (1–2): 65–68.

Curran, Kathryn, Barry Drust, and Dave Richardson. 2014. "'I Just Want to Watch the Match': A Practitioner's Reflective Account of Men's Health Themed Match Day Events at an English Premier League Football Club." *Soccer & Society* 15 (6): 919–933.

Curran, Kathryn, Daniel David Bingham, David Richardson, and Daniel Parnell. 2014. "Ethnographic Engagement from within a Football in the Community Programme at an English Premier League Football Club." *Soccer & Society* 15 (6): 934–950.

Dipasquale, Salvatore, Carmine M. Pariante, Paola Dazzan, Eugenio Aguglia, Philip McGuire, and Valeria Mondelli. 2013. "The Dietary Pattern of Patients with Schizophrenia: A Systematic Review." *Journal of Psychiatric Research* 47 (2): 197–207.

Firth, J., J. Cotter, R. Elliott, P. French, and A. R. Yung. 2015. "A Systematic Review and Meta-Analysis of Exercise Interventions in Schizophrenia Patients." *Psychological Medicine* 45 (7): 1343–1361.

Gardner-Sood, P., J. Lally, S. Smith, Z. Atakan, K. Ismail, K. E. Greenwood, A. Keen, et al. 2015. "Cardiovascular Risk Factors and Metabolic Syndrome in People with Established Psychotic Illnesses: Baseline Data from the IMPaCT Randomized Controlled Trial." *Psychological Medicine* 45 (12): 2619–2629. doi:http://dx.doi.org/10.1017/S0033291715000562.

Henderson, Claire, Stefanie O'Hara, Graham Thornicroft, and Martin Webber. 2014. "Corporate Social Responsibility and Mental Health: The Premier League Football Imagine Your Goals Programme." *International Review of Psychiatry* 26 (4): 460–466.

Holley, Jessica, Diane Crone, Philip Tyson, and Geoff Lovell. 2011. "The Effects of Physical Activity on Psychological Well-Being for Those with Schizophrenia: A Systematic Review." *British Journal of Clinical Psychology* 50 (1): 84–105.

Hulton, Andrew Thomas, David Flower, Rebecca Murphy, Dave Richardson, Barry Drust, and Kathryn Curran. 2015. "Effectiveness of a Community Football Programme on Improving Physiological Markers of Health in a Hard-to-Reach Male Population: The Role of Exercise Intensity." *Soccer & Society* 17 (2): 1–13.

Hunt, Kate, Sally Wyke, Cindy M. Gray, Annie S. Anderson, Adrian Brady, Christopher Bunn, Peter T. Donnan, Elisabeth Fenwick, Eleanor Grieve, and Jim Leishman. 2014. "A Gender-Sensitised Weight Loss and Healthy Living Programme for Overweight and Obese Men Delivered by Scottish Premier League Football Clubs (FFIT): A Pragmatic Randomised Controlled Trial." *The Lancet* 383 (9924): 1211–1221.

Hunter Institute of Mental Health. 2015. *Prevention First: A Prevention and Promotion Framework for Mental Health*. Newcastle: Hunter Institute of Mental Health.

Jayakody, K., S. Gunadasa, and C. Hosker. 2013. "Exercise for Anxiety Disorders: Systematic Review." *British Journal of Sports Medicine* 48 (3): 187–196.

Krustrup, P., P. Aagaard, L. Nybo, J. Petersen, M. Mohr, and J. Bangsbo. 2010. "Recreational Football as a Health Promoting Activity: A Topical Review." *Scandinavian Journal of Medicine & Science in Sports* 20 (s1): 1–13.

Krustrup, Peter, Morten B. Randers, Lars J. Andersen, Sarah R. Jackman, Jens Bangsbo, and Peter R. Hansen. 2013. "Soccer Improves Fitness and Attenuates Cardiovascular Risk Factors in Hypertensive Men." *Medicine & Science in Sports & Exercise* 45 (3): 553–561.

Lansley, Simon, and Daniel Parnell. 2015. "Football for Health: Getting Strategic." *Soccer & Society* 17 (2): 1–8.

Laursen, T. M., T. Munk-Olsen, and M. Vestergaard. 2012. "Life Expectancy and Cardiovascular Mortality in Persons with Schizophrenia." *Current Opinion in Psychiatry* 25 (2): 83–88.

Lawrence, David, Kirsten J. Hancock, and Stephen Kisely. 2013. "The Gap in Life Expectancy from Preventable Physical Illness in Psychiatric Patients in Western Australia: Retrospective Analysis of Population Based Registers." *British Medical Journal* 346: f2539-1.

Mammen, George, and Guy Faulkner. 2013. "Physical Activity and the Prevention of Depression." *American Journal of Preventive Medicine* 45 (5): 649–657.

Medicine, Society of Behavioral Meidicine & American College of Sports. 2015. "Increase United States Health Plan Coverage for Exercise Programming in Community Mental Health Programs for People with Serious Mental Illness." Available at: http://www.sbm.org/UserFiles/file/SBMandACSM_exerciseformentalhealthpositionstatement.pdf [Last accessed 20/03/16]

Notts County Football in the Community. 2016. *Working Age Dementia 20132016*.

Nyboe, L., and H. Lund. 2013. "Low Levels of Physical Activity in Patients with Severe Mental Illness." *Nordic Journal of Psychiatry* 67: 43–46.

Ottesen, Laila, Rikke Schou Jeppesen, and Birgitte R. Krustrup. 2010. "The Development of Social Capital through Football and Running: Studying an Intervention Program for Inactive Women." *Scandinavian Journal of Medicine & Science in Sports* 20 (s1): 118–131.

Parnell, D., and K. Curran. 2015. "Professional Football Clubs Could Deliver Pragmatic Physical Activity Interventions to Promote Mental Health." *British journal of sports medicine* 49 (15): 1026.

Parnell, Daniel, and Andy Pringle. 2016. "Football and Health Improvement: An Emerging Field." *Soccer & Society* 17 (2): 171–174.

Parnell, Daniel, Andy Pringle, Jim McKenna, Stephen Zwolinsky, Zoe Rutherford, Jackie Hargreaves, Lizzie Trotter, Michael Rigby, and David Richardson. 2015. "Reaching Older People with PA

Delivered in Football Clubs: The Reach, Adoption and Implementation Characteristics of the Extra Time Programme." *BMC Public Health* 15 (1): 1–12.

Parnell, D., and D. Richardson. 2014. "Special Issue: Football and Inclusivity." *Soccer and Society* 15 (6): 823–827.

Perez-Iglesias, Rocio, Benedicto Crespo-Facorro, Obdulia Martinez-Garcia, Maria L. Ramirez-Bonilla, Mario Alvarez-Jimenez, Jose M. Pelayo-Teran, Maria T. Garcia-Unzueta, Jose A. Amado, and Jose L. Vazquez-Barquero. 2008. "Weight Gain Induced by Haloperidol, Risperidone and Olanzapine after 1 Year: Findings of a Randomized Clinical Trial in a Drug-Naïve Population." *Schizophrenia Research* 99 (1-3): 13–22.

Pringle, A. 2009. "The Growing Role of Football as a Vehicle for Interventions in Mental Health Care." *Journal of Psychiatric and Mental Health Nursing* 16: 553–557.

Pringle, A., S. Zwolinsky, A. Smith, S. Robertson, J. McKennaand A. White. 2011. "The Pre-adoption Demographic and Health Profiles of Men Participating in a Programme of Men's Health Delivered in English Premier League football clubs". *Public health*, 125 (7): 411–416.

Pringle, Andy, Daniel Parnell, Stephen Zwolinsky, Jackie Hargreaves, and Jim McKenna. 2014. "Effect of a Health-Improvement Pilot Programme for Older Adults Delivered by a Professional Football Club: The Burton Albion Case Study." *Soccer & Society* 15 (6): 902–918.

Pringle, Andy, Daniel Parnell, Zoe Rutherford, Jim McKenna, Stephen Zwolinsky, and Jackie Hargreaves. 2015. "Sustaining Health Improvement Activities Delivered in English Professional Football Clubs Using Evaluation: A Short Communication." *Soccer & Society* 17 (2): 1–11.

Pringle, A., and P. Sayers. 2004. "It's a Goal!: Basing a Community Psychiatric Nursing Service in a Local Football Stadium." *The Journal of the Royal Society for the Promotion of Health* 124 (5): 234–238.

Pringle, Andy, Stephen Zwolinsky, James McKenna, Steven Robertson, Andy Daly-Smith, and Alan White. 2014. "Health Improvement for Men and Hard-to-Engage-Men Delivered in English Premier League Football Clubs." *Health Education Research* 29 (3): 503–520.

Rebar, Amanda L., Robert Stanton, David Geard, Camille Short, Mitch J. Duncan, and Corneel Vandelanotte. 2015. "A Meta-Meta-Analysis of the Effect of Physical Activity on Depression and Anxiety in Non-Clinical Adult Populations." *Health Psychology Review* 9 (3): 1–78.

Rosenbaum, S., A. Tiedemann, C. Sherrington, J. Curtis, and P. B. Ward. 2014. "Physical Activity Interventions for People with Mental Illness." *The Journal of Clinical Psychiatry* 75 (9): 964–974.

Rosenbaum, S., A. Tiedemann, Philip B. Ward, Jackie Curtis, and Catherine Sherrington. 2015. "Physical Activity Interventions: An Essential Component in Recovery from Mental Illness." *British Journal of Sports Medicine* 49 (24): 1544–1545.

Rutherford, Zoe, Brendan Gough, Sarah Seymour-Smith, Christopher R. Matthews, John Wilcox, Dan Parnell, and Andy Pringle. 2014. "'Motivate': The Effect of a Football in the Community Delivered Weight Loss Programme on over 35-Year Old Men and Women's Cardiovascular Risk Factors." *Soccer & Society* 15 (6): 951–969.

Schuch, Felipe Barreto, Andrea Camaz Deslandes, Brendon Stubbs, Natan Pereira Gosmann, Cristiano Tschiedel Belem da Silva, and Marcelo Pio de Almeida Fleck. 2016. "Neurobiological Effects of Exercise on Major Depressive Disorder: A Systematic Review." *Neuroscience & Biobehavioral Reviews* 61: 1–11.

Snethen, Gretchen A., Bryan P. McCormick, and Paul H. Lysaker. 2014. "Physical Activity and Psychiatric Symptoms in Adults with Schizophrenia Spectrum Disorders." *The Journal of Nervous and Mental Disease* 202 (12): 845–852.

Stanton, Robert, and Peter Reaburn. 2014. "Exercise and the Treatment of Depression: A Review of the Exercise Program Variables." *Journal of Science and Medicine in Sport* 17 (2): 177–182.

Stanton, Robert, Simon Rosenbaum, Megan Kalucy, Peter Reaburn, and Brenda Happell. 2015. "A Call to Action: Exercise as Treatment for Patients with Mental Illness." *Australian Journal of Primary Health* 21 (2): 120–125.

Stanton, Robert, Simon Rosenbaum, Peter Reaburn, and Brenda Happell. 2014. "A Multidisciplinary Approach to Aerobic Exercise Prescription for Mental Illness." *Sport Health* 32 (3): 58–61.

Stubbs, Brendon, Simon Rosenbaum, Davy Vancampfort, Philip B. Ward, and Felipe B. Schuch. 2016. "Exercise Improves Cardiorespiratory Fitness in People with Depression: A Meta-Analysis of Randomized Control Trials." *Journal of Affective Disorders* 190: 249–253.

Thompson, Paul D., David Buchner, Ileana L. Piña, Gary J. Balady, Mark A. Williams, Bess H. Marcus, Kathy Berra, Steven N. Blair, Fernando Costa, and Barry Franklin. 2003. "Exercise and Physical Activity in the Prevention and Treatment of Atherosclerotic Cardiovascular Disease a Statement from the Council on Clinical Cardiology (Subcommittee on Exercise, Rehabilitation, and Prevention) and the Council on Nutrition, Physical Activity, and Metabolism (Subcommittee on Physical Activity)." *Circulation* 107 (24): 3109–3116.

Thornicroft, G. 2011. "Physical Health Disparities and Mental Illness: The Scandal of Premature Mortality." *British Journal of Psychiatry* 199 (6): 441–442.

Vancampfort, D., M. De Hert, L. H. Skjerven, A. L. Gyllensten, A. Parker, N. Mulders, L. Nyboe, F. Spencer, and M. Probst. 2012. "International Organization of Physical Therapy in Mental Health Consensus on Physical Activity within Multidisciplinary Rehabilitation Programmes for Minimising Cardio-Metabolic Risk in Patients with Schizophrenia." *Disability and Rehabilitation* 34 (1): 1–12.

Vancampfort, Davy, and Guy Faulkner. 2014. "Physical Activity and Serious Mental Illness: A Multidisciplinary Call to Action." *Mental Health and Physical Activity* 7 (3): 153–154.

Vancampfort, Davy, Jan Knapen, T. Michel Probst, Sander Remans Scheewe, and Marc De Hert. 2012. "A Systematic Review of Correlates of Physical Activity in Patients with Schizophrenia." *Acta Psychiatrica Scandinavica* 125 (5): 352–362.

Vancampfort, Davy, Tomas Madou, Herman Moens, Tanja De Backer, Patrick Vanhalst, Chris Helon, Pieter Naert, Simon Rosenbaum, Brendon Stubbs, and Michel Probst. 2015. "Could Autonomous Motivation Hold the Key to Successfully Implementing Lifestyle Changes in Affective Disorders? A Multicentre Cross Sectional Study." *Psychiatry Research* 228 (1): 100–106.

Vancampfort, Davy, Michel Probst, Liv Helvik Skjaerven, Daniel Catalán-Matamoros, Amanda Lundvik-Gyllensten, Antonia Gómez-Conesa, Rutger Ijntema, and Marc De Hert. 2012. "Systematic Review of the Benefits of Physical Therapy within a Multidisciplinary Care Approach for People with Schizophrenia." *Physical Therapy* 92 (1): 11–23.

Vancampfort, Davy, Michel Probst, Jan Knapen, Attilio Carraro, and Marc De Hert. 2012. "Associations between Sedentary Behaviour and Metabolic Parameters in Patients with Schizophrenia." *Psychiatry Research* 200 (2-3): 73–78.

Vancampfort, D., S. Rosenbaum, M. Probst, A. Soundy, A. J. Mitchell, M. De Hert, and B. Stubbs. 2015. "Promotion of Cardiorespiratory Fitness in Schizophrenia: A Clinical Overview and Meta-Analysis." *Acta Psychiatrica Scandinavica* 132 (2): 131–143.

Vancampfort, D., S. Rosenbaum, P. B. Ward, and B. Stubbs. 2015. "Exercise Improves Cardiorespiratory Fitness in People with Schizophrenia: A Systematic Review and Meta-Analysis." *Schizophrenia Research* 169 (1): 453–457.

Vancampfort, D., B. Stubbs, A. J. Mitchell, M. De Hert, M. Wampers, P. B. Ward, S. Rosenbaum, and C. U. Correll. 2015. "Risk of Metabolic Syndrome and Its Components in People with Schizophrenia, Bipolar and Major Depressive Disorders: A Large Scale Meta-Analysis of 198 Studies." *World Psychiatry* 14 (3): 339–347.

Vancampfort, D., B. Stubbs, P. B. Ward, S. B. Teasdale, and S. Rosenbaum. 2015a. "Integrating Physical Activity as Medicine in the Care of People with Severe Mental Illness." *Australian and New Zealand Journal of Psychiatry* 49 (8): 681–682. doi:http://dx.doi.org/10.1177/0004867415590831.

Vancampfort, Davy, Brendon Stubbs, Philip B. Ward, Scott Teasdale, and Simon Rosenbaum. 2015b. "Why Moving More Should Be Promoted for Severe Mental Illness." *The Lancet Psychiatry* 2 (4): 295.

Vancampfort, Davy, Brendon Stubbs, Sumanth Kumar Venigalla, and Michel Probst. 2015. "Adopting and Maintaining Physical Activity Behaviours in People with Severe Mental Illness: The Importance of Autonomous Motivation." *Preventive Medicine* 81 (2015): 216–220.

White, A., S. Zwolinsky, A. Pringle, J. McKenna, A. Daly-Smith, S. Robertson, and R. Berry. 2012. *Premier League Health: A National Programme of Men's Health Promotion Delivered in/by Professional Football Clubs, Final Report 2012*. Leeds, UK: Centre for Men's Health & Centre for Active Lifestyles, Leeds Metropolitan University.

Sport policy and English primary physical education: the role of professional football clubs in outsourcing

Daniel Parnell, Ed Cope, Richard Bailey and Paul Widdop

ABSTRACT

Sports policy in England has led to considerable recent investment in Primary Physical Education (PE) via the 'PE and Sport Premium'. An outcome of this has been growth in the outsourcing – handing over control of services to external agencies – of PE, including sport coaches from professional football clubs' community programmes. Despite the growing research on healthy stadia, we know very little about the work performed by community arms of professional clubs in relation to delivering Primary PE. This article discusses the challenges of outsourcing PE to coaches who work for professional football clubs, while offering some evidence related to the employment and development of sports coaches. Given that the evidence of sport coaches' involvement in Primary PE is limited and that funding and outsourcing it likely to continue England until (at least) 2020, it is important and timely to discuss critically the role of professional football clubs within the current sport policy.

Introduction

Professional football clubs via their community programmes have featured as a key deliverer on the healthy stadia agenda (Parnell and Pringle 2016; Curran et al. 2014; Hunt et al. 2014). As part of this work, these community programmes deliver a range of school-based sport provision, including Primary Physical Education (PE). The role of external providers of Primary PE, specifically sports coaches, has come under increasing scrutiny. Indeed, many clubs deliver Primary PE services through school-based coaching. As a result of government policy and funding from the English Premier League, the outsourcing of Primary PE to coaches has grown, while research in this area is lacking. As a result, this article aims to explore current sport policy and critically discuss how professional football clubs and sport coaches, within the healthy stadia agenda, are delivering Primary PE.

In May 2010, a Conservative Party-led coalition government assumed political leadership of the United Kingdom (UK). In response to (real and perceived) debt incurred by the previous Labour administration, the new government initiated considerable cuts to public spending, including a raft of austerity measures in its 'Comprehensive Spending Review', which outlined £81 billion cuts to government departments. This spending review ensured that public spending was reduced on a national scale, leaving few government departments untouched. As part of the spending review, local governments had to launch their own reductions (Commission 2011; DCLG 2010). The Department of Communities and Local Government delivered funding cuts of 51% between 2010 and 2015, resulting in grants to local government falling by 27% (Parnell, Widdop, and King 2015). As a consequence, discretionary services, such as sport, leisure and culture faced uncertainty (Collins and Haudenhuyse 2015; Local Government Association 2013; Parnell, Millward, and Spracklen 2014; Parnell et al. 2015). Despite this lack of protection for sport provision in the run up to the London 2012 Olympic and Paralympic Games (hereafter Olympic Games), it was anticipated that funding support for sport would continue. The 2012 Olympic Games aspired to stimulate political and national interest in sport. Indeed, the 2012 Olympic Games would – it was claimed – act as a vehicle to endorse and promote sports participation for all social groups, particularly children and young people (Department for Culture Media and Sport 2008; London Organising Committee of the Olympic and Paralympic Games 2007). On securing the bid to host the Olympic Games, Public Service Agreement Target 22 aimed to deliver a successful Olympic Games with a sustainable legacy, which included getting more young people taking part in PE and sport (National Audit Office 2010).

The Olympic legacy narrative was explicitly associated with PE, school sport, and talent development and built on earlier policies that sought to transform radically the state and status of these activities for young people (Cale, Harris, and Duncombe 2016; Phillpots 2013; Weed et al. 2012). Talent in schools had been, by and large, little more than the locally networked PE teacher offering direction to more able students towards the nearest community sports club (Bailey 2006). Despite this, Primary School settings have seen a policy shift and financial investment in identifying and developing gifted and talented pupils, including those in PE and school sport. In order to support talented students with PE and school sport, a new contributory initiative emerged, the PE, School Sport and Club Links (PESSCL) scheme (DES/DCMS 2003). This programme involved eight initiatives to increase levels of participation and was predominantly funded by the Treasury (at the time, Labour), who committed £459 million to transform PE and school sport, with an additional allocation of £686 million to improve school sport facilities across England (DES/DCMS 2003), when it was launched in 2002[1]. The strands of PESSCL included, gifted and talented activities, competition managers in schools, multi-skills clubs, academies and camps in Primary Schools and specific jobs with the remit of talent identification, based within new Specialist Sports Colleges as part of School Sport Partnerships (Flintoff 2003; YST 2004). The approach was intended to complement existing talent development strategies, building a stronger school-to-club system in collaboration with national governing bodies (NGBs), and necessitated much closer interaction between schools and external coaches. Through distinct curricular and extra-curricular programmes, the scheme aimed to promote a cultural shift towards a system whereby excellence and outstanding achievement were identified, developed and celebrated (Bailey 2007), although it is uncertain whether the objectives of these have been fully realized (Parnell et al. 2016).

Following the 2010 coalition's comprehensive spending review, reduced public spending challenged the maintenance of support for PE and school sport (Parnell et al. 2016).

Almost immediately, the new Secretary of State for Education informed the Youth Sport Trust, previously the agency given responsibility for PE and school sport (Department for Culture Media and Sport /Strategy Unit 2002), that the £162 million ring-fenced funding for School Sport Partnerships would end in order to give schools the time and freedom to focus on providing competitive sport (Parnell et al. 2016). A new youth sport policy document, 'Creating a sporting habit for life: a new youth sport strategy' was introduced that called for a new approach to policy and practice that would be a more rigorous and targeted way of thinking focusing on results within grassroots sport and school-club links (Department for Culture Media and Sport 2012). This policy set out to improve links between schools and community sports clubs (Department for Culture Media and Sport 2012) and introduce a new funding initiative.

In 2012, the UK Government announced the launch of 'Primary PE and Sport Premium' funding (amounting to £450 million) for English schools, initially for three years. This equated to an approximate payment of £9250 per school. The fund, it was claimed, would support the improvement of the quality of PE and sport. The fund would allow Head Teachers to invest in activities such as providing enhanced teacher professional development, increased children's competitive sport, additional education for teachers, and activities for children to recognize the value and benefit of high-quality PE and how it can help deliver whole school improvement (Cope, Bailey, and Parnell 2015). The result of these developments led some stakeholders, most notably Head Teachers, to use the Premium to employ Primary PE specialists as members of staff, offer existing staff professional development opportunities and delivering sport competitions or buying new equipment (such as specialist facilities) (Cope, Bailey, and Parnell 2015). In many cases, however, the Premium was spent hiring external sports coaches (Department for Education 2014), which reflected a shift in focus from central management, to a competitive, decentralized environment. A range of deliverers moved in to take advantage of the new funding space, including small businesses, social entrepreneurs and charities, including the community programmes attached to professional football clubs.

Professional football clubs as deliverers

The focus of professional football clubs' work initially targeted children in community and school settings through their community programmes, and had two objectives. First, it sought to engage and connect with children through football to create lifelong supporters; second, it tried to establish talent identification across local communities (Mellor 2008; Parnell et al. 2013). Since the establishment of similar activities in the 1970s, through the national 'Football in the Community' scheme, and the role of football clubs in addressing social issues and the healthy stadia agenda has continued to grow. Football clubs now work with a number of key target groups in addition to children, including adult men and women, families and older adults for several key policy agendas, including health-enhancing physical activity, social inclusion and general health (Parnell, Millward, and Spracklen 2014). As a result of this, professional football clubs have developed a range of stadia-based and outreach programmes. To date, research on this area has been limited with only preliminary evidence about how this type of work is delivered by professional sport clubs (Drygas et al. 2013). Exploring healthy stadia extends beyond a settings-based approach to health promotion, to include community outreach, such as school-based programmes (Drygas et al. 2013;

Parnell, Pringle, Mckenna et al. 2015; Parnell et al. 2016). The growing body of evidence on the role of professional football clubs in delivering interventions in the community has been mainly concerned with health improvement programmes for men and women (Bingham et al. 2014; Curran et al. 2014; Hunt et al. 2014; Parnell and Richardson 2014; Rutherford et al. 2014; Parnell et al. 2015; Parnell and Pringle 2016). There is, however, limited evidence available about child- and youth-focused interventions (Parnell et al. 2013). In the light of the appearance of increasing opportunities for professional football clubs working in Primary PE settings, the urgency of such research is considerable.

Professional football clubs operate a broad range of activities and services broadly housed within Primary PE and school sport. This includes the provision of football/sport coaches for PE, breakfast and after-school clubs, reading and literacy programmes, and appearances by professional football players. For example, Premier League Reading Stars is delivered in a partnership between the Premier League, associated clubs, and the National Literacy Trust. It is claimed that this project helped three out of four children make at least six months' progress in reading over a ten-week period. Added to this, two-thirds of child participants reported that seeing a Premier League footballer read made them want to read more (Pabion 2015). Another example is the Premier League 4 Sport initiative, which aimed to contribute to the legacy of the 2012 Olympics Games (from September 2009) by helping young people get involved in sport in their local community (Premier League 2016). This was a collaborative project between the Premier League, Sport England and the Youth Sport Trust, and was funded by a £3.8-million partnership with the UK Government. The project aimed to facilitate Premier League clubs to become hubs linked to community sport facilities and local secondary schools to create satellite sport centres (Premier League 2016). The scope and purpose of professional football clubs working and delivering community programmes within their stadia through outreach within Primary PE settings has clearly grown in both investment and scope, making clubs a considerable provider to schools.

The growth of professional football clubs delivering sport in schools is no doubt a result of the 2014 announcement that the English Premier League would launch of a substantial investment in a 3-year programme of support and delivery of Primary PE. This funding was generally welcomed insofar as it aimed to increase the quality of Primary PE, improve sports participation, increase physical activity, provide talent development and identification pathways, and build connections between clubs and their local communities. While this appears laudable, the academic community has offered a more critical perspective within wider discussions of the state and of Primary PE, and the use of sport coaches. Zwolinsky et al. (2016, 242–245) have challenged the claims attached to this activity (such as improved concentration, behaviour, educational attainment and overall physical health), stating that little is known about whether these outcomes actually happen as a consequence of delivery. This suggests that more work must be delivered by strategic stakeholders to capitalize on such investments, to enhance the system from a strategic and operational level in terms of evidenced-based practice and research. It does, however, ignore the substantial evidence base suggesting associations between these and other participation in sport and other physical activities, and that many of these outcomes do not appear to be affected in any way by the employment status of the teacher or coach (Bailey 2006; Bailey et al. 2012).

Critical discussion of outsourcing in Primary PE

External providers, in the form of football and sports coaches, are now established stakeholders in the delivery of Primary PE in England. This has led to intensification of the discussion surrounding their employment. To summarize, research in this area has focused on: (1) the appropriateness of coaches' skill and knowledge to deliver high-quality PE; (2) the impact coaches have on assisting in the professional development of generalist teachers; and (3) generalist teachers' competence, confidence and enthusiasm to deliver Primary PE. The following section will discuss the current state of knowledge in each of these sub-areas before a more general discussion highlighting the need for future work in this field of study.

The appropriateness of coaches' skill and knowledge to deliver high-quality PE

A frequently mentioned concern has been that football and sports coaches have been given responsibility to deliver Primary PE without a recognized formal teaching qualification. The minimum statutory requirement to coach within English Primary Schools is a Level Two qualification for each sport delivered. Therefore, if a school employed a professional football club's services to deliver football and hockey, the expectation is that the coaches delivering these sports will have a Level Two qualification in both. Typically, Level Two courses require coaches to engage with 30–40 h of face-to-face delivery, with a similar quantity of hours of home study and/or evidence of coaching practice, and qualifies the coach to plan, lead and review coaching sessions and programmes independently. These courses are relatively short in duration, which is perhaps not conducive for optimal professional learning (Armour and Yelling 2004). Furthermore, there is an overriding focus on developing coaches' content knowledge (Cushion, Armour, and Jones 2003; Nelson and Cushion 2006). This means that coaches have a highly developed understanding of 'what' to coach, but not necessarily 'how' to coach.

The courses that have previously been prescribed for sport coaches were not developed with Primary PE delivery in mind, and so a focus on developing coaches' knowledge and skills in delivery of this subject in this context were without precedent. The extent to which these courses, alone, would be able to contribute towards preparing coaches to deliver the entirety of Primary PE has been questioned (Blair and Capel 2011; Parnell et al. 2013, 2016), leading to specific question being raised over coaches' abilities to plan and assess effectively (Griggs 2010). In some cases, coaches themselves have acknowledged how little they know about curriculum requirement (Blair and Capel 2011). Furthermore, Rainer et al. (2012, 429–446) found many of the head teachers in their sample were dissatisfied with the coaches they had employed as they were 'inexperienced', 'inconsistent in their delivery', and only interested in 'self-promotion'.

Shifting the focus from sport coaches to Primary teachers, it is important to acknowledge their limited preparation to teach the subject, too. English Primary teachers are generalists and have very little time in their training allocated to learning how to deliver high-quality PE. It has been reported that Primary teachers receive between 6 and 9 h of face-to-face content dedicated solely towards learning how to teach Primary PE (Talbot 2008). So, while there is no doubt that teachers will often enjoy greater opportunities than coaches to develop a wide suite of pedagogical knowledge and accompanying skills than coaches, the extent to which these could be applied within a PE context is uncertain. Delivering quality

PE requires different pedagogical knowledge and skills than teaching in a classroom. For example, the way the lesson is structured is obviously different, as are lesson progressions and assessment (Bailey 2001). What is needed is *pedagogical content knowledge*, which is knowledge of both *what* to deliver and *how* to deliver it (Cassidy, Jones and Potrac 2009; Herold and Waring 2016).

The impact coaches have on assisting in the professional development of generalist teachers

The Association for Physical Education (AfPE) – the subject association for PE in the UK – have argued that outsources provision is most effective when coaches working in Primary Schools do so alongside teachers, rather than displace or replace them. This seems a plausible option, as the potential shortfalls in coaches' professional training could be balanced by the generalist teachers' knowledge and understanding. A supplementary argument could also be made, namely that the collaborative model of delivery offers a degree of sustainability if cuts were made to government funding, or the Primary PE and Sport Premium funding was abolished altogether, as teachers would have had the opportunity to improve their professional knowledge in PE by working with specialist coaches. There is some evidence to suggest that this already happens, and even providing teachers with the opportunity to observe coaches delivering PE can be beneficial for their professional development (Harris, Cale, and Musson 2012). Given the limited evidence base, it is difficult to make judgements on whether or not teachers and coaches working alongside each other is typical within English schools; our suspicion is it is not.

These changes for funding and delivery have resulted in the development of an additional qualification, designed by AfPE, to provide coaches with a greater understanding of National Curriculum for PE programmes of study, as well as the wider educational and statutory environment in which they will be operating. The Advanced Level Certificate in 'Supporting the Delivery of Physical Education and School Sport' quickly became a requirement for external providers of Primary PE. While the qualification was not equivalent of a teaching qualification, it was a clear move towards providing coaches with a firmer educational foundation of knowledge, skills and understanding.

Generalist teachers' competence, confidence and enthusiasm to deliver Primary PE

Evidence suggests that Primary PE is mainly taught by generalists teachers (Hunter 2006), and that it is often of poor quality (Kirk 2005). This situation seems to be the result of a combination of factors, including: insufficient teacher training; limited subject knowledge and the necessary pedagogy in PE; and limited professional development opportunities once initial training is completed (Hunter 2006; Kirk 2005; McKenzie and Kahan 2008). It is hardly surprising, therefore, that a significant number of Primary School teachers have low levels of confidence and do not feel competent teaching PE (Decorby et al. 2005; Morgan and Bourke 2005; Morgan and Hansen 2008; Sloan 2010). This situation raises an interesting question for educational leaders: is it better that children are introduced to formal physical activities by a qualified, generalist teacher who has no in-depth knowledge of that subject, or by a coach who has sport-specific knowledge, but a limited understanding of wider educational issues? Few would deny the potential problems that result from wide-scale replacement of Primary School teachers by sport coaches in PE, yet the absence of confidence and competence of generalist teachers in the current situation is also problematic.

Summary

Given the current evidence base, it is unclear who is best placed to deliver Primary PE. On the one hand, it seems reasonable to assume that teachers will generally better understand the learning and developmental needs of children; on the other hand, football and sport coaches are more likely to have an enthusiasm and expertise to teach sporting activities. To be clear, this argument is not a condemnation of the practices of generalist teachers. On the contrary, it is important to acknowledge their broad base of knowledge and skills required to teach the whole curriculum and the pressures associated with this. It also does not follow that from the evidence cited above, as a matter of policy, sports coaches ought to replace generalist teachers in the delivery of Primary PE lessons. Despite the evident difficulties experienced by Primary School teachers, there are many who do feel confident and competent to teach PE, and some are genuine specialists, with highly developed and practised skills. However, as Zwolinsky et al. (2016, 242–245) highlighted, while there is much acclaim attached to Primary PE, especially by those offering sport coaching services (but including those in education), few have been able to evaluate and articulate evidence of success. There is a deficit in our understanding of the effective delivery of Primary PE (Kirk 2005; and Parnell et al. 2016; Zwolinsky et al. 2016), and it is necessary to avoid speculation of the impact of such delivery and partnership working. Furthermore, sport coaches, teachers, head teachers, managers and policy-makers (and researchers) need to understand more about which parts of Primary PE work, who they work for and in which circumstances they work (Parnell et al. 2016; Zwolinsky et al. 2016), which will only be achieved through evidence and evaluation.

It is also important to consider the present political and sport policy landscape. The Conservative Party won the 2015 general election, taking full control and leadership. The public and politicians were left in no doubt about whether the reduction in public spending would continue. The Prime Minister David Cameron stated that there was a need for 'a leaner, more efficient state' in which 'we need to do more with less. Not just now, but permanently' (quoted in Krugman 2012: 1). Indeed, what would be termed 'an age of austerity' would continue in an attempt to manage national economic recovery. Conn (2015) noted that local government spending had been cut from £1.4 billion in 2009–10 to £1 billion in 2013–14. The impact of austerity and now super austerity on sport is largely unknown, however there is preliminary research highlighting that there could be significant repercussions (Parnell, Millward, and Spracklen 2014).

In late 2015, a new spending review was announced by the Chancellor of the Exchequer (the Finance Minister), George Osborne, which would influence a number of departments, including the DfE (which was responsible for PE and school sport) and the Department for Culture, Media and Sport (which was responsible for other aspects of sport). The DCMS was delivered administration budget cuts of 20% of its funding, as part of the the Government's new Sporting Future strategy in December 2015, However, the strategy outlined five claimed contributions that sport can make to wider society. Interestingly the DfE highlighted a key leadership role in school sport policy for Primary PE (Parnell, Widdop, and King 2015). However, there was little detail about how this unspecified commitment would be implemented or fulfilled. The positivity of such a loose commitment within a quickly developed strategy documents threatened to be overshadowed by the continued and growing uncertainty surrounding Primary PE. The announcement in the Chancellor's budget of 2016 that a sugar tax levy on sugar in drinks would be used to double investment in the Primary PE and Sport Premium from £150 million to £320 million per year by 2018 is a huge nod in the direction of continued and growing outsourcing of Primary PE (YST 2016).

It seems likely that there will be continued growth of outsourcing Primary PE throughout the duration of the next sport strategy. It might also be expected that the English Premier League will grow as one of the main providers. Indeed, the English Premier League has recently announced that, in partnership with the Government, it will reach every child in the country through the delivering of Primary PE. The partnership seeks to double the Premier League's current reach from 4158 schools to 10,000 schools over three years and extend it to all Primary Schools within six years in England and Wales (Wintour 2015). As such, professional football clubs both from the English Premier League and English Football League will have a major role to play and a responsibility to improve the quality of children's sporting experiences and contribute to getting children more physically active. The challenges observed in the provision of football will no doubt resemble the experiences of other NGBs wishing to participate in the delivery of Primary PE, and wish to access part of the Sport Premium funding, and potentially boost their sport's participation figures. Indeed, challenges will include upskilling sport coaching staff (Parnell et al. 2013). Recent years have witnessed significant changes to international standards in coach education, and this has partially addressed concerns related to the adequacy of coaches' skill for the delivery of Primary PE (Cope, Bailey, and Parnell 2015).

Moving forward, English Premier League clubs have an opportunity to address concerns related to coaches delivering Primary PE within the broad healthy stadia agenda. This includes investing in a broad and Primary PE-specific professional development programme for coaches and investing in research and evaluation. This will not only attend to issues of quality and effectiveness, but would offer programme feedback on practice and guidance for improvements alongside offering strategic leadership in this unique element of the sports industry when other professional sports, NGBs and in some regard the DfE have remained quiet. Through engagement in the delivery of Primary PE, professional sport clubs have an opportunity to positively affect the quality of provision in sporting activities for large numbers of children. In recognition of the critical debate in this area, it is important for future research to offer greater rigour and insight into the effectiveness of the delivery of Primary PE before making any substantive claims associated with the impact of Primary PE. The importance and potential impact of this opportunity is substantial. Such changes and research could contribute to the healthy stadia agenda in terms of both community outreach and engagement, creating local impact and enhancing sporting and education outcomes for children.

Note

1. Education in England is overseen by the departments within the UK Government. The equivalent systems in the other three home countries are the responsibility of the legislatures in Scotland, Wales or Northern Ireland.

Disclosure statement

No potential conflict of interest was reported by the authors.

References

Armour, K. M., and M. R. Yelling. 2004. "Continuing Professional Development for Experienced Physical Education Teachers: Towards Effective Provision." *Sport, Education and Society* 9 (1): 95–114.

Bailey, R. 2001. *Teaching Physical Education: A Handbook for Primary & Secondary School Teachers*. London: Kogan Page.

Bailey, R. 2006. "Physical Education and Sport in Schools: A Review of Benefits and Outcomes." *Journal of School Health* 76 (8): 397–401.

Bailey, R. 2007. "Talent Development and the Luck Problem." *Sport, Ethics and Philosophy* 1 (3): 367–377.

Bailey, R. P., C. Hillman, S. Arent, and A. Petitpas. 2012. "Physical Activity: An Underestimated Investment in Human Capital." *Journal of Physical Activity and Health* 10 (3): 289–308.

Bingham, D. D., D. Parnell, K. Curran, R. Jones, and D. Richardson. 2014. "Fit Fans: Perspectives of a Practitioner and Understanding Participant Health Needs within a Health Promotion Programme for Older Men Delivered within an English Premier League Football Club." *Soccer and Society* 15 (6): 883–901.

Blair, R., and S. Capel. 2011. "Primary Physical Education, Coaches and Continuing Professional Development." *Sport, Education and Society* 16 (4): 485–505.

Cassidy, T., R. Jones, and P. Potrac. 2009. *Understanding Sports Coaching: The social, cultural and pedagogical foundations of sports practice*. London: Routledge.

Cale, L., J. Harris, and R. Duncombe. 2016. "Promoting Physical Activity in Secondary Schools Growing Expectations: 'Same Old' Issues?" *European Physical Education Review*. http://epe.sagepub.com/content/early/2016/01/06/1356336X15623774.abstract.

Collins, M., and R. Haudenhuyse. 2015. "Social Exclusion and Austerity Policies in England: The Role of Sports in a New Area of Social Polarisation and Inequality?" *Social Inclusion* 3 (3): 5–18.

Commission, Audit. 2011. *Tough times: Councils' Responses to a Challenging Financial Climate*. London: AC.

Conn, D. 2015. "Olympic Legacy Failure: Sports Centres under Assault by Thousand Council Cuts." *The Guardian*, 5 July. Accessed December 20, 2015. http://www.theguardian.com/sport/2015/jul/05/olympic-legacy-failure-sports-centres-council-cuts

Cope, E., R. Bailey, and D. Parnell. 2015. "Outsourcing Physical Education: A Critical Discussion." *International Journal of Physical Education* 52 (4): 2–11.

Curran, K., D. Bingham, D. Richardson, and D. Parnell. 2014. "Ethnographic Engagement from within a Football in the Community Programme at an English Premier League Football Club." *Soccer and Society* 15 (6): 934–950.

Cushion, C. J., K. M. Armour, and R. L. Jones. 2003. "Coach Education and Continuing Professional Development: Experience and Learning to Coach." *Quest* 55 (3): 215–230.

Decorby, K., J. Halas, S. Dixon, L. Wintrup, and H. Janzen. 2005. "Classroom Teachers and the Challenges of Delivering Quality Physical Education." *The Journal of Educational Research* 98 (4): 208–221.

Department for Communities and Local Government (DCLG). 2010. *Local Government Finance Report 2010/11*. London: Author.

Department for Culture Media and Sport. 2008. *Playing to Win: A New Era for Sport*. London: Department for Culture Media and Sport.

Department for Culture Media and Sport. 2012. *Creating a Sporting Habit for Life: A New Youth Sport Strategy*. London: Department for Culture Media and Sport.

Department for Culture Media and Sport /Strategy Unit. 2002. *Game Plan: A Strategy for Delivering Government's Sport and Physical Activity Objectives*. London: Cabinet Office.

Department for Education. 2014. "PE and Sport Premium: An Investigation into Primary Schools." *Department for Education.* 17 January. Accessed November 30, 2014 www.gov.uk/government/collections/dfe-annual-reports

Department for Education and Skills/Department for Culture Media and Sport. 2003. *Learning through PE and Sport: A Guide to the Physical Education, School Sport and Club Link Strategy.* London: Department for Education and Skills.

Drygas, W., J. Ruszkowska, M. Philpott, O. BjÖrkstrÖm, M. Parker, R. Ireland, and M. Tenconi. 2013. "Good Practices and Health Policy Analysis in European Sports Stadia: Results from the 'Healthy Stadia' Project." *Health Promotion International* 28 (2): 157–165.

Flintoff, A. 2003. "The School Sport Co-Ordinator Programme: Changing the Role of the Physical Education Teacher?" *Sport, Education and Society* 8 (2): 231–250.

Griggs, G. 2010. "For Sale–Primary Physical Education. £ 20 per Hour or Nearest Offer." *Education 3–13* 38 (1): 39–46.

Harris, J., L. Cale, and H. Musson. 2012. "The Predicament of Primary Physical Education: A Consequence of 'Insufficient' ITT and 'Ineffective' CPD?" *Physical Education and Sport Pedagogy* 17 (4): 367–381. http://www.tandfonline.com/doi/abs/10.1080/13573322.2015.1127802?journalCode=cses20.

Herold, F., and M.Waring. 2016. "An Investigation of Pre-Service Teachers' Learning in Physical Education Teacher Education: Schools and University in Partnership." *Sport, Education and Society,* 1–13.

Hunt, K., S. Wyke, C. M. Gray, A. S. Anderson, A. Brady, C. Bunn, P. T. Donnan. 2014. "A Gender-Sensitised Weight Loss and Healthy Living Programme for Overweight and Obese Men Delivered by Scottish Premier League Football Clubs (Ffit): A Pragmatic Randomised Controlled Trial." *The Lancet* 383 (9924): 1211–1121. doi: http://dx.doi.org/10.1016/S0140-6736(13)62420-4

Hunter, L. 2006. "Research into Elementary Physical Education Programs." In *Handbook of Physical Education,* edited by D. Kirk, D. Macdonald and M. O'Sullivan, 580–595. London: Sage Publications.

Kirk, D. 2005. "Physical Education, Youth Sport and Lifelong Participation: The Importance of Early Learning Experiences." *European Physical Education Review* 11 (3): 239–255.

Krugman, P. 2012. "The Austerity Drive in Britain Isn't Really about Debt and Deficits at All; It's All about Using Deficit Panic as an Excuse to Dismantle Social Programs." *New York times.* June 01. Accessed December 20, 2015. http://www.nytimes.com/2012/06/01/opinion/krugman-the-austerity-agenda.html

Local Government Association. 2013. *Future Funding Outlook for Councils from 2010/11 to 2019/20.* London: LGA.

London Organising Committee of the Olympic and Paralympic Games. 2007. "Olympic Games Concept and Legacy." *London 2012.* Accessed November 30, 2015. http://www.london2012.com/publications/theme-1-olympicgames-concept-and-legacy.ph

McKenzie, T., and D. Kahan. 2008. "Physical Activity, Public Health, and Elementary Schools." *The Elementary School Journal* 108 (3): 171–180.

Mellor, G. 2008. "'The Janus-Faced Sport': English Football, Community and the Legacy of the 'Third Way.'" *Soccer and Society* 9 (3): 313–324.

Morgan, P., and S. F. Bourke. 2005. "An Investigation of Pre-Service and Primary School Teachers' Perspectives of PE Teaching Confidence and PE Teacher Education." *ACHPER Healthy Lifestyles Journal* 52 (1): 7–13.

Morgan, P. J., and V. Hansen. 2008. "Classroom Teachers' Perceptions of the Impact of Barriers to Teaching Physical Education on the Quality of Physical Education Programs." *Research Quarterly for Exercise and Sport* 79 (4): 506–516.

National Audit Office. 2010. "Measuring up: How Good Are the Government's Data Systems for Monitoring Performance against Public Service Agreements?" *Review of the Data Systems for Public Service Agreement.* Accessed November 20, 2015. http://www.nao.org.uk/publications/1011/review_data_systems_for_psa_22.aspx

Nelson, L. J., and C. J. Cushion. 2006. "Reflection in Coach Education: The Case of the National Governing Body Coaching Certificate." *Sport Psychologist* 20 (2): 174.

Pabion, C. (2015). "Premier League Reading Stars 2013/14. Evaluation Report." *London: National Literacy Trust*. Accessed December 10. http://www.literacytrust.org.uk/premier_league_reading_stars/impact

Parnell, D., S. Buxton, D. Hewitt, M. J. Reeves, E. Cope, and R. Bailey. 2016. "The Pursuit of Lifelong Participation: The Role of Professional Football Clubs in the Delivery of Physical Education and School Sport in England." *Soccer and Society* 17 (2): 225–241.

Parnell, D., P. Millward, and K. Spracklen. 2014. "Sport and Austerity in the UK: An Insight into Liverpool 2014." *Journal of Policy Research in Tourism, Leisure and Events* 7: 200–203. doi: http://dx.doi.org/10.1080/19407963.2014.968309.

Parnell, D., and D. Richardson. 2014. "Introduction." *Soccer and Society* 15 (6): 823–827.

Parnell, D., and A. Pringle. 2016. "Football and Health Improvement: An Emerging Field." *Soccer and Society* 17 (2): 171–174.

Parnell. D., A. Pringle, J. McKenna, S. Zwolinsky, Z. Rutherford, J. Hargreaves, L. Trotter, M. Rigby, and D. Richardson. 2015. "Reaching Older People with PA Delivered in Football Clubs: The Reach, Adoption and Implementation Characteristics of the Extra Time Programme." *BMC Public Health 15, 220.* doi: http://dx.doi.org/10.1186/s12889-015-1560-. http://www.biomedcentral.com/1471-2458/15/220

Parnell, D., A. Pringle, P. Widdop, and S. Zwolinsky. 2015. "Understanding Football as a Vehicle for Enhancing Social Inclusion: Using an Intervention Mapping Framework." *Social Inclusion* 3 (7): 200–203.

Parnell, D., G. Stratton, B. Drust, and D. Richardson. 2013. "Football in the Community Schemes: Exploring the Effectiveness of an Intervention in Promoting Healthful Behaviour Change." *Soccer and Society* 14: 35–51.

Parnell, D., P. Widdop, and N. King. 2015. "Local Authority Cuts Loom Large over Community Sport." *ConnectSport*, December 13. Accessed December 20, 2015. http://www.connectsport.co.uk/academic-research/local-authority-cuts-threaten-community-sport

Phillpots, L. 2013. "An Analysis of the Policy Process for Physical Education and School Sport: The Rise and Demise of School Sport Partnerships." *International Journal of Sport Policy and Politics* 5 (2): 193–211.

Premier League. 2016. "Premier League for Sport." *The Premier League*, January 2. Accessed January 20. http://www.premierleague.com/engb/communities/2011-12/premier-league-4-sport.html

Rainer, P., B. Cropley, S. Jarvis, and R. Griffiths. 2012. "From Policy to Practice: The Challenges of Providing High Quality Physical Education and School Sport Faced by Head Teachers within Primary Schools." *Physical Education & Sport Pedagogy* 17 (4): 429–446.

Rutherford, Z., B. Gough, S. Seymour-Smith, C. Matthews, J. Wilcox, and D. Parnell. 2014. "'Motivate': The Effect of a Football in the Community Delivered Weight Loss Programme on over 35-Year Old Men and Women's Cardiovascular Risk Factors." *Soccer and Society* 15 (6): 951–969.

Sloan, S. 2010. "The Continuing Development of Primary Sector Physical Education: Working Together to Raise Quality of Provision." *European Physical Education Review* 16 (3): 267–281.

Talbot, M. 2008. "Ways Forward for Primary Physical Education." *Physical Education Matters* 3 (1): 6–8.

Weed, M., E. Coren, J. Fiore, I. Wellard, L. Mansfield, D. Chatziefstathiou, and S. Dowse. 2012. "Developing a Physical Activity Legacy from the London 2012 Olympic and Paralympic Games: A Policy-Led Systematic Review." *Perspectives in Public Health* 132 (2): 75–80.

Wintour, P. 2015. "Premier League to Expand Primary School Sport Scheme." *The Guardian*, October 3. Accessed November 20. http://www.theguardian.com/education/2015/oct/03/premier-league-to-expand-primary-school-sport-scheme

YST (Youth Sport Trust). 2004. *Multi-Skill Academies for Gifted and Talented Pupils – Information and Guidance*. Loughborough: Youth Sport Trust.

YST (Youth Sport Trust). 2016. "Budget Announcement Has Potential for Transformational Change." Accessed March 16. https://www.youthsporttrust.org/news/budget-announcement-has-potential-transformational-change

Zwolinsky, S., J. McKenna, D. Parnell, and A. Pringle. 2016. "Can 'English Premier League' Funding for PE and School Sport Achieve Its Aims?" *Soccer and Society* 17 (2): 242–245.

'It brings the lads together': a critical exploration of older men's experiences of a weight management programme delivered through a Healthy Stadia project

Lorena Lozano-Sufrategui, Andy Pringle, David Carless and Jim McKenna

ABSTRACT
Older men whose weight is considered unhealthy may experience particular barriers that can restrict their adoption of health improvement interventions. Despite promising findings recommending the use of sports settings to facilitate health promotion with men, little evidence has addressed older men's health needs for, or experiences of, these settings. Using a qualitative methodology, this study explored the experiences of 14 ageing men attending a football-led weight management programme delivered at a community sports setting. The thematic analysis of semi-structured interviews elucidates important insights regarding the provision of sports-led health improvement interventions for this population. Men especially valued the opportunity to play sports and do physical activity in an environment that promotes 'inclusive' competition and caring interpersonal relationships. Implicit in the findings is the key role of practitioners in promoting social engagement. We conclude the paper with key practical implications of this research.

Introduction

Older men (OM) previously classed as 50 years of age or older and whose weight is considered unhealthy are a concern for Public Health policy (Harris et al. 2009; NICE 2014; Salihu, Bonnema, and Alio 2009). This population presents a higher risk of developing poor lifestyle behaviours, such as reduced physical activity (PA) levels and unhealthy diets (Department of Health 2011). This can result in an increased risk of developing non-communicable diseases, including coronary artery disease, stroke and type 2 diabetes (White et al. 2011). Arguably, these health outcomes may explain why obese UK men over 40 die 5.8 years younger than their thinner peers (Logue et al. 2010).

OM are known to experience particular barriers that may restrict their adoption of lifestyle improvement interventions, including PA-based programmes (NICE 2008). These barriers include (i) feelings of insecurity stemming from fear of falls and injury (Booth et al. 2000), (ii) lack of energy (King et al. 2000), (iii) pain and (iv) tiredness (Sallinen et al.

2009). These factors may explain why PA participation decreases with advancing age (BHF (British Heart Foundation) 2015), and place OM as a key priority group for Public Health (Rutherford et al. 2014).

A promising approach to engage men with their health involves the adoption of a settings approach for the delivery of PA interventions (Brown et al. 2012; Clark et al. 2012; Royal Society for Public Health 2014). In particular, previous authors have advocated for the delivery of lifestyle programmes in sports clubs and sporting settings (Johnman, Mackie, and Sim 2013). This approach to health improvement in the UK has resulted in the emergence of Healthy Stadia concept (Haigh and Crabb 2006), which refers to a stadium that 'promotes the health of visitors, fans, players, employees and the surrounding community. It is a place where people can go to have a positive, healthy experience playing or watching sport' (Crabb and Ratinckx 2005). Echoing Hirt and Clarkson (2011), these facilities provide a sense of group affiliation that facilitates connectedness between men. Moreover, these settings hold great potential to connect with the interests of OM (Pringle et al. 2014). Promising initiatives have also started to explore the possibility of delivering men-only weight management programmes (WMPs) through professional sports clubs (Witty and White 2011) and with older adults (Hunt et al. 2014; Krustrup et al. 2010).

Although the use of sports in male-specific contexts (i.e. football clubs, stadia) may facilitate health promotion in men (Pringle et al. 2014), including older men (Andersen et al. 2014; Bingham et al. 2014; Parnell et al. 2015; Schmidt et al. 2014), the active construction of a particular form of masculinity emphasising competition, aggression and personal dominance over others may exclude other 'non-hegemonic' men (Robertson 2003; Spandler and McKeown 2012). These can include OM, who often find difficulties in joining the competitive performance of team sports and may feel anxious about engaging in sports (Nielsen et al. 2014). Hence, it is important to acknowledge the health potential of recreational sport, to avoid the proliferation of 'divisive social practices' (Kelly 2011) that portray the dominant performance narrative in sport (Douglas and Carless 2014).

Given that men will attend health interventions that are deemed acceptable to them (Pringle et al. 2014), it remains important to understand how sports settings relate to the needs of OM to ensure optimum provision. With these thoughts in mind, our study aims to answer the following research question: How do OM experience their attendance at a football-led WMP delivered in a community sport setting? Whilst this WMP is not a project delivered by an amateur or professional sports club, its focus on men, health and sports can help inform those working in and around the Healthy Stadia agenda in this growing area of health promotion. Therefore, by presenting this programme and the findings of this research, we will aid those delivering health-improvement interventions in a number of contexts across the Healthy Stadia agenda, including health improvement programmes for OM delivered by professional sports clubs.

Methods

Intervention context

This study took place in a WMP that works in partnership with the Wigan Borough Healthy Stadia and Sports Club Network to deliver health and well-being messages. This is the first borough wide partnership to include professional and amateur sports clubs set up and launched in the UK. The Network endorses partners and other local services with 60–80%

of clubs becoming actively involved with a number of health improvement programmes (Wigan Borough 2015). One of the local partners is Tackling the Pounds (this is a pseudonym, because ethical permissions prevent naming the programme), a men-only WMP that aims to help men lose 5% of their body weight through participation in PA and sport and education on healthy lifestyles. Each weekly session lasts 90 min, with 60 min of PA – often circuit training and sport, mainly football during the last 20–30 min of the session. This is followed by 30 min of education.

TtPs was gender-sensitized in terms of context (delivered in environments men are familiar with), content (information about the science of weight loss was kept practical), and style of delivery (flexible and non-regimental approach that encouraged social interaction and humour). The sessions were delivered by qualified practitioners, who had a background in health promotion, nutrition and exercise and tailored the activities for each participants' ability.

Weekly sessions took place in the town's soccer dome. This is a sports setting with 12 football pitches, a sports shop and a fitness club. It is located close to the town's football stadium which has held Premier League Status in recent years.

Research Context

This study forms part of a larger investigation that explores men's experiences of weight management before, during and after attending TtPs. Ethical approval was obtained from Leeds Beckett University and NHS Research Ethics Committees.

The research is based on the experiences of 14 men taking part in a WMP delivered in a community sports setting. To protect their identities, we present age groups instead of specific ages. Eight participants were OM (two men were aged between 50 and 59 years old; three were between 60 and 69; two were in the range of 70–79, and one was 80+). We also include the experiences of six participants who, despite not being classified chronologically as OM according to previous definitions (Harris et al. 2009; Salihu, Bonnema, and Alio 2009), they provided relevant information to answer the research question. All participants were categorized as overweight or obese according to Body Mass Index (BMI) classifications. Their mean BMI was 32.4 kg/m^2.

This study focuses on 14 semi-structured interviews conducted by LL, whilst men attended TtPs. Interviews were conducted in a quiet room at the programme venue immediately after an intervention session, lasting 30 to 120 min. Interviews were audio recorded and transcribed verbatim.

Data Analysis and Representation

Data analysis was conducted using Braun and Clarke's (2006) approach to thematic analysis (TA). This is a qualitative analytic method for identifying, analysing and reporting themes across a data-set. Themes were selected if they captured something important about the research question. An inductive approach, where themes identified are strongly linked to the data themselves (Patton 1990), is used to provide a rich description of the data. We addressed Guba's (1981) criteria to ensure the trustworthiness of the data: (a) credibility was established, in part, by triangulating the data from different informants; ensuring honesty in informants by building trust and rapport between LL and participants through extensive fieldwork; and examining previous research to frame findings; (b) by providing thorough background data to establish the context of the study, we aimed to ensure the transferability of the findings; (c) we have also provided an in-depth methodological description of the study, to ensure dependability; and (d) two researchers have taken part in the analytical stage of the study to enhance the confirmability of the findings.

All participants were given pseudonyms to maintain their anonymity. Participants' age group and initial BMI are indicated in brackets. Descriptors are used to identify the number of men who articulated each theme, including: *few* (0–5 respondents), *some* (5–10) and *many* (10+). Yet, the *keyness* (Braun and Clarke 2006, 82) of a theme not only depended on its prevalence, but also on how well it captured something important in relation to the research question.

Results

Findings are presented using an organizing framework of five themes which support critical reflection on the key experiences of 14 men attending TtPs. These themes include the following: ageing, opportunity, inclusive competition, caring interpersonal relationships and the role of practitioners in promoting engagement.

Ageing

Many men in this study reported an increase in physical limitations as a result of an ageing body. Some participants talked about the irreversibility of this process, which increasingly placed them at a higher risk of injury. This was illustrated by Dermot (70–79, 28.9 kg/m^2):

> I have a little bit of arthritis in my knee, and it will get worse, it's bound to do. But at the moment I've just got to be a bit careful really, which I am [...] Because somebody three weeks ago tried too hard, and he tore his calf muscle. And he's been told it's a four to six months recovery. So that's focused my mind a little bit.

Although (fear of) being injured limited men's participation in sports, at the same time, being physically active was valued by participants as a way to gain better health. For some, increasing activity could delay the decline they associated with the ageing process. Predicting the physical decline related to ageing, Connor (40–49, 32.7 kg/m^2) believed that attending the programme was the right thing to do before the decline started. For him, intervening sooner rather than later was important:

> The only reason I've started to think about it [doing PA] the last sort of six months is because I am getting older now. And you do think about things like grandchildren, stuff like that. You know, you gotta do something before it is too late really. It just comes to the point where you are not gonna be active or you are not gonna be physically active, are you? And not gonna do stuff like this, so sort of get up and do something now.

Likewise, for Adam (50–59, 27.3 kg/m^2), getting older signified the end of the young, seemingly imperishable body, and the beginning of a new stage in his life, where he felt the need of looking after a vulnerable body:

> Well for me I was just getting older and I could tell that I wasn't a teenager anymore so it was just look after yourself. Basically, I think what appeals more as you are getting older as a young man you are indestructible you can do anything, eat anything [...] For me it was just you know getting older and look after myself better.

Opportunity

Ageing was associated with an increase in the number of structural barriers to participate in organized sports. As a result, many participants welcomed the opportunity of playing sport with the other men who were attending TtPs. For many participants, being offered the opportunity to play sport was more valuable than the sport being played, as Ralph (60–69, 45.4 kg/m^2) said:

> To be honest I'm not keen on football but at least I play it, which I am quite surprised at, you know. I never thought I would have played football, not at my age, but I did it.

Likewise, Alan (40–49, 39.5 kg/m^2) expressed his surprise when talking about the opportunity to take part in 'real' sport with other men:

> Lorena: What do you like the most in the programme?
>
> Alan: I'll be honest, the football. I quite enjoyed today's exercise and the game of football, because everyone is involved […] Because it's a team sport, and we're playing together, it's good, you're taking part with other people, which I never thought I would. The last time I played football must have been 15, 20 years ago, in the back yard garden. Not real football, just passing to my nephew. And after being the size I was [pause] I didn't think I would be playing football. I've still got a long way to go, but I feel better every time we play, and I couldn't run a single yard I don't think 12 months ago, so even if it's just jogging around [pause] I'll never be the fastest runner, but it is an improvement really, and it's good.

Although there may be more opportunities for younger men to take part in competitive sport, these are lost as men age. For Craig (40–49, 28 kg/m^2), older men's involvement in sports needed to be promoted more effectively, with the focus shifting from competitiveness to participation:

> Craig: I just think it's very very important and it's a great opportunity for people who can't go out and play top level, or can't go and play rugby or football anymore because they are 40 or 50 […] For example, [name] he's 76 or something like that and he's absolutely amazing, unbelievable. But I think it's an opportunity for people who've passed the age of playing competitive sport to come and have a go and not feel the odd one out. Because there's a lot of elitism in sport, because you don't pass to, or you are not good enough, all that […] And I think there should be more things like that. I'd like to help other people myself, I think is good. Why can't you do it [sport]? There's people telling you you've past it when you are like 30, whatever, you are too old, but why? No! You're not, you're not! You are probably too old to compete with 25 year old, but you're not too old to have a kick around.

In this excerpt, Craig distinguishes between traditional competition in sport – an oppositional and confrontational activity that may discourage participation – and 'having a kick around' – an activity that encompasses positive involvement and social interactions with other peers. This distinction was common across our data, and therefore constitutes the focus of the next section.

Inclusive competition

Craig's excerpt above suggests that traditional modes of competition – what we identify as 'exclusive' competition – can discourage participation for some. However, him, and other men, also talked about a different type of competition – 'inclusive' competition – where participation in cooperative and collaborative activities was supported and valued. When participants referred to this type of competition, the notion of 'everybody is involved' was recurrent in their accounts. Mike's (80+, 27.1 kg/m^2) point illustrated it:

Lorena: What would you say to your friends about the programme?

Mike: I would say it's very satisfactory, I would say once a week is not enough, whether we do it here or do it ourselves, your needs are at least twice a week, better, if you did it three times and do the exercises at home. But [at home] you don't have the impetus that you get here, because everybody is doing their best here.

However, the degree of inclusivity of activities that involved competition varied among different subgroups of men. Often, this depended on participants' level of fitness, not just age. To demonstrate this, Ian (40–49, 46.3 kg/m^2) talked about competition as a bond within the team, where 'everybody passes to everybody else' (Ian), highlighting the enjoyment of playing as an essential quality of football. However, these signals of good bonding vanished when other men adopted a different, less inclusive attitude. Ian said:

> Normally it's fun, you know, we don't compete. We compete but everybody passes to everybody else, like err you know what I mean. Because we are not footballers, we are just doing it for the fun afterwards, you know what I mean. But when you get five or six that play five-a-side football and they sort of err it's like: 'I don't wanna know', it's like: 'Pass, pass, pass, pass, bang!' And you think to yourself: 'Yeah, but we are here just for a bit of fun'. They take it a bit too serious, and they get in with the tackles sometimes and I am thinking: 'I don't need to sort of get [injured], that's why I stay out at the wing, because I am not getting involved in the tackles and pushing myself up just for a bit of a knock about.

Again, this excerpt suggests that activities where confrontation or opposition between individual men or teams is accentuated may jeopardize the elements of 'inclusive' competition that men valued, such as fun, enjoyment, involvement and safety. This concern was not only raised by men who were affected by it, but also by other often younger and physically fitter men. To counteract the negative effects of 'exclusive' modes of competition, these participants adapted their involvement in the sport to make it more inclusive and to safeguard the fun element Ian referred to in the excerpt above. Balancing game intensity, speed and forceful contacts was important for Crispin (29–39, 27.5 kg/m^2), a young participant who adopted a willing attitude to help others enjoy the games:

> When we do, say if we play football, I try to take it easy on the older guys. I don't play as well as I would if I was against similar people, you know, people of similar age and similar ability. I don't want the other guys to go out and think: 'Oh, I am not going there next week because there is this one guy, half our age, he takes it too seriously, runs round tackling, hurting people'. You know, I don't wanna upset anyone; I want everyone to enjoy it. I enjoy it, but I don't want people not to come again because of me.

For some men, football was an opportunity to legitimize and promote mutual caring behaviours with other men. To exemplify this point, Pierce (50–59, 37.8 kg/m^2) talked about how he used sports to promote inclusivity in the programme:

Lorena: Do you feel that it can get a bit too competitive sometimes?

Pierce: That's a different sort of competitive. That's competitive within the spirit of the game of football, yeah.

Lorena: As a team?

Pierce: Yes, that's a team competitive aspect, which is brilliant, because everybody encourages everybody else, from the oldest to the youngest, everybody. You know, if somebody

> is not getting a pass of the ball, you'll try and get the ball to them so they do become involved, they don't get left out. Uhm but that's in that scenario or in that setting, that team competition is brilliant, because it is good fun, and everybody has a laugh.

What is implied here is that 'inclusive' competition that encouraged a sense of team spirit, enjoyment and participation was different from the form of competition often found in elitist and professional sport.

Caring interpersonal relationships

It is likely that men's degree of involvement in physical activities and sports often depended on the social environment that prevailed within the programme. As suggested above, men's attitudes towards one another facilitated participation. This created an opportunity for men to 'do' things together, which resulted in a stronger 'bond' between the men and promoted inclusivity. Even men who were confident about their physical abilities stressed the importance of the social component of sport. For Miles (40–49, 29.7 kg/m^2), a supportive atmosphere was an opportunity for participants to demonstrate competence, and this enhanced the relevance and meaningfulness of their participation in sports:

> I think the first session I was a little bit daunted about it, a bit nervous. I wasn't sure what I was letting myself in for, again because I've always been quite physically fit and I know I am decent footballer and I am decent at most sports, I can put my hand to it, so I am never gonna feel out of place in somewhere like this, so therefore is very much in my confidence. But it wasn't, I think it was more the meeting people thing, I think that was my concern. Although I was overweight, I've never felt that fat or grossly overweight. So it was a great opportunity for me to come and do something that I knew I would enjoy. Once I got here I found there was a great camaraderie between the lads, everybody seems to really encourage each other, which I didn't think would happen. I thought it would still be a case of it's you, versus the next, versus the next. But it's not, it's very much pat on the back, well done, you've played well, you really pushed yourself there.

Again, Miles' excerpt suggests that cooperation, care and relationships – as opposed to oppositional activities – were the elements that made the programme meaningful for him. Through the programme, men also found and engaged in other sport-related activities. These other activities were a springboard to establishing closer links with other men, within and outside the programme. Namely, men frequently mentioned the football games they played with other men's health services, organized by the programme. Ian (40–49, 46.3 kg/m^2) said:

> We played football against other men's health services like in [place], we played football against them, there's Fit Fans in [place], you know that's along with the football, you know we try to move it forward, as you know we're going away for the weekend at the end of August doing some canoeing and stuff and it's like err we are going on the Saturday we are gonna have lunch there and we're gonna go out and try to do canoeing and team building, and then an evening meal. And then you know they've got a social club there, you know, and things like that […] So that's good because it gets people having a chance to having a laugh and a joke, and working together with one another, building up. You know, that bond and teamwork and friendship. I found that when we went to [place], that was good, I enjoyed that, you know what I mean, things like that. But you know, it brings the lads together, so they build mates and that sort of thing.

For some men, it was these caring interpersonal relationships are what made participation in sports meaningful, despite their preference for other types of sport. Alan (40–49, 39.5 kg/m^2), a rugby fan, said:

> Even though I'm not very good, I enjoy taking part, because it's just a team game and you're having a err you're getting involved, you know. I do enjoy playing the football at the end. I never thought I would say this, [but I enjoy it] more than the rugby, yeah yeah.

The role of staff in promoting engagement

The sections above imply that men valued and enjoyed the competitive element of the sessions as long as this occurred in a supportive environment that promoted participation and caring interpersonal relationships. Similar to previous research (e.g. Bingham et al. 2014; Curran et al. 2014), the role and skills of the practitioners facilitated the development of the above outcomes. A key skill that characterized the deliverers of the sessions was their ability to adapt the physical activities and sports to the needs of the group. Bert's (60–69, 27.5 kg/m^2) first day experience highlights what happens when this is not well handled; in this case at another programme:

Lorena: Can you remember the first session you attended?

Bert: Yeah, because I was with some rugby lads and it was absolutely knackered at the end of it. That was my very first one, that was in [place] which is supposed to be very [hard]. So Luke suggested coming here, because they are all my age, because in [place] they are all 30 odd year olds, 40. They were just killing me.

Lorena: so how did you feel the first time you saw all of them kind of fit and it was your first and you were a bit older?

Bert: I just thought well this is not for me because I'll never get to their level of fitness and they will just keep walking all over me, so I was a bit unsure as well as whether to carry on or not […] I think that could put some people off. Whereas if they were given an alternative, so if someone is coming, I think you should try to match their age to the age groups that are ran around the area.

Similarly, Abraham (60–69, 29.2 kg/m^2) found it difficult to participate in some activities due to his limited functionality. Participants like Abraham said that the sessions were 'too vigorous' for them, which placed him at a higher risk of relapse:

> I think myself, the exercises are getting too vigorous, I really do, because an awful lot of people, who are not coming now, are getting old. And I don't think it's been taken into consideration the limitations, you know, because Chris [a participant who dropped out], when I said: 'Are you coming back?' he said: 'Well I'll go to the Tuesday one, because that's all games and you can do your own pace sort of thing, you know, table tennis, football or whatever. But I don't want to do this one because it's too much'. So it's quite, if you take notice, most of the people who did come, were more or less retired, I was retired. There weren't many who weren't. I think it's got to that stage, although he's trying to make you fit, I think it's a bit too strenuous.

Again, in the above excerpt, Abraham warns about the inappropriateness of some forms of competition. More successful outcomes emerged when practitioners were original, creative and offered a variety of both individual and group activities that promoted inclusivity and enjoyment. Participants particularly referred to the deliverers' ability to modify some aspects of a game. This promoted inclusion because participants' different levels of ability were less discordant in the playing field. Also, this generated a type of humour that was important for engagement and inclusion. The following interaction with Ian (40–49, 46.3 kg/m^2) demonstrates this point:

Ian: I was saying to them the other week what we do at [place] is like play football with a rugby ball.

Lorena: [laughs]

Ian: If you have never tried it, try it sometime, and it's really good fun. Because it's a laugh because the ones who are good at football doesn't make no bloody difference whatsoever because that ball just goes where it wants to go, and it just means that you are running a bit more for it and you're sort of chasing the ball, you know […] It just adds a bit of fun to the game.

Another activity that was introduced in the programme was walking football. This is similar to normal football, but running is banned, with or without the ball. Observations of the sessions suggest that this adapted activity promoted inclusivity that was not evident in normal football, where some players stayed 'out at the wing waiting for the ball to come to us' (Ian): in walking football, everybody was involved in the game. For instance Ross (70–79, 27 kg/m^2), who suffered from a degenerative disease, talked about walking football as the only sport he could participate in. As a result, he missed playing it when it was not available: 'I like all the exercises, but what I do miss is the football, the walking football'.

Discussion

Emerging outcomes and practical implications

In this paper, we have explored older men's experiences of participating in sport, specifically football, in a male-only WMP that works in partnership with the Wigan Borough Healthy Stadia and Sports Club Network to deliver health and well-being messages. Although this WMP was not delivered by an amateur or professional sports club, it is part of the aforementioned Network and as such uses sports to engage men with their health. In line with NICE guidance (NICE 2008), we have taken seriously OM's needs and views regarding intervention delivery in sports settings and engaged men as influential shapers of service provision. By doing so, we tried to generate a sense of engagement among participants and possibilities for ownership of services delivered in a local community sporting setting. In what follows, we would like to consider how our findings inform service delivery across the Healthy Stadia agenda, including health improvement programmes for OM delivered by professional sports clubs.

Tailoring provision around men's needs is an important aspect in the design and delivery of programmes. For example, participants reported being at different stages of fitness, functional capacity and readiness to engage in sport-led programmes. To provide these individuals with an enjoyable and achievable experience, key characteristics of PA – such as frequency, intensity, time and type – need to be considered (Barisic, Leatherdale, and Kreiger 2011). This is not only important for new recruits, but also for more experienced and longer term engagers, who may have advanced their fitness and ability and as a result require more frequent and longer activity sessions. TtPs was not age-specific, meaning that men of different ages and presenting with differences in PA characteristics needed to be balanced by practitioners, whose ability to understand and navigate men's needs and wants were key to the success of the intervention.

Pringle et al. (2014) recommended building mediators for change in PA interventions, such as social support, enjoyment, achievement, fitness and fun. In response to this, our research has illustrated some of the key elements that facilitated behaviour change in a sample of OM. The findings suggest that programmes were effective when they directly – and indirectly – fostered social support. The social opportunities arising from the programme provided a source of enjoyment that was especially valued by men who were hesitant about their ability to play sport. Another aspect that the men enjoyed was the maintenance of aspects of the competitive element that characterizes many sports. However, the type of 'competition' that participants valued was a *work of inclusion* that promoted caring interpersonal relationships through humour, support and encouragement. These requisites were promoted not only by the men who attended the sessions, but also by the practitioners. Previous researchers have suggested that practitioners who are personable, respectful, empathic, supportive and caring play a key role in contributing to participants' positive experiences of programmes (e.g. Bingham et al. 2014; Curran et al. 2014).

A number of men reported engaging in the processes of change described by Marcus et al. (2000). These processes are 'the strategies and techniques that people use to modify their behaviour' (16), and can be deconstructed into cognitive and behavioural processes. In our study, we came across men who *became aware of the risks* and *comprehended the benefits* of being more active. For example, men reported the need to change their lifestyles so they could be more active to fulfil immediate tasks, such as looking after their grandchildren, and in the future – thus demonstrating their aspiration of lifelong fitness. Similarly, men *reminded themselves* of how to best sustain their activity levels. Participants gave accounts of how the competitive element of sports became either too dangerous or too vigorous for them or others. In doing this, men talked about *safeguarding* from injury or over-exertion. By making the case that participants needed to consider how their overzealous and competitive nature could have a detrimental impact on others, they *cared about the consequences to others* and *offered alternative* activities for them.

With these considerations in mind, it is important that practitioners and managers working on projects associated with the Healthy Stadia agenda understand the practical considerations of implementing such programmes. Two key practical implications emerge from this research. First, since some men may be discouraged to take part in sport-led interventions that appear to promote confrontational and oppositional activities, it is important that managers prepare practitioners to deal with these occurrences during interventions. One way of doing this is to include clear and inclusive messages such as 'all ages welcome' or 'open to all levels of ability' during promotions of programmes and in the implementation phase. Second, whilst previous authors such as Curran et al. (2014) have called for more appropriate professional development for practitioners, these recommendations have focused on sport-based qualifications. In addition to this knowledge, it would also be valuable for practitioners working in healthy stadia to use other resources that provide specific directions on how to work with older men. For example, the *Active for Later Life* resource of the British Heart Foundation (BHF) toolkit for planning PA programmes provides specific evidence and recommendations with regards to the development of PA programmes for older people. Similarly, some charities such as Age Concern have provided training to football club community trusts and training on working with men.

It is also worth stressing that OM can present with specific barriers related to age, including disability and threat of injury, as well as particular motives for engagement, such as the importance of building a routine around programme attendance. Additionally, this research has emphasized how practitioners can enhance the attractiveness of health improvement programmes for older men. To replicate this, it is important that practitioners working on this type of interventions display a caring attitude towards participants, show creativity with regards to tailoring the sport to the needs of OM, handle exercise intensity and promote the integration of all participants. These aspects clearly enhanced the attractiveness of TtPs for OM.

Conclusion

This research has explored the use of football as a tool for engaging older men in a weight management programme delivered at a sports venue. Although this community project is not specifically delivered by an amateur or professional sports club, its context is important for those working in and around the Healthy Stadia agenda, given the scope of programmes undertaken by the clubs. Specifically, this research has offered some interesting insights for practitioners working in promoting public health at sports stadia. The primary learning to be taken from this research relates to the experience of older men engaged through physical activity sessions delivered through football, and relative barriers and enabling factors within the context of male identity. Within these, this research has suggested that inclusive competition, caring relationships and the role of the practitioners play an important part in participants' experience and engagement in this type of programmes. Further, whilst this research acknowledges that facilities such as sports stadia have meaning for most men (Hirt and Clarkson 2011), far more important for improving human functioning is not just the setting, but also *what people do* – individually and collectively – in that particular environment to make things better. Therefore, if stadia-based programmes are to thrive, it makes sense to make a greater effort to understand what men do in those settings, and share that evidence with relevant parties. This research, using a qualitative methodology, has been an attempt to undertaking such endeavour.

Disclosure statement

No potential conflict of interest was reported by the authors.

References

Andersen, Thomas Rieks, Jakob Schmidt, Jessica Nielsen, Markus Randers, Emil Sundstrup, Michael Jakobsen, Lars Andersen, et al. 2014. "Effect of Football or Strength Training on Functional Ability and Physical Performance in Untrained Old Men." *Scandinavian Journal of Medicine and Science in Sports* 24 (S1): 76–85. doi:http://dx.doi.org/10.1111/sms.12245.

Barisic, Andriana, Scott T. Leatherdale, and Nancy Kreiger. 2011. "Importance of Frequency, Intensity, Time and Type in Physical Activity Assessment for Epidemiological Research." *Canadian Journal of Public Health* 102 (3): 174–175.

BHF (British Heart Foundation). 2015. *Physical Activity Statistics 2015*. London: BHF.

Bingham, Daniel, Daniel Parnell, Kathryn Curran, Roger Jones, and Dave Richardson. 2014. "Fit Fans: Perspectives of a Practitioner and Understanding Participant Health Needs within a Health Promotion Programme for Older Men Delivered within an English Premier League Football Club." *Soccer & Society* 15 (6): 883–901. doi:http://dx.doi.org/10.1080/14660970.2014.920624.

Booth, Michael, Neville Owen, Adrian Bauman, Ornella Clavisi, and Eva Leslie. 2000. "Social-cognitive and Perceived Environment Influences Associated with Physical Activity in Older Australians." *Preventive Medicine* 31 (1): 15–22.

Borough Wigan. 2015. *Healthy Stadia® & Sports Club Network*. Accessed November 9, 2015. http://wiganhealthystadia.org.uk/wp-content/uploads/2012/05/8410-HoM-Healthy-Stadia-4pp-A4.pdf

Braun, Virginia, and Victoria Clarke. 2006. "Using Thematic Analysis in Psychology." *Qualitative Research in Psychology* 3 (2): 77–101. doi:http://dx.doi.org/10.1191/1478088706qp063oa.

Brown, Wendy J., Deirdre McLaughlin, Janni Leung, Kieran A. McCaul, Leon Flicker, Osvaldo P. Almeida, Graeme J. Hankey, Derrick Lopez, and Annette J. Dobson. 2012. "Physical Activity and All-cause Mortality in Older Women and Men." *British Journal of Sports Medicine* 46 (9): 664–668. doi:http://dx.doi.org/10.1136/bjsports-2011-090529.

Clark, Florence, Jeanne Jackson, Mike Carlson, Chih-Ping Chou, Barbara J Cherry, Maryalice Jordan-Marsh, Bob G Knight, et al. 2012. "Effectiveness of a Lifestyle Intervention in Promoting the Well-being of Independently Living Older People: Results of the Well Elderly 2 Randomised Controlled Trial." *Journal of Epidemiology and Community Health* 66 (9): 782–90. doi: http://dx.doi.org/10.1136/jech.2009.099754.

Crabb, Judy, and Linda Ratinckx. 2005. *The Healthy Stadia Initiative: A Report for North West Public Helath Team*. London: Department of Health.

Curran, Kathryn, Daniel D. Bingham, David Richardson, and Daniel Parnell. 2014. "Ethnographic Engagement from within a Football in the Community Programme at an English Premier League Football Club." *Soccer & Society* 15 (6): 934–950. doi:http://dx.doi.org/10.1080/14660970.2014.920627.

Department of Health. 2011. *Start Active, Stay Active: A Report on Physical Activity for Health from the Four Home Countries' Chief Medical Officers*. London: Department of Health.

Douglas, Kitrina, and David Carless. 2014. *Life Story Research in Sport: Understanding the Experiences of Elite and Professional Athletes through Narrative*. London: Routledge.

Frith Hannah, and Kate Gleeson. 2004. "Clothing and Embodiment: Men Managing Body Image and Appearance." *Psychology of Men & Masculinity* 5 (1): 40–48.

Guba, Egon G. 1981. "Criteria for Assessing the Trustworthiness of Naturalistic Inquiries." *Educational Communication and Technology* 29 (2): 75–91. doi:http://dx.doi.org/10.1007/BF02766777.

Haigh Matthew, and Judy Crabb. 2006. *Healthy Stadia Report 2005/06*. http://www.heartofmersey.org.uk/uploads/documents/nov_06/hom_1162977236_Healthy_Stadia_Report_2005-200.pdf

Harris, Tess J., Christopher G. Owen, Christina R. Victor, Rika Adams, and Derek Gordon Cook. 2009. "What Factors Are Associated with Physical Activity in Older People, Assessed Objectively by Accelerometry?" *British Journal of Sports Medicine* 43 (6): 442–450. doi:http://dx.doi.org/10.1136/bjsm.2008.048033.

Hirt, Edward R., and Joshua J. Clarkson. 2011. "The Psychology of Fandom: Understanding the Etiology, Motives, and Implications of Fanship." In *Consumer Behavior Knowledge for Effective Sports Marketing*, edited by Lynn R. Kahle and Angeline Close, 59–85. New York: Routledge.

Hunt, Kate, Sally Wyke, Cindy M. Gray, Annie S. Anderson, Adrian Brady, Christopher Bunn, and Peter T. Donnan. 2014. "A Gender-sensitised Weight Loss and Healthy Living Programme for Overweight and Obese Men Delivered by Scottish Premier League Football Clubs (FFIT): A Pragmatic Randomised Controlled Trial." *The Lancet* 383 (9924): 1211–1221. doi:http://dx.doi.org/10.1016/S0140-6736(13)62420-4.

Johnman, Cathy, Penelope Mackie, and Fiona Sim. 2013. "The Beautiful Game." *Public Health* 127 (8): 697–698. doi:http://dx.doi.org/10.1016/j.puhe.2013.07.008.

Kelly, Laura. 2011. "'Social Inclusion' through Sports-based Interventions?" *Critical Social Policy* 31 (1): 126–150. doi:http://dx.doi.org/10.1177/0261018310385442.

King, Abby C., Cynthia Castro, Sara Wilcox, Amy A. Eyler, James F. Sallis, and Ross C. Brownson. 2000. "Personal and Environmental Factors Associated with Physical Inactivity among Different Racial-ethnic Groups of U.S. Middle-aged and Older-aged Women." *Health Psychology* 19 (4): 354. doi:http://dx.doi.org/10.1037/0278-6133.19.4.354.

Krustrup, Peter, Per Aagaard, Lars Nybo, Jeffrey Petersen, Magni Mohr, and Jens Bangsbo. 2010. "Recreational Football as a Health Promoting Activity: A Topical Review." *Scandinavian Journal of Medicine & Science in Sports* 20 (1): 1–13. doi:http://dx.doi.org/10.1111/j.1600-0838.2010.01108.

Logue, Jennifer, Lorna Thompson, Finn Romanes, David C. Wilson, Joyce Thompson, and Naveed Sattar. 2010. "Management of Obesity: Summary of SIGN Guideline." *BMJ* 340: c1295. doi:http://dx.doi.org/10.1136/bmj.c154.

Marcus, Bess H., Leigh Ann H. Forsyth, Elaine J. Stone, Patricia M. Dubbert, Thomas L. McKenzie, Andrea L. Dunn, and Steven N. Blair. 2000. "Physical Activity Behavior Change: Issues in Adoption and Maintenance." *Health Psychology* 19 (1, Suppl): 32. doi:http://dx.doi.org/10.1037/0278-6133.19.

NICE (National Institute for Health and Care Excellence). 2008. *Occupational Therapy and Physical Activity Interventions to Promote the Mental Wellbeing of Older People in Primary Care and Residential Care. NICE Guidelines [PH16]*. Accessed July 23, 2015. https://www.nice.org.uk/guidance/ph16

NICE (National Institute for Health and Care Excellence). 2014. *Managing Overweight and Obesity in Adults – Lifestyle Weight Management Services. Clinical Guidleline 53*. Accessed July 22, 2015. https://www.nice.org.uk/guidance/ph53

Nielsen, Glen, Johan Michael Wikman, Christian Jais Jensen, Jakob Friis Schmidt, L. Gliemann, and T. R. Andersen. 2014. "Health Promotion: The Impact of Beliefs of Health Benefits, Social Relations and Enjoyment on Exercise Continuation." *Scandinavian Journal of Medicine & Science in Sports* 24 (1): 66–75. doi:http://dx.doi.org/10.1111/sms.12275.

Parnell, Daniel, Andy Pringle, James McKenna, Stephen Zwolinsky, Zoe Rutherford, Jackie Hargreaves, Lizzie Trotter, Michael Rigby, and David Richardson. 2015. "Reaching Older People with PA Delivered in Football Clubs: The Reach, Adoption and Implementation Characteristics of the Extra Time Programme." *BMC Public Health* 15 (220): 1–12. doi:http://dx.doi.org/10.1186/s12889-015-1560-5.

Patton, Michael Quinn. 1990. *Qualitative Evaluation and Research Methods*. Oxford: Sage.

Pringle, Andy, Stephen Zwolinsky, James McKenna, Steven Robertson, Andy Daly-Smith, and Alan White. 2014. "Health Improvement for Men and Hard-to-engage-men Delivered in English Premier League Football Clubs." *Health Education Research* 29 (3): 503–520. doi:http://dx.doi.org/10.1093/her/cyu009.

Robertson, Steve. 2003. "If I Let a Goal in, I'll Get Beat Up: Contradictions in Masculinity, Sport and Health." *Health Education Research* 18 (6): 706–716. doi:http://dx.doi.org/10.1093/her/cyf054.

Royal Society for Public Health. 2014. *The RSPH Guide to Commissioning for Health Improvement*. Accessed July 10. https://www.rsph.org.uk/download.cfm?docid=AC19A7F2-5899-4087-92BAC242A8E6D6DA

Rutherford, Zoe, Brendan Gough, Sarah Seymour-Smith, Christopher R. Matthews, John Wilcox, Dan Parnell, and Andy Pringle. 2014. "'Motivate': The Effect of a Football in the Community Delivered Weight Loss Programme on over 35-year Old Men and Women's Cardiovascular Risk Factors." *Soccer & Society* 15 (6): 951–969. doi:http://dx.doi.org/10.1080/14660970.2014.920628.

Salihu, Hamisu M., Sarah M. Bonnema, and Amina P. Alio. 2009. "Obesity: What is an Elderly Population Growing into?" *Maturitas* 63 (1): 7–12. doi:http://dx.doi.org/10.1016/j.maturitas.2009.02.010.

Sallinen, Janne, Raija Leinonen, Mirja Hirvensalo, Tiina-Mari Lyyra, Eino Heikkinen, and Taina Rantanen. 2009. "Perceived Constraints on Physical Exercise among Obese and Non-obese Older People." *Preventive Medicine* 49 (6): 506–510. doi:http://dx.doi.org/10.1016/j.ypmed.2009.10.001.

Schmidt, Jakob, Peter Reinhard Hansen, Thomas Rieks Andersen, Lars Andersen, Thomas Hornstrup, Peter Krustrup, and Jens Bangsbo. 2014. "Cardiovascular Adaptations to 4 and 12 Months of Football or Strength Training in 65- to 75-year-old Untrained Men." *Scandinavian Journal of Medicine & Science in Sports* 24 (S1): 86–97. doi:http://dx.doi.org/10.1111/sms.12217.

Spandler, Helen, and Mick McKeown. 2012. "A Critical Exploration of Using Football in Health and Welfare Programs Gender, Masculinities, and Social Relations." *Journal of Sport & Social Issues* 36 (4): 387–409. doi:http://dx.doi.org/10.1177/0193723512458930.

White, Alan, Bruno De Sousa, Richard De Visser, Richard Hogston, Svend Aage Madsen, Péter Makara, Martin McKee, Gary Raine, Noel Richardson, and Nicholas Clarke. 2011. "Men's Health in Europe." *Journal of Men's Health* 8 (3): 192–201. doi:http://dx.doi.org/10.1136/bmj.d7054.

Witty, Karl, and Alan White. 2011. "Tackling Men's Health: Implementation of a Male Health Service in a Rugby Stadium Setting." *Community Practitioner* 84 (4): 29–32.

Lessons from the field for working in Healthy Stadia: physical activity practitioners reflect on 'sport'

Jim McKenna, Thomas Quarmby, Nicky Kime, Daniel Parnell and Stephen Zwolinsky

ABSTRACT

Drawing on four areas of our ongoing work, each with its own distinctive relevance to the Healthy Stadia agenda, this paper addresses the tension inherent to programmes aiming to promote physical activity through sport. Our experiences highlight often unresolved, but certainly resolvable, tensions between the aspirations of the respective agendas. These are not small matters; better Public Health is a powerful driver of the Healthy Stadia agenda. In particular, we notice that the desire for sporting, over health, improvement can be an important challenge point. In the hard-to-reach groups we work with, sport often has strong – and only occasionally positive – connotations. Equally, the importance of generating powerful social experiences is seen in the PA 'camp' as being an imperative for encouraging the involvement of hard-to-reach groups. In contrast, in sport-oriented programmes, this is more likely to be seen as a happy bi-product of a good sport experience.

Introduction

In this paper, physical activity (PA) specialists from academia gathered to discuss the role that sport plays in one of the key areas of Healthy Stadia activity. Sport, in particularly football is now well evidenced in preventing and treating non-communicable diseases (Hunt et al. 2014; Krustrup and Bangsbo 2015). Professional sport clubs play an increasingly acknowledged role in enhancing Public Health (Martin et al. 2016; Parnell and Richardson 2014; Pringle et al. 2014). This health promoting activity is delivered through the community engagement programmes of professional sport clubs and through their stadia (or settings-based) activity.

Professional sport clubs through their community engagement initiatives tackle a breadth of health-oriented interventions. This covers a wide spectrum of the lifespan; including children (Parnell et al. 2013, 2016); men (Curran et al. 2014; Pringle et al. 2014); women (Rutherford et al. 2014) and older adults (OA) (Parnell et al. 2015; Pringle et al. 2014). The evidence is growing for this setting-based approach, which offers a potentially attractive vehicle for policy-makers and practitioners alike to attend to Public Health – including those working on and towards the Healthy Stadia agenda.

The Healthy Stadia agenda places the emphasis on supporting, exploring and understanding the potential of sport venues. Three cross-cutting themes underpin this work: healthy stadium environments for fans and non-match day visitors, e.g. healthier food options; active travel options; healthy club workforces, e.g. annual health checks; PA programmes; and healthy populations in local communities, e.g. men's weight loss programmes; PA interventions (Martin et al. 2016). It has been the latter of which that has received the most attention from policy-makers, practitioners and researchers in recent times.

One fundamental underpinning philosophy of this approach is that funding sport is a trustworthy and credible approach for making PA consumable for individuals and community populations. This article seeks to articulate the challenges we experience with integrating sport into PA promotion, which is where much of the main funding currently lies in the UK. We also discuss issues emerging from ongoing work in four communities with complex needs. The paper draws on our research with four groups; Looked After Children (LAC), Adult Diabetes, OA and Low Socio-Economic Status communities across a variety of community sport and professional sport club-based settings.

Collectively, these contributions highlight our experiences of the principle and prominent challenges associated with pursuing sport to deliver PA-oriented interventions. This is particularly important for putting flesh on the bones of what the Healthy Stadia focus means on a day-to-day basis, especially in terms of engaging the local community. We have learned that, in their own right, stadia offer very little that is meaningful in behaviour change terms. More important are the things that people experience while in those stadia and how these community outreach programmes from stadia can facilitate positive health changes in local communities. That reality requires an increased focus of attention on the actions of the people who commission services, work in delivering programmes or develop policy surrounding community-based interventions focused on the Healthy Stadia agenda.

Looked after children

Even though sport is often seen as a panacea for addressing a host of social ills (Coalter 2007), the beneficial link between sport and PA is unclear for marginalized young people, including LAC. LAC includes those who have been removed from their family and placed in state care and their number is increasing. Of the 68,840 LAC in England in 2014 (Department for Education 2014), many suffer poor physical and mental health, have difficulties with social and emotional well-being and lack stable relationships. All this produces problems with attachment and individual resilience (Simkiss 2013).

UK policy calls for all LAC children to engage in sport and PA 'equal to their peers' to overcome earlier disadvantage and enhance their physical and psychological well-being (Department for Education and Skills 2007). Yet, recent evidence highlighted that sport is rarely a central feature of their daily lives, with most of their sport experience being confined to school-based PE (Quarmby 2014). LAC often experience multiple placements, making their initial sporting experiences disrupted and limited. This lack of regular experience is only likely to contribute to their low self-competence and self-confidence in sport.

Their lack of stable placements often results in a disrupted schooling and Physical Education (PE) experiences; this runs counter to the narrative that youth sport offers a universally positive social experience. Combined with an uncritical and/unrefined promotion of sport within PE, this compounds the problems LAC face in making and maintaining friendships. LAC have reported being picked last for teams, explaining this socially; they didn't know anyone in their PE lessons.

Arguably, limited experiences within and beyond school will impact on the development of physical capital ('ability'), potentially building a negative cycle of sport experiences. As such, sport – however it is encountered – highlights differences and alienates these individuals even further. Sport clearly has its benefits but by delivering competitive sport through PE in a wholly uncritical way, it is likely to have a negative impact on LAC's engagement in lifelong PA. While research evidence constantly suggests that regular engagement in PA may produce a variety of benefits that help some of the most marginalized and disadvantaged groups of young people in particular, we know little about how this group of young people view, access and experience PA.

So far, the LAC experience of sport has been underwhelming, but visionary clubs, like West Bromwich Albion and Tottenham Hotspur (and funding agencies like the British Academy) are making positive strides in redressing these shortcomings. These clubs offer LAC-specific programmes that aim to improve educational attainment, develop skills and, importantly, promote healthy active lifestyles. The 'wow' factor of the club helps to attract LAC but the attraction of doing sport rarely matters to them. Instead, it is the experience of positive, supportive, social environments that ensures their engagement. Once that's in place, many then opt for do more PA, mainly because they expect it to be similarly positive, supportive and social. Although some – mostly boys – do eventually adopt sport, few are as positive about what that might offer them.

Adult diabetes

There are 3.9 million people in the UK with undiagnosed diabetes (Diabetes UK 2012); a further 2.9 million are diagnosed (Diabetes UK 2012). Numbers are expected to increase to 5 million by 2025, which makes its management a major Public Health priority (Diabetes UK 2012). Assuming that recruitment into any Healthy Stadia programme will reflect this prevalence, at least 1 in 16 attendees will have diabetes, whether diagnosed or not.

Although most health systems aim to treat diabetes locally, using medication, evidence increasingly confirms the value of PA-based approaches (Avery et al. 2012). However, this means that the strategies mostly used to promote PA can focus on the single message of 'sport equals PA'. For some people with diabetes, this may be inappropriate and ill-advised. This undifferentiated message can be promoted when staff are ill-informed and/or under-trained. As a result, these staff may also ignore prior health status and/or, misunderstand the secondary complications associated with diabetes. Equally, important issues may go unaddressed regarding individuals' knowledge of their own diabetes. Further, focusing on sport needs to be understood against the common personal histories of many clients with diabetes; this includes low self-efficacy and motivation resulting from negative experiences associated with earlier involvement in sport (Edmunds, Roche, and Stratton 2010).

Yet, PA promotion also requires care. For those who have diabetes and who do not engage in recommended levels of PA, there is often a fear of hypoglycemia, compounded by the perception that to be active invariably requires engagement in sport (Brazeau et al. 2014). Equally, diabetes has two main forms with distinctive PA issues. Those with type 1 diabetes need to know how to control their diabetes *before* they participate in sport; this requires sophisticated self-management skills (American Diabetes Association 2004). The variability of exercise intensity generates additional complications and when this is not handled properly, it can end with emergency admission to hospital. For those with type 2 diabetes, regular participation in sport can help with metabolic control, but equally may be unfavourably compared to the ease of dietary change and taking medications (Di Loreto et al. 2003).

Many newly diagnosed individuals are surprised to learn that only a small increase in light intensity, day-to-day activity, equivalent to casual walking, will improve their metabolic control (Healy et al. 2007). Therefore, for the least active people in the diabetes community, the promotion of PA as 'everyday activity' is usually a more useful strategy than the promotion of PA as 'sport and fitness'. Indeed, from a Public Health perspective, recommending individuals to lead a more active lifestyle, rather than encouraging them to participate in sport, is more achievable for most inactive individuals. Given the negative connotations of sport held by some individuals with diabetes, this factor alone may act as a disincentive for engaging in any form of PA (Blair, Cheng, and Holder 2001). Public health messages that reflect this understanding may be more successful in sustaining long-term behaviour change, which is central to improving health status in people with diabetes.

Older adults

OA represent a core priority group for PA and Public Health policy (Department of Health 2011). As a result, significant interest is placed on how to optimize adherence to interventions promoting these approaches (Short, Vandelanotte, and Duncan 2014). Sport, specifically football – and more specifically, professional football clubs – has featured in many approaches to tackle Public Health priorities in this group (Bingham et al. 2015; Pringle et al. 2014).

For example, Extra Time (ET) is a national programme of PA interventions delivered in professional football clubs for OA aged 55+ years. In ET, each club took its own approach to addressing the complex health needs of this target group. While the results and outcomes associated with ET have already been reported (Parnell et al. 2015), OA also offered their perspective on what 'worked' for them. The key design characteristic of ET that the OA endorsed included the 2 h-long weekly classes, no admission costs and a broad menu of physical and social activities, delivered within and external to the football stadia. ET offered exercise to music, indoor bowls, cricket, new age curling, walking football, alongside traditional board games, bingo, table tennis, Zumba and skittles. This content matches that of other football-led health improvement interventions for OA (Pringle et al. 2014).

From 985 recruits, over 400 provided useable questionnaires detailing their responses to ET. From these people, 80.2% reported that the link to the professional football club made ET more appealing. Yet, semi-structured interviews with regular attenders identified that the appeal of the football club was only important in initial recruitment. Importantly, for programmers, relatively few recruits ever took up the opportunity to play football, and almost always these were men with histories of involvement with football. For the majority, adherence to ET was more strongly linked to participating in enjoyable activities and enriching social opportunities, than to any sport offering. These two features were inseparable, whereas sport, particularly football, was mostly seen as offering neither. Indeed, most sports-based options were met with widespread disinterest, with obvious implications for ET staff, most of whom had strongly sporting backgrounds.

Once alternative activities were offered OA willingly flocked to participate in – and continued to prefer – them. These activities involved light-to-moderate intensity exertion, with modest skill demands (but with a significant opportunity to acquire competence), delivered alongside social activities. It took a while for some club staff to register this need, but once they did, more successful engagement followed.

Inactive low socio-economic status communities

Leeds is one of the most active big cities in the UK (Robinson 2014). Despite this, over 40% of Leeds' residents engage in no sport, and ≥60% fail to meet current PA recommendations (Sport England 2013). To address this, 'Leeds Let's Get Active' (LLGA) was developed as part of Sport England's 'Get Healthy, Get into Sport' funding stream. LLGA aimed to recruit inactive participants from low SES neighbourhoods to 'do something'. LLGA participants had free access to around 150 h of gym and swim sessions at 17 leisure centres across the city. This has strong resonance with the Healthy Stadia agenda because it links local people to local resources to focus on improving health behaviour. Our evidence gives powerful insights into issues affecting recruitment, retention and overall programme success.

In two years, more than 64,000 participants registered, presenting a wide range of baseline PA (Zwolinsky and McKenna 2015). This reach is testament to the potential impact of carefully targeted recruitment. However, and notwithstanding its already impressive scale, this reach will only be optimized when interventions can be promoted with relevant messages about sport and PA. The LLGA communities we spoke to held divergent – and often contradictory – views about these respective elements of programme content (Zwolinsky and McKenna 2015). Indeed, while there were 64,000 recruits, less than 50% activated their registration by attending a first session. This gives an important lesson; neither local reputation nor attractiveness will ensure attendance.

Equally, LLGA delivery staff were initially uncertain of the interests and capacities of their 'non-regular' clients; the assumption was that motivation for both sport and PA behaviour was universal. The most effective LLGA deliverers adopted a proactive approach to recruitment to ensure that inactive people felt confident in taking the first steps across the thresholds of these venues. The implication here – for Healthy Stadia – is that it is not sufficient to rely on assumptions about the 'power' of the stadium; more is needed to engage potential beneficiaries of programmes. Equally, once participants actually attend, any power linked to the stadium is quickly forgotten; recruits expect to experience something that meets their direct needs.

In LGGA, the most successful staff acknowledged that many potential clients assumed that the centres were 'home' to intimidating people who were 'nothing like me'; they were thin, attractive, popular, skilled and competitively successful. Each of these notions, let alone their combination, can be sufficient to prevent many inactive people from taking the first steps to involvement, even though the buildings were well-established locations within the community.

Baseline LLGA data also signal that recruits into programmes having widely variable PA backgrounds. For example, just over half (55%) of participants who were identified as 'sufficiently active for health' (≥150 min of MVPA per week) in their baseline questionnaires reported involvement in sport at least once each week. Among participants who were 'inactive' at baseline (<30 of minutes of MVPA per week) sport was less prominent; 15% (Zwolinsky and McKenna 2015). Therefore, to help increase PA levels, it is important that community providers move beyond the assumption that active = sporty and the equally ill-founded corollary that inactive = non-sporty. Further, talking to recruits confirmed their highly variable PA and sporting histories; many had periods that featured (in) activity and others characterized by (non) sporty behaviour.

By responding to these, and many other similar ideas, LLGA generated over 135,000 gym and swim sessions in inactive participants. This is important; it shows that inactive people can be effectively integrated into conventional venues. Overall, an additional 799 MET-minutes/week were reported by participants at follow-up. However, within this figure, sport participation increased by only 5 min. Worse, only 28% of recruits achieved an additional 30+ minutes of sport each week at follow-up; twice as many (55%) achieved similar or greater increases through PA (Zwolinsky and McKenna 2015). These findings question the efficacy and effectiveness of using sport to deliver on the implicit social contract underpinning Public Health to reduce illness and preventable death and to improve quality of life (Fineberg 2012).

Among these participants, PA seemed better suited than sport for improving activity and health profiles. Moreover, our experience suggests that health professionals working with similarly inactive clients are likely to achieve better results by placing PA, rather than sport, at the heart of the intervention to deliver on the Healthy Stadia agenda.

Summary

These accounts, and our subsequent reflections on them, underline the fractious relationship that prevails around using 'sport' to promote PA. Clearly, inactive people hold strong and varied notions about (i) sport-based venues, (ii) sport and (iii) their relevance to personal needs. Overall, in three of these communities – excluding LACs – the notion of sport appeals, and continues to be made appealing, to a sizeable group. However, they are predominantly males and they are (usually) in the minority.

While sport is often understood ambiguously, so too were sport-oriented venues. On the one hand, sports venues can be very appealing. Yet, inactive adults in LLGA recognized the presence of local recreational centres but felt that the traditional sport that went on there was too physically demanding for them. This dissuades some from joining and others from sustaining involvement; the low uptake in LLGA is ample evidence that any reliance on ideas linked to the 'build it and they will come' mentality (in LLGA that link might be expressed as 'It's there so they will come'), is unlikely to be effective in client groups who are as suspicious of sports venues as they are of sport-based programmes.

On the other hand, for other people, sport provides a meaningful and valuable challenge. Thus, sport is a double-edged sword; what is powerfully engaging for some is overwhelmingly counterproductive for others. Sport seems most acceptable to inactive people when it is used to prioritize and meet their social needs. At this point, for many 'traditionalists', that form of sport has lost much of its 'real' meaning.

Achieving the potential benefits associated with playing sport relies on the flexibility and variability that it affords. Yet, deliverers of sport are often under-prepared, and sometimes unwilling, to offer what works best for inactive people. These clients can be confused by the contradictions around high level sport; we regularly see inactive people, drawn in by the allure of elite level sport, but who are rarely able or willing to participate in those sports. What is more, when participation is PA-oriented, some sports advocates regard it as diluted and not 'the real deal'. For these individuals, sport engagement is the single yardstick of programme effectiveness. However, when so few inactive people achieve these goals – as seen in our ongoing work – it can be enormously dispiriting for programme staff.

Given this lack of agreement and understanding between practitioners apparently 'in the know', it's no surprise that inactive people so readily lump sport together with PA. They often describe both their experience and expectations with a single, negative, judgement. Yet, when we can get them to disaggregate their experiences, it is sport that draws the most bitter, and predominantly childhood-based, accounts. Rarely does walking, dancing or gardening draw such negativity, although cycling – and road accidents involving cyclists – sometimes does.

Crucially, the assumption that sport generates PA is as strongly endorsed by sport advocates as it continues to be rejected by PA advocates. Crucially, that rejection is often deeply held by the least active individuals. Even after all this time, we – those who variously represent either the sport or the PA constituencies – still seem to be sleeping in the same bed, but dreaming different dreams. For this reason, we suggest that it is essential for all those working within and around the Healthy Stadia agenda become fluent with these issues. Sport and PA represent inherently different behaviours, with distinctive challenges, incentives and meanings for every potential recruit. Responding to such diversity requires that practitioners deploy an equally diverse repertoire of skills to meet clients' preferences.

Acknowledgments

The authors wish to thank all the individuals and agencies who partnered these programmes and all the organizations who supported this work.

Disclosure statement

No potential conflict of interest was reported by the authors.

References

American Diabetes Association. 2004. "Physical Activity/Exercise and Diabetes." *Diabetes Care* 27: S58–S62.

Avery, L., D. Flynn, A. van Wersch, F. F. Sniehotta, and M. I. Trenell. 2012. "Changing Physical Activity Behavior in Type 2 Diabetes: A Systematic Review and Meta-analysis of Behavioral Interventions." *Diabetes Care* 35 (12): 2681–2689. doi:http://dx.doi.org/10.2337/dc11-2452.

Bingham, D., D. Parnell, K. Curran, R. Jones, and D. Richardson. 2015. "Fit Fans: Perspectives of a Practitioner and Understanding Participant Health Needs within a Health Promotion Programme for Older Men Delivered within an English Premier League Football Club." *Soccer & Society* 15: 883–901.

Blair, S. N., Y. Cheng, and J. S. Holder. 2001. "Is Physical Activity or Physical Fitness More Important in Defining Health Benefits?" *Medicine & Science in Sports & Exercise*, 33 (6 Suppl): S379–S99; discussion S419-20.

Brazeau, A. S., V. Gingras, C. Leroux, C. Suppère, H. Mircescu, K. Desjardins, P. Briand, J. M. Ekoé, and R. Rabasa-Lhoret. 2014. "A Pilot Program for Physical Exercise Promotion in Adults with Type 1 Diabetes: The PEP-1 Program." *Applied Physiology, Nutrition, and Metabolism* 39 (4): 465–471. doi:http://dx.doi.org/10.1139/apnm-2013-0287.

Coalter, F. 2007. *A Wider Social Role for Sport: Who's Keeping the Score?* New York: Routledge.

Curran, K., D. Bingham, D. Richardson, and D. Parnell. 2014. "Ethnographic Engagement from within a Football in the Community Programme at an English Premier League Football Club." *Soccer & Society* 15 (6): 934–950.

Department for Education. 2014. *Children Looked after in England (including Adoption and Care Leavers) Year Ending 31 March 2014*. London: Department for Education.

Department for Education and Skills. 2007. *Care Matters: Time for Change*. London: Department for Education and Skills.

Department of Health. 2011. *Start Active, Stay Active: A Report on Physical Activity for Health from the Four Home Countries. Chief Medical Officers*. London: Department of Health.

Di Loreto, C., C. Fanelli, P. Lucidi, G. Murdolo, A. De Cicco, N. Parlanti, F. Santeusanio, P. Brunetti, and P. De Feo. 2003. "Validation of a Counseling Strategy to Promote the Adoption and the Maintenance of Physical Activity by Type 2 Diabetic Subjects." *Diabetes Care* 26 (2): 404–408.

Diabetes UK 2012. *State of the Nation 2012*. London: Diabetes UK.

Edmunds, S., D. Roche, and G. Stratton. 2010. "Levels and Patterns of Physical Activity in Children and Adolescents with Type 1 Diabetes and Associated Metabolic and Physiologic Health Outcomes." *Journal of Physical Activity and Health* 7 (1): 68–77.

Fineberg, H. V. 2012. "Shattuck Lecture. A Successful and Sustainable Health System – How to Get There from Here." *New England Journal of Medicine* 366 (11): 1020–1027. doi:http://dx.doi.org/10.1056/NEJMsa1114777.

Healy, G. N., D. W. Dunstan, J. Salmon, E. Cerin, J. E. Shaw, P. Z. Zimmet, and N. Owen. 2007. "Objectively Measured Light-intensity Physical Activity is Independently Associated with 2-H Plasma Glucose." *Diabetes Care* 30 (6): 1384–1389. doi:http://dx.doi.org/10.2337/dc07-0114.

Hunt, Kate, Sally Wyke, Cindy M. Gray, Annie S. Anderson, Adrian Brady, Christopher Bunn, Peter T. Donnan, et al. 2014. "A Gender-sensitised Weight Loss and Healthy Living Programme for Overweight and Obese Men Delivered by Scottish Premier League Football Clubs (FFIT): A Pragmatic Randomised Controlled Trial." *The Lancet* 1211–1221. doi:http://dx.doi.org/10.1016/S0140-6736(13)62420-4.

Krustrup, P., and J. Bangsbo. 2015. "Recreational Football is Effective in the Treatment of Non-communicable Diseases." *British Journal of Sports Medicine* 49 (22): 1426–1427. doi:http://dx.doi.org/10.1136/bjsports-2015-094955.

Martin, A., S. Morgan, D. Parnell, M. Philpott, A. Pringle, M. Rigby, A. Taylor, and J. Topham. 2016. "A Perspective from Key Stakeholders in Football and Health Improvement." *Soccer & Society* 17 (2): 175–182. doi:http://dx.doi.org/10.1080/14660970.2015.1082751.

Parnell, D., S. Buxton, D. Hewill, M. Reeves, E. Cope, and R. Bailey. 2016. "The Pursuit of Lifelong Participation: The Role of Professional Football Clubs in the Delivery of Physical Education and School Sport in England." *Soccer & Society.* 17 (2): 225–241. doi:http://dx.doi.org/10.1080/14660970.2015.1082752.

Parnell, D., A. Pringle, J. McKenna, S. Zwolinsky, Z. Rutherford, J. Hargreaves, L. Trotter, M. Rigby, and D. Richardson. 2015. "Reaching Older People with PA Delivered in Football Clubs: The Reach, Adoption and Implementation Characteristics of the Extra Time Programme." *BMC Public Health* 15: 25. doi:http://dx.doi.org/10.1186/s12889-015-1560-5.

Parnell, D., and D. Richardson. 2014. "Introduction: Football and Inclusivity." *Soccer & Society* 15 (6): 823–827.

Parnell, D., G. Stratton, B. Drust, and D. Richardson. 2013. "Football in the Community Schemes: Exploring the Effectiveness of an Intervention in Promoting Healthful Behaviour Change." *Soccer & Society* 14 (1): 35–51.

Pringle, A., D. Parnell, S. Zwolinsky, J. Hargreaves, and J. McKenna. 2014. "Effect of a Health-improvement Pilot Programme for Older Adults Delivered by a Professional Football Club: The Burton Albion Case Study." *Soccer & Society* 15 (6): 902–918.

Pringle, A., S. Zwolinsky, J. McKenna, S. Robertson, A. Daly-Smith, and A. White. 2014. "Health Improvement for Men and Hard-to-Engage-Men Delivered in English Premier League Football Clubs." *Health Education Research* 29 (3): 503–520. doi:http://dx.doi.org/10.1093/her/cyu009.

Quarmby, T. 2014. "Sport and Physical Activity in the Lives of Looked-after Children: A 'Hidden Group' in Research, Policy and Practice." *Sport, Education and Society* 19: 944–958.

Robinson, S. 2014. *Sports and Leisure Survey Sees Leeds Sitting Top of the Table*. Leeds: Press Release Leeds City Council.

Rutherford, Z., B. Gough, S. Seymour-Smith, C. Matthews, J. WIlcox, D. Parnell, and A. Pringle. 2014. "'Motivate': The Effect of a Football in the Community Delivered Weight Loss Programme on over 35-Year Old Men and Women's Cardiovascular Risk Factors." *Soccer & Society No.* 16 (5): 951–969.

Short, C. E., C. Vandelanotte, and M. J. Duncan. 2014. "Individual Characteristics Associated with Physical Activity Intervention Delivery Mode Preferences among Adults." *International Journal of Behavioral Nutrition and Physical Activity* 11 (1): 25. doi:http://dx.doi.org/10.1186/1479-5868-11-25.

Simkiss, D. 2013. "Looked-after Children and Young People." In *Annual Report of the Chief Medical Officer 2012 – Our Children Deserve Better: Prevention Pays*, edited by Department of Health. London: Department of Health.

Sport England. 2013. *Active People Survey 7–12 Months Rolling Results: April 2012–April 2013*. Sport England 2013. Accessed August 3, 2013. http://www.sportengland.org/research/who-plays-sport/national-picture/

Zwolinsky, S., and J. McKenna. 2015. *Leeds Let's Get Active: Final Report, August 2015*. Centre for active Lifestyles, Leeds: Leeds Beckett University.

Index

Note: Page numbers in *italics* refer to figures
Page numbers in **bold** refer to tables